D1628442

THE LIFE CYCLE
OF STRUCTURES IN
EXPERIMENTAL
ARCHAEOLOGY

Sidestone Press

THE LIFE CYCLE OF STRUCTURES IN EXPERIMENTAL ARCHAEOLOGY

AN OBJECT BIOGRAPHY APPROACH

edited by
**Linda Hurcombe and
Penny Cunningham**

© 2016 Individual Authors

Published by Sidestone Press, Leiden
www.sidestone.com

Imprint: Sidestone Press

Lay-out & cover design: Sidestone Press
Photographs cover: Reconstructed Uimaranta house, Saarijärvi Stone Age Village
    (Finland) by Eero Muurimäki; Thatching using reeds, Kierikki Stone Age
    Village (Finland) by Inga Nieminen; Hut rebuilding, Pietraperzia, Enna,
    (Sicily, Italy) by Kati Caruso & Claudia Speciale; Thatching using reeds
    Kierikki Stone Age Centre (Finland) by Inga Nieminen; The Main House,
    after its collapse in 2009, Irish National Heritage Park, Ferrycarrig, Co.
    Wexford (Ireland) by Tríona Sørensen.

ISBN 978-90-8890-365-6 (softcover)
ISBN 978-90-8890-389-2 (hardcover)
ISBN 978-90-8890-366-3 (PDF e-book)

This project has been funded with support from the
European Commission. This publication reflects the
views only of the authors, the commission cannot be
held responsible for any use which may be made of the
information contained therein.

Contents

CONSTRUCTION

STRUCTURES IN LIFE

DECLINE OF STRUCTURES

List of Figures, Graphs and Tables

Brian Cumby making a logboat at Kierikki Stone Age Centre, Finland, 2013.

Brian Cumby, shipwright: born 9th October 1950, died 26th February 2015

Brian had over 30 years experience as a shipwright and was involved in building reconstructions of historical vessels including being one of several shipwrights to create the replica of the Matthew, the ship in which John Cabot sailed from Bristol to North America in AD 1497. Brian was involved in the two events which gave rise to this book: the workshop in Exeter in May 2013 and the conference in Kierikki, Finland in June 2014. During two visits to Kierikki in 2013 and 2014 he worked with the Exeter team to repair existing logboats and create a new one. During an earlier Exeter workshop in October 2012 OpenArch participants also visited the National Maritime Museum (Cornwall) in Falmouth, UK, when Brian was leading the project to build a Bronze Age sewn plank boat. Building the boat was an experiment in an unfamiliar technology of stitching massive shaped oak timbers together using yew withies, and an experiment in relying on volunteers to complete such a challenging project. It was also an experiment in conducting the construction inside the museum and building publicity over the construction phase. The boat, Morgawr, was successfully launched 6th March 2013. His intimate involvement with the OpenArch project has led the editors to dedicate this volume to him.

Preface

Linda Hurcombe[1], Penny Cunningham[1],
Leena Lethinen[2]

1 University of Exeter, Department of Archaeology (UK)
2 Director of Kierikkikeskus/Kierikki Stone Age Centre (Finland)

OpenArch: Dialogue with Science, Work package 5

The papers collected here result from discussions within the OpenArch Project, supported by the Culture Programme of the European Union. OpenArch is a European Culture project (2010-2015) whose members consist of eleven partners from European archaeological open-air museums (AOAMs), the University of Exeter (UK) and EXARC. OpenArch aims to build a permanent partnership of AOAMs, raise standards among participants and improve the visitor experiences across Europe. The focus of AOAMs is to present both the tangible and intangible past to the public. The tangible parts of AOAMs are the archaeological remains and the reconstructions of structures (i.e. houses, ships, logboat). The intangible and, in some respects the most interesting part of an AOAM, is the story of the people that once lived there. One of the strongest themes across the partnership is the role of structures: what kinds of houses, storage facilities, kilns, boats and boundaries did people use; how were they made and maintained? Scientific evidence from artefacts and sites provides the basis for the reconstructions, but these need testing and critical reflection as they are made and used. In this way, the structures become part of the dialogue with science.

OpenArch is divided into Work Packages. All Work Packages are the responsibility of the entire partnership, but one or two OpenArch partners coordinate each work package. The Dialogue with Science (work package 5) is coordinated by University of Exeter (UK) and Kierriki Stone Age Centre (Finland) and focuses on experimental archaeology and, in particular, larger-scale experiments to demonstrate how co-operation between scientists and AOAMs can contribute to improving the visitor experience.

This volume is the result of this sharing of research and experience. Its aim is to benefit both the science and the visitor experience across the archaeological spectrum. Archaeological experiments help us to understand how structures were constructed, and perhaps what they looked like, how they performed, and just as importantly, how people used these structures in the past.

Experiments within OpenArch and the Dialogue with Science work package have been defined in cooperation with craftspeople, archaeologists, experimental archaeology experts and universities, so that the experiments of this project add value to the visitor experience and to archaeology. Broad experimental themes include structures for different purposes, as dwellings, as pyrotechnical aids for the production of metals and wood tar and pitch, for storage, and for water transport.

The papers in this volume result from two very successful Dialogue with Science Work Package events: a workshop held in May 2013 at the University of Exeter (UK), and a conference at Kierikki Stone Age Museum (Finland), in June 2014. Participants from Austria, Denmark, Finland, Germany, Italy, The Netherlands, Norway, Serbia, Sweden and the UK, who are either working on experimental research projects or at AOAMs met to discuss the birth, life and death of various structures and to discuss the value and scale of the experimental archaeology approach in studying and presenting the past to the public.

The May 2013 workshop explored the research and visitor agendas of structures and their life cycles as they are experienced by experimental archaeology projects and AOAMs. The structures are not static entities but change through time going through a life cycle, thus key themes considered were the birth, life and death of structures explored through the planning phase, the assembling of materials, the construction period, and then the maintenance and repair needs and the change of use of structures as they age. Followed, ultimately, by some combination of the decay, dilapidation, dismantling and destruction of these experimental structures. The conference also considered the structure's life cycle as performance where the visitor is drawn into a dynamic interaction and relationship with the life cycle of a structure.

During the May 2013 workshop it became clear from discussions that there was a wealth of knowledge and experience represented. Furthermore a number of common problems surrounding the creation and upkeep of archaeological structures experienced by both experimental archaeologists and AOAMs were identified and through discussions some solutions were established. The wide range of papers presented at the conference highlighted the diversity of experimental structures – these are not just houses but also include boats, furnaces, and other diverse constructions.

To develop some of the key themes further a conference was held in June 2014 at Kierikki Stone Age Village (Finland). Papers focused on house constructions, ceramics, iron smelting, reconstructing Bronze Age tools as the means to make structures, and pitch and glue making experiments. These were followed by a series of papers relating to house reconstructions at AOAMs focusing on issues such as the compromises that need to be considered when designing a new reconstruction in light of large visitor numbers, the knowledge and skills required for successful thatching and insights concerning health and safety issues (for staff and visitors) whilst also trying to create and maintain the 'right' ambience for visitors at AOAMs.

The Kierikki conference highlighted the scope of experimental work being undertaken by the OpenArch partners and how these are not only contributing to our understanding of the past and the archaeological record but also really enhancing the visitor experience.

Both the conference and the workshop demonstrated the wealth of experience and knowledge that has been created through an understanding of the life cycle of structures in a variety of formats. As a natural extension of these two events, the University of Exeter, with the co-operation of Kierikki Stone Age Centre, set the agenda to integrate research and practice in a single volume. Although a life cycle approach may appear subjective, through accounts of individual experiences of designing, planning and constructing structures, they relate to solving problems as they arise, testing ideas and evaluating performance. In sharing the insights and experiences of those who are working in the fields of experimental archaeology and open-air museums this volume not only adheres to the ethos of the OpenArch Project but also presents the results from an academic research perspective. We hope that the academic and museum communities will both recognise the value of the approach presented here.

OpenArch Bibliography

This volume is one contribution to a series of printed material arising from the OpenArch project, most of which is available on the web: www.openarch.eu.

Gómez Gutiérrez, M. 2015. *Archaeological Open-Air Museums and the dialogue with the museum community.* OpenArch. (handbook available at http://openarch.eu/work-packages/products/wp6-publication-aoams-and-dialogue-museum-community).

Kelm, R. (ed.) 2015. *Archaeology and Crafts: experiences and experiments of traditional skills and handicrafts in archaeological open-air museums in Europe.* Proceedings of the VI. OpenArch Conference in Albersdorf, Germany, 23-37 September 2013. Husum.

Jakobsen, B. and Burrow, S. 2015. *Handbook: Management of Open-Air Museums.* OpenArch. (Handbook available at http://openarch.eu/work-packages/products/management-open-air-museums).

Paarderkooper, R. and Zielińska, M. 2013. *Communication Strategy: Strategic Public Relations for Archaeological Open-Air Museums.* OpenArch. (Handbook available at http://openarch.eu/work-packages/products/2013-pr-book-communication-strategy-available-online.

van Hasselt, M. 2015. *Live interpretation in Archaeological Open-Air Museums: Do's and Don'ts of including live interpretation.* OpenArch (handbook available at http://openarch.eu/work-packages/products/guidebook-live-interpretation-aoam.

An introduction to the life cycle and object biography approach to structures in experimental archaeology

Linda Hurcombe and Penny Cunningham

Experimental archaeology

This volume focuses on experimental archaeology but the term is not always uniformly applied. The term experimental archaeology is understood differently by the archaeological and lay communities. The Popperian view of science stresses that the ideas can come from any source but that scientific knowledge and understanding progresses by framing these ideas as hypotheses and then testing them to show not that they are right, but that they remain valid. Many authors have presented an overview of these issues and tried to refine understanding by reserving the use of the term experimental archaeology for this scientific approach while others have taken a pragmatic line on this and accepted that in academic contexts the term should be used in this way but that popular understanding may vary (e.g. Hurcombe 2004; Outram 2008; Kelterborn 2005).

The division between experiment, experience, and demonstration is a relatively straightforward one but experiences are acknowledged as contributing towards the ideas for experiments and as exploratory pathways to formulating scientific experiments. The experiences are also an important means of gaining the expertise which the scientific experiment often requires (Petersson and Narmo 2011; Cunningham *et al.* 2008). The problem of forming a full scientific experiment is exacerbated when the variables are difficult to control and when the experiment is potentially costly of time, materials and expertise, and where the results might be most usefully monitored over long timescales spanning many years (Jewel 1963; Bell *et al.* 1996). Many experimental archaeological structures are just such complex projects. Several good debates have been presented focussing on the terminology, style, and study of building structures (Beck 2011; Rasmussen 2007, 2011; Reynolds 1999, Schmidt 2000, Schöbel 2004). The discussions have suggested that reconstructions should be full-scale but that terms such as model and construct, or (re)construction could replace words such as reconstructions because, it is acknowledged, that it is not possible to exactly copy, replicate or reconstruct. The past is gone and we build our 'reconstructions' in the present with modern minds and furthermore often compromise or make reasoned guesses to fill in gaps in the evidence. Rasmussen (2007, 7-9) makes a good case for substituting the term reconstruction, which can describe both a process and a product, with 'full-scale model' and reserving this term for structures arising from archaeological evidence rather than from generalised ideas. This has merit but the use of the word 'model' alone can in the English language also imply an 'idealised aspirational perfection', or a 'smaller-scale copy' as well as a theorised model which is the sense in which Rasmussen uses the word. Thus abbreviating the term to FSM might be the way forward. In addition there are reconstructions for different needs and Demant's (2009) discussion of three standards of replication for textiles could be applied more widely to include structures as well.

In a volume such as this, where many communities might make use of the content and where the contributors are drawn from a wide variety of languages and backgrounds, the pragmatic approach has been adopted. The key issue is honesty and clarity. None of the present authors are discussing anything other than full size structures and most fulfil the FSM definition. All are research-based at some level: but the level does vary, but not through choice. Some FSMs have had to draw more widely from the ethnographic record, or draw in archaeological evidence from other periods or from different regions, and take in more reasoned guesswork, all due to evidence constraints. The earlier periods, in particular, are faced with a paucity of evidence.

The focus in this volume is on 'structures' as this word allowed houses, granaries, storage pits, furnaces and many other structures to be considered. The term structures also has no overtones of replication and so avoids some of the problems associated with other terminology. The value of the FSMs is that they are some form of reconstruction and that the reflective critiques presented in the chapters offer clarification and insightful ways of contributing to scientific research even if they are not always themselves framed as fully scientific experiments. Experiences have a value and role in the formulation of experimentation as this volume shows. In light of this clarifying statement the term reconstruction has been retained.

Experience as a research resource

The contributors to this volume are drawn from a variety of communities from the research, museum, and live interpretation fields. The intended audience is similarly diverse and we are aware that some would-be users do not have good access to research libraries and some do, but will be unfamiliar with the practical experiences of creating and using structures. The choice of Sidestone Press as publisher was made to ensure that the physical volume or e-volume can be purchased but that anyone with access to the web can read it online and that the images which are so important for conveying details are available in colour. Throughout this volume the role of Archaeological Open-Air Museums is stressed. This term and its acronym AOAMs has been widely adopted following Paardekooper (2012) to include many organisations named as 'centres', 'parks' and 'open-air museums' with variations across different languages but all serving as interpretation centres.

The style of this volume reflects a key issue of the experimental archaeology of structures. There are two pathways to dealing with structures arising from two funding sources; these are research and public presentation. Over the course of interactions and discussions spanning many years, both during the five year OpenArch project and beforehand, it is evident that they both have advantages and disadvantages. The OpenArch project has shown some good examples and many of the conferences and workshops have provided useful resources (Kelm 2015; Gómez Gutiérrez 2015; Jakobsen & Burrow 2015). Research projects normally include provision for publication but usually have a specific focus and a defined time span. While five years is a long time for a funded project, it is not a long period in the life cycle of many structures such as houses, granary stores or boats. In contrast, the AOAMs would want most of their structures to last as long as possible and their funding sources may even require longevity for the finished structures. The funding focus is the finished product and its use and there may be no money set aside for research or publication. Furthermore, most museums do not have time set aside for writing up a research project. There is little point in bemoaning the different agendas but there is much to be learnt from bringing these two aspects into firstly, a better understanding of one another's key operating parameters and secondly, for research-style information to be gleaned from multiple experiences of structures amassed over many years. This volume attempts to do exactly that, by bringing together experiences as much as direct hypothesis-testing experiments. For this reason many of the papers record experiences in the hope of informing further research and assist reflection on the practical experiences of structures. The authors often use photos or sketch diagrams rather than line drawings and the references may include websites and videos. There are often few published sources and the papers come across as very 'pure', i.e. they are the result of the authors intense practical experience or, the summation of experiences over many years/decades of thought, practice and discussions with colleagues working in the same field.

Many of the experiments or experiences reported here are very individual because they are built from raw materials with natural variation. The full scientific ideal of hypothesis testing and replicability is inherently difficult where so few variables can be tightly controlled and the structures are too large for a laboratory approach. Instead, most large scale structures can be seen as actualistic experiments. This term has been used to denote a style of experiments with more realistic 'in life' conditions. Where these kinds of experiments are part of funded research they are undertaken with as much documentation as possible (Jewell 1963; Bell *et al.* 1996). Experimentation with structures can also inform via individual experiences as these are often individually repeated following common principles with learning and understanding accumulating over time. The latter situation is often the style of experimentation which is the least well published but, the experiences are nonetheless valuable. The concept of experience as a research resource runs throughout much of this volume which tries to encapsulate and publish this set of tacit knowledge and demonstrate the value of this resource at a research level.

Life cycles and object biographies as theoretical frameworks

The structures which form the stage and setting in AOAMs can themselves be full scientific experiments or solely educational. Neither role sees them as static. The key issue emerging from the OpenArch debates was change. Any discussions of structures feature a sense of purpose and functionality. The partners had between them structures standing for several decades some of which were in need of repair or in an advanced state of deterioration, or structures that were in the planning or idea phase. The latter were in some cases replacements for structures which had deteriorated and the new version directly built on the success and problems of the first structure.

The structures had one common structuring principle, a chronological existence which went through phases and could best be described as a life cycle. For different kinds of structures the life expectancy differed but phases described by terms such as conception, birth, life and death were common to all and easily understood. However, the life cycle is set within a social and individual framework. This volume presents the best theoretical framework for setting discussion on structures in experimental archaeology as a combination of a life cycle and object biography approach.

Both life cycles and object biographies are useful approaches. Life cycle can be seen as a generalised set of phases which have a broadly linear trajectory moving from conception, birth, life, and death, with life featuring periods of growth, adulthood, and decline. Object biographies (Gosden and Marshall 1999; Dant 2001) emphasise the social contexts of the changes and the term can be applied to a category of objects, or to an individual structure. This is the theoretical framework that archaeologists would use when talking about this kind of concept. The archaeological understanding of an object biography is that it concentrates on the relationship between objects, social context and people in ways that see modifications, changes in social meanings and associations, by acknowledging that value can shift as the social relationships between object and people shift (Hurcombe 2007, 41). The story of the houses are not presented as static entities but as things that have changed and that have perhaps a very punctuated, sharp 'end of life' deliberately caused by humans, including the burning of some of the houses, as well as a slow steady decline (Rasmussen 2007).

For the public visiting the structures it seems that the life cycle stories are important as they can see that the structures change, which may include elements of deterioration and/or repair. These changes and the stories they create can be publicised at events, be part of the social media profile and invite public participation whilst also having a research value. Life cycles and object biographies offer change and social context to the public and researchers alike.

Structures: Examples of above ground extrapolation

'Creating and building' activities draw people in as visitors and as volunteers. Is the visitor going to be excluded or involved in acts of construction as part of that dialogue? Are volunteers going to be used and, if so, once people are drawn into the project what makes them want to stay? Where involvement works successfully it can also provide a ready pool of volunteers to take that construction into the next phase of its life in use. Both St. Fagan's (UK) 'Bryn Eryr' building, and building the bronze age boat, *Morgawr*, have drawn in volunteers and shown the social draw of the construction phase of the object biography of structures (Jakobson and Burrow 2015: 98; van de Noort *et al.* 2014). This concept was so marked

Figure 1.1: 'Construction as performance': Brian Cumby working on the bronze age boat Morgawr in full public view (The Morgawr reconstruction project was funded by AHRC and National Maritime Museum, Cornwall, UK). Source: Linda Hurcombe.

that in the *Morgawr* boat project it was termed 'construction as performance' with the whole reconstruction taking place in front of the public within the museum workshop (Figure 1.1, and see p. 83-89, this volume).

An object biography approach to structures, with its stress on social contexts lends itself to the consideration of modern dilemmas of reconstruction.

Figure 1.2. is an example prepared by Bryony Coles (1992, 148, Fig. 16.1) which is based on a drawing and evidence from the Circum Alpine lake villages by Arnold (1990, Fig. 6.9). With each annotation she is trying to explain why all these elements above ground are reasoned guesswork. There is not necessarily concrete evidence for all of them (Drury 1982). On the other hand there is a reasoned supposition for those elements and the annotations are based on archaeological evidence from similar sites (Figure 1.2). That approach could form something which is a dialogue with the visitors i.e. a story about what reasoned guesses were made and what was solid evidence. In this way the structures in AOAMs are about the dialogue with science and authenticity. Keeping a photographic record, with annotated notes of the processes of construction, helps to record the decision making process related to both construction and the materials used as well as a way of explaining the process to volunteers, seasonal staff and visitors.

Why 'Structures?'

The broad term 'structures' has been used in this volume in order to encompass different kinds of 'houses' (hall, villa, tents, longhouse, hut, roundhouse) and also include; sheds, wind breaks, boat houses, partitions, granaries, drying racks, workshops, sweat lodges, kilns, smoke houses, forges, furnaces, mills, bread ovens,

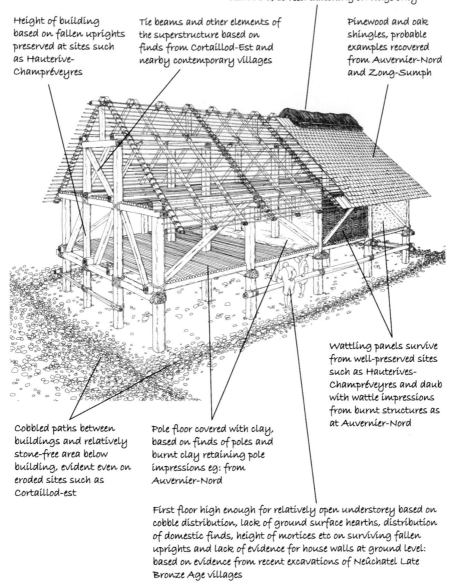

Pollen and macro remains indicate that relatively little reed fringed the lake c.1000BC, so reed thatching on ridge only

Height of building based on fallen uprights preserved at sites such as Hauterive-Champréveyres

Tie beams and other elements of the superstructure based on finds from Cortaillod-Est and nearby contemporary villages

Pinewood and oak shingles, probable examples recovered from Auvernier-Nord and Zong-Sumph

Wattling panels survive from well-preserved sites such as Hauterives-Champréveyres and daub with wattle impressions from burnt structures as at Auvernier-Nord

Cobbled paths between buildings and relatively stone-free area below building, evident even on eroded sites such as Cortaillod-est

Pole floor covered with clay, based on finds of poles and burnt clay retaining pole impressions eg: from Auvernier-Nord

First floor high enough for relatively open understorey based on cobble distribution, lack of ground surface hearths, distribution of domestic finds, height of mortices etc on surviving fallen uprights and lack of evidence for house walls at ground level: based on evidence from recent excavations of Neûchatel Late Bronze Age villages

Figure 1.2: An example of how reasoned annotations might be useful features of reconstructed buildings based on a reconstruction drawing by Béat Arnold (1990, Fig. 69), after Coles (1992: 148, Fig. 16.1).

tanneries, docks, boats, walls, banks and defences, burial mounds, weirs and traps, storage pits and many others. Some structures can be permanent, seasonal or transient. Some of the topics omitted from this volume include field systems, walls and hedges and the structures involved in growing plants and in the use of plants for structures (Jewell 1963; Bell *et al.* 1996). These have formed part of OpenArch partner's activities (growing vines, Ilić and Tapavički-Ilić, Ćirić, 2014; growing a crop of spelt with the straw used for thatching, Burrow 2015; and clearing an area of woodland to plant a cereal crop and then using the plot to create the concept of a forest garden at AÖZA).

Structures as a stage for presenting the past?

For OpenArch the question of the role of structures is highly relevant across the very diverse character in the 11 partners. They all engage with the presentation of the past and they each have different structures. Some have whole villages, others have just one of two houses. In each case we are looking at engaging with the visitors' dialogue with science and creating new ways of opening up that dialogue, enriching the visitor experience and, in addition, enriching the research opportunities.

The structures create a setting, presenting possibilities and opportunities. In some cases they are simply scenery, they are an aesthetic tableau, in others they are a very immersive experience where interpreters in costume play a role and keep in character all of the time that the visitor is with them. In other cases, researchers use these centres because they offer opportunities for larger time scale integration of different types of activities and often spaces or facilities for activities which might not be available in their own university environment.

Many of the OpenArch partners have engaged with the life cycle in interesting ways providing many different aspects and a diversity of approaches.

Viminacium

In keeping with the complexity of a Roman city, the AOAM at Viminacium (Serbia) shows multiple strands of experiment, experience and ethos, all of which can be seen under the object biography framework. The ethos aspect of the object biography framework makes an interesting starting point.

Buildings constructed on archaeological sites as part of AOAMs often have to serve several agendas. The Roman town of Viminacium, was situated on the Danube and was at one stage on the same kind of scale as Rome with 30,000 inhabitants, but it now forms part of an AOAM with an ethos of modern buildings offering interpretations of the Roman experience (Nikolić 2013; Nikolić *et al.* 2011; Ilić and Nikolić 2015). Several of the buildings offer a very different style of reconstruction. The villa building complex in Viminacium, known as the *Domus Scientarium Viminacium*, is not designed as a reconstruction or a full scale model in the archaeological sense but instead forms a modern interpretation of the spirit and atmosphere of Roman life in the villa and provides accommodation and a restaurant for some visitors and also a library and study hub for the scientific community. The modern bedrooms have en-suite bathrooms but they are spaced around a small peristyle (colonnaded inner yard).

The amphitheatre had to be built over the ancient building (any other footprint will simply affect other Roman buildings of this extensive Roman town). It was originally planned to be rebuilt as a reconstruction in wood and stone, but plans changed because it was never going to be possible to make an archaeologically ideal reconstruction, especially because the ancient building had three phases of use and

Figure 1.3: The wooden amphitheatre on modern stone foundations (top) and the amphitheatre in use during a production of Aida (bottom). Source: Viminacium.

a mixture of materials which changed over the three phases. It was decided instead to reconstruct it in wood as this was used in all phases for the auditorium and because a wooden building is not such a permanent structure as one of stone. If ideas about the reconstruction changed, the wooden building would be easier to replace or modify. The wooden structure still had to have modern foundations and the wooden construction used modern techniques although a future idea would be to have a section which showed the carpentry and finishing techniques and treatments that were relevant to the ancient way of building. In other words, the modern building would reflect better the ancient one, and also fit better with the ethos of modern reconstruction ethics (Figure 1.3). The idea was to make a building that could be used for modern spectacles and so some compromises were made. For example, the modern construction has wider, more comfortable seats but the Roman ways of creating the flow of people to allow a crowd to move away quickly at the end of a performance or in the event of fire was followed. These modern routes also had to conform to modern health and safety constraints (Figure 1.3).

The OpenArch participants all enjoyed staying in and using the modern villa which though not a direct reconstruction nonetheless provided food for thought about ideas for such buildings in life from a variety of perspectives: past inhabitants, modern researcher, tourist, architect and archaeologist. The modern interpretation can be viewed as a reincarnation or second life of this kind of structure referring back to its antecedents.

In another strand the individual components of the original structure have been analysed as closely as possible, but the composite relationships still require a reasoned best compromise to achieve a viable solution. Research into the components of buildings is provided by the work at Viminacium on binding materials for buildings which covers mortars with different functions such as plaster, rendering, and bedding mortars (Nikolić and Bogdanović 2012; Nikolić et al. 2014, 2015). The research was directly based on the archaeological evidence from the site and was conducted in order to inform the restorations of existing archaeological building and also to investigate raw materials for construction and the supply routes for these. The mortar is important because it is a composite. Stones are easily researched as they are one material, brick is usually also straightforward, but mortar is the most difficult because it is made from so many different components in different quantities and the process itself is also important to achieve the right mixture and effect. The Romans generally used what they found near to the site and used more distance sources only rarely. In Viminacium it was particularly difficult to decide on the mortar mixture because in the surrounding area there were no natural pozzolanic deposits available today for exploitation. Artificial pozzolanic additions in the mortar were known to be used in the past, usually brick which is now easily recognised if the mortar is red, but some other additions would not leave such obvious traces. When deciding the composition of the new mortar they had to consider the weakness of new mortar if the mix was made without any modern pozzolanic additions, or whether to add pozzolocin in order to make the mortar behave with greater strength. In the end they used the pozzolanic addition of a zeolithic tuff as this would provide a more durable mortar which met better the preservation and longevity principles of the restorations.

This is a common dilemma for conservation of ancient mortars as the chemical components are only an outcome of the mortar as a whole mixture and cannot always be traced back to the exact material component available on site originally so there is only a best guess using the combined information from mineralogists and petrologists. The restorations made on site used the new mortar.

The research has mostly been disseminated at a scientific level although visitors do ask about it on occasion. The experiments were first conducted in the lab then undertaken on site. The mortar has only been on site for two years and as mortars gain strength over time, in the future it is planned to take new samples from the new mortar to make a direct comparison with the ancient mortar. This additional phase of experiments may suggest further refinements and is a good example of the longevity of some of the experimental work necessary to understand fully the roman construction processes and skills.

The third strand of experiments at Viminacium was focused on cremation structures and arose directly from the archaeological evidence (Ilić *et al.* 2014, 127-134; Tapavicki-Ilic & Mrdic, 2015). A single cremation experiment using an animal carcass was planned to demonstrate the viability of the hypothesis that the cremations could occur above the pits. The condition of the bone allowed the time and temperature to be known and different accelerators of olive oil and pork fat were tested but with no difference observed. The experiment demonstrated that the larger pit features could once have had the cremation occurring directly over them with the remains reducing to the approximate size of the archaeological cremations deposits. Here the object biography approach allows the burial context of the pit and burnt debris to be interpreted as a single sharply punctuated event in the life cycle of both the deceased and the formation of a funeral pyre and burial rite together.

Hunebedcentrum

The Hunebedcentrum Centre (Netherlands) has in recent years developed a completely new set of buildings themed on different periods. For each structure there is an information board nearby which identifies the archaeological site that has formed the basis of the full scale model. The buildings highlight subtle differences in design between the different periods and there is also a clear plan for making appropriate furniture and artefacts to go with them (Figure 1.4). As the centre develops a community of volunteers to staff the houses and make the objects, the buildings enter a new phase of life. The life cycle awareness ensures that maintenance issues are a part of future plans. In addition, they have made use of modern technology to take 3D scans of the new buildings. As the buildings begin to change, are repaired or altered, the 3D scans can be repeated as a set of records of the buildings, allowing direct comparisons (Klompmaker 2014a & b).

Foteviken

Foteviken (Sweden) also has a strong modern community. The buildings are all different and form a jumble of small streets and alleys which give the atmosphere of a village (Figure 1.5). As the houses face storms and are periodically lived in repairs are done as needed. Due to the close relationship of buildings and individuals they have taken a unique approach. The houses are given notional ownership with the owner taking responsibility for the cleaning and many other small tasks, including maintenance of the building, which enables the houses to function well. Furthermore, the notional ownership means that some houses can even be inherited.

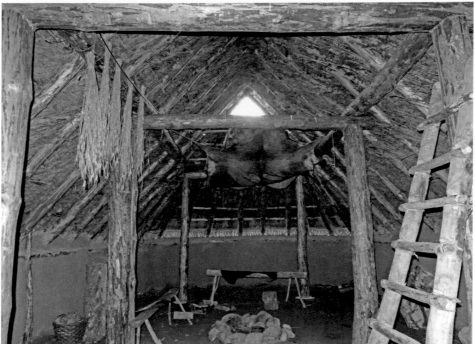

Figure 1.4: One of the new houses at Hunebedcentrum (above) and the interior of one of the furnished buildings (below). Source: Linda Hurcombe.

Figure 1.5: One of the many streets at Foteviken.

Figure 1.6: The clay roof tops of Calafell with the collapsed roof in the background.
Source: Linda Hurcombe.

Calafell

Each of the AOAMs in the OpenArch partnership have to work with different building traditions. At Calafell (Spain), on the shores of the Mediterranean, there are buildings with stone and clay walls, the rooves are flat and are supported by ceiling beams and rows of big cane *Arundo donax* which grows locally. They have experimented with different building techniques and systems for the rooves. Figure 1.6 shows a variety of rooves and the small area where one roof has been allowed to collapse as part of their investigations into how such rooves work.

St. Fagans

A contrasting case study of the complex object biography issue of structures is provided by St Fagans, National Museum of Wales (UK). Over the five years of the OpenArch project the first set of Iron Age houses at St Fagans have been pulled down and a new building to represent this period has been erected on a different part of the site. Both these experiences have featured strongly in all discussions on the management issues of reconstructed buildings (Jakobsen and Burrow 2015). The new buildings learn from the experiences of the old buildings. The well-illustrated extensive overview written by Burrow (2015) is one of the clearest reports on the object biography of structures and provides a wealth of life cycle information over a twenty-year period.

The old buildings had traditional reed thatch and were part of a set of buildings in which Peter Reynolds played a major role. OpenArch discussions have suggested that his experiences at Butser and influences on other roundhouse buildings amounts to a 'building tradition' or 'community of practice' within archaeological roundhouse reconstructions. In the case of the St Fagans houses there was some levelling of the site when they were originally built but, as the silting process occurs over a long timescale, and with many staff changes taking place, this was 'forgotten' over time and led to groundwater problems. There were other issues with the first set of buildings such as smoke not being drawn out of a building well and the deterioration of the thick *Phragmites* roof due to the houses being overshadowed by trees which reduced the wind and slowed the drying out of wet thatch, which added to problems caused by leaf debris.

In particular, the new Bryn Eryr building stays faithful to being a full scale model of an archaeological groundplan, but was selected partly because the two houses were close enough in ground plan to be joined to one another. This enabled some of the modern requirements of two access routes suitable for wheelchair access to be facilitated without compromising the archaeological groundplan. In keeping with most archaeological reconstruction buildings, the above ground evidence was less direct and reasoned assumptions were made. Here though Burrow and colleagues forged a new path by using different material for the roof: spelt. The story of the planting of the crop and its eventual harvest, threshing and storage before being able to be used for thatch gives a new dimension to experimental reconstructions and forms another OpenArch example of construction as performance, in this case both for the visitor and with the visitors' help (Figure 1.7). The thatch is also applied using two techniques and it will be the subject of ongoing observation and

Figure 1.7: (Top) A reaper binder cutting spelt to be used as thatch. (bottom) Bryn Eryr partially thatched with spelt. Source: Steve Burrow.

reports on maintenance issues. This object biography approach where the phases of the life cycle of a building are recognised and the biographical contextualisation of this particular building is so clearly outlined, is already making the Bryn Eryr house a stand out example of a modern approach to archaeological reconstruction buildings at AOAMs. The public as well as volunteers have helped move the thatch as well as participated in its harvest and preparation and visitors have seen the phases of work as part of an ongoing narrative about the building's biography.

Though the completed double house can now be 'staged' as an educational area and as a reconstructed interior complete with furniture and tools drawing on the archaeological evidence, the whole is an integrated story with time-depth. Both aspects can aid the communication to the visitor of the dialogue with science and also the value of the building to archaeological research contributing a different kind of experiment. If short reports and updates continue to provide the ongoing story, this building will not have 'forgotten' elements and its value to science and to public presentation will be considerable.

These reflections have contributed substantially to debates and benefitted from discussions within OpenArch on the kinds of new thinking that could go into newly-designed ancient buildings.

Bring structures to life with an object biography approach

The papers in the volume are aligned with the object biography approach. The organisation follows the path of the life cycle and draws out issues at each stage.

Brunning tackles the experiment and experience dichotomy of planning and executing a project. He focuses on the lessons learnt over 25 years from maintaining structures such as roundhouses, logboats and trackways and how these informed the planning of new reconstructions. Included in the discussion are the compromises that have to be made in relation to health and safety and the public interaction with the reconstructions. The introduction has outlined the way in which putting up structures is underpinned by ethnographic and craft traditions and that these skills and traditions are increasingly rare. Caruso and Speciale offer a key example of the way in which these rare skills can inform our understanding of aspects of the archaeological record. The 'living memory' provides a useful and timely piece of research in its own right as well as offering this ethnographic contribution to the experiment, experience and ethnography links of assembling materials and skills to make a building. The different elements all need to work into a composite structure.

Thinking through structures presents four very different articles in which each contributes in a different way towards extending ideas about structures beyond the better-known houses. Hurcombe and Emmerich Kamper emphasise the perishable elements of structures and present the diversity of plant and animal resources which can contribute as rooves, doors and walls to substantial but archaeologically ephemeral buildings, as well as form short-lived structures. The longevity of materials in the soil should not prevent archaeologists considering the importance of the 'missing majority'. They make the point that storage areas and space for drying materials can be important both within a building and outside as extra storage or drying or working spaces. Cunningham's article takes this further still by focussing on the structures built for food storage. In temperate regions with marked seasonal resources ethnographic evidence suggests a range of potential solutions. The need for stored food can vary from a safety-net in hard times to being part of an annual round of activity. As storage, both in pits and above ground, makes an important contribution to the success of any community, actively considering storage and the structures associated with this need enriches the way archaeologists think about structures and sites.

Many Archaeological Open-Air Museums (AOAMs) feature boats and these present special challenges. In this volume they are considered as another variation in the 'structures' category. Hurcombe and Cumby present some of their collaborative projects. Cumby offers the skills and insights of a shipwright on archaeological and present day issues of building and maintaining boats. The range of experiments and experiences offers a chance to consider the variety of materials used and the composite nature of some boats such as the full-scale replica of a Bronze Age boat built with stitches of yew withies – an example of a skill which had to be relearnt in the present day. The final contribution to this section is a different kind of missing skill relating to structures. Birch tar has to be distilled and in preceramic periods this has to be achieved by some form of structure. The archaeological evidence exists, but it is in the form of the product not the structure which allowed the distillation process to work. Pfeifer and Claußen present two structures which have allowed birch tar to be extracted. In both cases the structures are small, short-lived, and likely to prove difficult for archaeologists to identify, but these experiments offer up ideas for the interpretation and recognition of these essential structures.

The papers themed on the construction phase offer five different experiences of large buildings and furnace structures. Nieminen presents her experiences of learning to thatch as part of house building activites in Kierikki Stone Age Village (Finland), with a clear sense of reflection on the compromises and learning aspects of thatching. This contrasts with Lobisser's discussion of wood working techniques within the reconstruction of a massive timber structure from the Bronze Age Terramara culture at Parco Montale in Northern Italy. Karjalainen and Vattulainen, and Cañamero, Gutiérrez and Vallès similary offer contrasts. The latter use furnace structures for experiments in making and working with iron focused on Celtic Iberian iron practice. Whereas the former try to understand the slab furnaces of the Finnish Iron Age which uses bog iron and the authors assess whether such structures are reusable. Process and product are both part of the assessment of the structures. In this section the experiment and experiences are intertwined with skills being developed alongside the scientific aspects of the projects. Van Gijn and Pomstra offer another approach to construction. A Neolithic style house is built using a range of period-relevant tools with the function history of each individual tool documented as part of a joint experiment.

In many cases the maintenance of the building is a crucial factor in its longevity. Strategies for dealing with repairs and storm damage in a timely way prevent more rapid deterioration. In all cases and throughout the OpenArch experience the role of a fire to drive off damp has been emphasised. The air quality issues of gas and particles caused by the fire are balanced against the lack of fire allowing cold and damp conditions and the growth of mould. Considering living standards within structures offer insights and opens up new questions especially as the structures in AOAMs are also workplaces for staff and volunteers with health and safety responsibilities in the modern world. Christensen tests the indoor environment in a reconstructed Viking Age houses (Denmark) during the winter to offer a different view on how elements such as hearth and roof work together in a living environment. Ambient heat and overnight conditions are as important as day time ones. Muurimäki's experiences are a contrast as they are the result of many years of experimentation in the construction and roof design of buildings relevant to Finland's archaeological past. The long-term nature of Muurimäki's reflections adds to archaeological understanding alongside the targeted scientific data collection of Christensen's work.

The decline of structures features another highly contrasting pair of articles. Bradley takes a whole biography approach to his reconstruction of a North American ancestral Pueblo style structure. As a subterranean structure, the access routes, fall of light, the wall and roof deterioration are all covered. All these factors offer potential insights into the way archaeologists have to decide whether the evidence is due to deliberate acts or abandonment, and the way the building may take on other roles over time is part of the object biography approach to understanding them and their social context. Sørensen's article builds on these themes using the case study of the deterioration and collapse of roundhouses. The failure of the roof by 'sitting down' i.e. slumping and twisting, meant the building switched use, not that it died. In all her discussions the building is personified making 'the day the house sat down' a fitting closing chapter for the object biography approach to the life cycle of structures.

Bibliography

Arnold, B. 1990. *Cortaillod-Est et les villages du lac de Neuchâtel au Bronze final: Archéologie Neuchâteloise 6*, Sainte Blaise: Ed. du Ruau.

Beck, A.S. 2011.Working in the borderland of experimental archaeology: on theoretical perspectives in recent experimental work. In Petersson, B. and Narmo, L.E. (eds.) *Experimental Archaeology: between enlightenment and experience*. Acta Archaeologica Lundensia Series 8:62: Lund University: Norway. pp. 167-194.

Bell, M., Fowler, M.J. & Hillson, S.W. 1996. *The Experimental Earthwork Project, 1960-1992*. Council for British Archaeology: York.

Burrow, S. 2015. From Celtic village to Iron Age Farmstead: Lessons learnt from twenty years of building, maintaining and presenting Iron Age roundhouses at St Fagans National History Museum. *Exarc Journal Digest 2*: 6-11. (Full article available at http://journal.exarc.net/issue-2015-4/aoam/celtic-village-iron-age-farmstead-lessons-learnt-twenty-years-building-maintaining-and-presenting).

Coles, B.J. 1992. *The wetland revolution in prehistory*. The Prehistoric Society and WARP: Southampton.

Cunningham, P., Heeb, J. and Paardekooper, R. (eds.) 2008. *Experiencing archaeology by experiment*. Oxbow Books: Oxford.

Dant, T. 2001. *Fruitbox/toolbox: biography and objects. Auto/Biography 9 (1 & 2)*:11-20.

Demant, I. 2009. Principles for reconstruction of costumes and archaeological textiles. In Alfaro, C., Tellénbach, M. and Ferrero, R. (eds.) *Textiles y Museologia: Aspects of study, analysis and exhibition of ancient textiles and textile tools. Clothing and textiles, new perspectives on textiles in the Roman Empire*. pp. 143-153.

Drury, P.J. 1982. *Structural reconstruction: approaches to the interpretation of excavated remains of buildings*. BAR British Series 110: Oxford.

Gosden, C. and Marshall, Y. 1999. The cultural biography of objects. *World Archaeology 31(2)*: 169-178.

Gómez Gutiérrez, M. 2015. *Archaeological Open-Air Museums and the dialogue with the museum community*. OpenArch (handbook available at http://openarch.eu/work-packages/products/wp6-publication-aoams-and-dialogue-museum-community).

Hurcombe, L. 2004. Experimental Archaeology, in Renfrew C. and Bahn, P. (eds.) *Archaeology: The Key Concepts*, London: Routledge. pp. 110-115.

Hurcombe, L. 2007. *Archaeological Artefacts as Material Culture*. London: Routledge.

Ilić, O., Tapavički-Ilić, M., Ćirić, Đ. 2014. The OpenArch Project: archaeological experiment of planting grapevine in Viminacium. *Archaeology and Science 9*:127-134.

Ilić, O., and Nikolić, N. 2015. Archaeological Park Viminacium: Cultural-historical heritage in the Jubilee year of Christianity. *Archaeology and Science 10*: 231-244.

Jakobsen, B. and Burrow, S. 2015. *Handbook: Management of Open-Air Museums*. OpenArch: (Handbook available at http://openarch.eu/work-packages/products/management-open-air-museums).

Jewell, P.A. (ed.) 1963. *The experimental earthwork on Overton Down, Wiltshire 1960*. The British Association for the Advancement of Science: London.

Kelm, R. 2015. The Stone Age Park Dithmarschen (Steinzeitpark Dithmarschen) – concepts and development of a visitor orientated educational centre for sustainable development. In Kelm, R. (ed.) *Archaeology and Crafts: experiences and experiments of traditional skills and handicrafts in archaeological open-air museums in Europe*. Proceedings of the VI. OpenArch Conference in Albersdorf, Germany, 23-37 September 2013. Husum. pp. 13-25.

Kelm, R. (ed.) 2015. *Archaeology and Crafts: experiences and experiments of traditional skills and handicrafts in archaeological open-air museums in Europe*. Proceedings of the VI. OpenArch Conference in Albersdorf, Germany, 23-37 September 2013. Husum.

Kelterborn, P. 2005. *Principles of experimental research in archaeology*. euroREA 2: 120-122.

Klompmaker, H. 2014a. *Reconstruction/Building an Iron Age house*. (http://OpenArch.eu/work-packages/activities/reconstructionbuilding-iron-age-house).

Klompmaker, H. 2014b. *Reconstruction/Building an Bronze Age house*. (http://OpenArch.eu/work-packages/activities/reconstructionbuilding-bronze-age-house).

Nikolić, E. 2013. Contribution to the study of Roman architecture in Vimincium construction materials and building techniques, *Archaeology and Science 8*: 21-48.

Nikolić, E., Anđelković, J., and Rogić, D. 2011. Archaeological Parks as production of emotional design: Design organisation of a park based on the exploration of visitors' emotions. *Archaeology and Sciences 6*: 259-270.

Nikolić, E. and Bogdanović, I. 2012. Study of mortar from the Viminacium amphitheater as the basis for its future conservation and restoration. *Archaeology in Serbia: Projects Archaeological Institute* pp. 58-61.

Nikolić, E. and Bogdanović, I. 2012. Proučavanje maltera iz viminacijumskog amfiteatra kao osnova za njegovu buduću konzervaciju i restauraciju / Viminacium Amphitheatre Mortar Research as a Basis for its Conservation and Restoration. In V. Bikić, S. Golubović, D. Antonivić (eds.). *Arheološki institut Godišnjak*, 2011. godina. Beograd: Arheološki institut, 2012, pp. 58-61.

Nikolić, E., Rogić, D., and Milovanović, 2015. Role of brick in hydraulicity of Viminacium mortars: Decorative mortars of thermae. *Archaeology and Science 10*: 71-92.

Outram, A. 2008. Introduction to experimental archaeology. *World Archaeology 40:1*: 1-6.

Paardekopper, R. 2012. *The value of an Archaeological Open-Air Museum is in its use: understanding Archaeological Open-Air Museum and their visitors.* Sidestone Press: Leiden.

Petersson, B. and Narmo, L.E. (eds.) 2011. *Experimental Archaeology: between enlightenment and experience.* Acta Archaeologica Lundensia Series 8:62: Lund University: Sweden.

Rasmussen, M. 2007. *Iron Age Houses in flames: Testing house reconstructions at Lejre.* Studies in technology and Culture 3: Lejre.

Rasmussen, M. 2011. Under the same roof: experimental research and interpretation with examples from the construction of house models. In Petersson, B. and Narmo, L.E. (eds.) *Experimental Archaeology: between enlightenment and experience.* Acta Archaeologica Lundensia Series 8:62: Lund University: Sweden. pp. 167-167.

Reynolds, P.J. 1999. The nature of experiment. In archaeology Harding, A.F. (ed.) *Experiment and design: archaeological studies in Honour of John Coles.* Oxbow Books: Oxford. pp. 156-162.

Schmidt, M. 2000. Fake! Haus-und Umweltrekonstruktionen inarchäologischen Freilichtmuseen. In Kelm, R. (ed.) *Vom Pfostenloch zum Steinzeithaus. Archäologische Forschung und rekonstruktion jungsteinzeitlicher Haus-und Siedlungsbefunde im Nordwestlichen Mitteleuropa.* Heide: Ärchaeologisch-Ökologisch Zentrum Albersdorf. pp. 169-177.

Schöbel, G. 2004. On the responsibility of accurately interpresting prehistoric life in full scale. *EuroREA* 1:150-160.

Tapavicki-Ilic, M. and Mrdic, N. 2015. Roman burial rite in Viminacium: the latest discovery. In Zerbini, L. (ed.) *Culti e religiostià nelle province danubiane, Atti del II Convegno Internazonale Ferrara 20-22 Novembre 2013*, Bologna: pp. 483-495.

Van de Noort, R., Cumby, B., Blue, L., Harding, A., Hurcombe, L., Hansen, T.M., Wetherelt, A., Wittamore, J. and Wyke, A. 2014. Morgawr: an experimental Bronze Age-type sewn-plank craft based on the Ferriby boats. *International Journal of Nautical Archaeology* 43 (2): 292-313.

Part One

Planning structures

Hands on Heritage

Experimental and experiential archaeology in the Avalon Marshes, Somerset, UK

Richard Brunning

Introduction

The Avalon Marshes area is a floodplain in the central Brue west of Glastonbury in Somerset (UK), composed of a mixture of wet grassland, arable and a mosaic of reedbeds and wet woodland. Deep Holocene peat deposits there have preserved an internationally important collection of prehistoric organic objects and structures. This remarkable preservation, coupled with the public invisibility of the monuments themselves, has stimulated the reconstruction of wooden trackways, dugout canoes and Iron Age roundhouses over the last 25 years. None of this work qualifies as pure experimental archaeology although very valuable insights have been gained into the operation and maintenance of the original structures. The true value of the reconstructions lies in the opportunities they have given to archaeologists, the general public and school groups to gain intimate 'hands on' experience of prehistoric life. The direct interaction of over 200,000 people with the different reconstructions, not to mention the numerous times that they have been used in television programmes, suggests that there is great public benefit to be gained from such projects. Several new reconstructions are planned over the next two years that will hopefully build on the lessons learnt to provide both experiential and experimental archaeology over the next two decades.

The archaeology of the marshes

The deep deposits of Holocene peat in the central Brue valley have been exploited for fuel since the Roman period. Archaeological discoveries have been recorded from these peat excavations from the mid 19th century onwards (Stradling 1849 and 1851). The waterlogged peat excluded oxygen and thus allowed the preservation of organic materials, especially wood, for thousands of years. Both individual artefacts and wooden structures have been discovered and excavated by a series of archaeologists beginning with John Morland, Arthur Bulleid and Harold St George Gray in the late 19th and early 20th century, Sir Harry Godwin in the 1930s to 1960s and, most productively, the Somerset Levels Project run by John and Bryony Coles between 1973 and 1989.

The first reported discovery was a dugout canoe known as 'Squire Phippen's Big Ship' (Stradling 1849, 52). Since then four other canoes have been found in the area, one of which has been dated to the Iron Age (Godwin 1967) and another is from the same period as it was discovered in the foundations of Glastonbury Lake Village (Bulleid and Gray 1911, 114 and 333).

The most numerous structures are the prehistoric wooden trackways that allowed communication between the islands of hard geology in the valley and from those islands to the surrounding 'dryland' on the Polden hills and Wedmore. Over 43 trackways have been investigated, ranging in date from the early Neolithic to the early Iron Age (Bulleid 1933, Godwin 1960, Coles and Coles 1986). The earliest are the Post and Sweet Tracks that were constructed over the same route in 3838 BC and 3807/6 BC respectively. These are the oldest wooden trackways known from the UK and the Sweet Track is also the oldest religious monument in the country as, in addition to its role as a communication route, it was also the focus for the votive deposition of a wide range of artefacts including pottery, flint, stone axes, and wooden objects including bowls, stirrers, pins, beaters, a possible bow and a toy axe.

Figure 2.1:
Reconstruction of
the Sweet Track by
E. Mortlemans.

The Sweet Track (Figure 2.1) provides the most complete representation of Neolithic material culture of any archaeological site in the UK. For the Iron Age, the famous 'lake villages' of Meare and Glastonbury are the best preserved later prehistoric settlements in the country and have produced the most complete representation material culture from that period (Bulleid and Gray 1911 and 1917, Gray and Bulleid 1953, Gray 1966, Coles 1987, Coles, Coles and Morgan 1988 and Coles and Minnitt 1995).

Although the Avalon Marshes area has produced some internationally important archaeological discoveries there is very little for the general public to see on the ground. The excavated remains have been conserved and are either in store or on display in local museums and the sites still *in situ* are covered by peat. For this reason there has been a long tradition of creating reconstructions of some of the structures for the public to experience. This began with the Somerset Levels Project that made reconstructions of some of the prehistoric trackways alongside archaeology displays in a local garden centre and in the nearby Shapwick Heath National Nature Reserve. The reserve had the advantage of containing extensive areas of wetland vegetation that closely correspond to prehistoric environments, specifically the reedswamp of the early Neolithic and the wet fen woodland of the later Neolithic.

Trackways

Reconstructions of brushwood, corduroy (logs laid edge to edge), hurdle and plank trackways have been built for the public to walk on in the Avalon Marshes area since the 1980s, generally corresponding quite closely to the archaeological evidence, although usually not in their appropriate wetland setting. The exceptions are two reconstructions of the Sweet Track, both prompted by the needs of filmmakers. In 1983 a short (10 m) stretch was built by the Somerset Levels Project in an old peat cutting (Coles and Orme 1984a) and in 1997 the Somerset County Council Heritage Service made a 30 m length in a reedbed on Shapwick Heath NNR (Figure 2.2) that closely resembled the environment that the original Neolithic trackway traversed (Coles and Brunning 2009). The latter used materials of the right size, species and method of manufacture as the original trackway. The use of narrow, thin radially split planks for the walkway allowed a true appreciation of the inherent instability of the structure, and the efficacy of the different methods of stabilising it could be tested.

By using a combination of the stratagems recorded from the original build, a reliable walking surface could be achieved. Notching the planks so that they fitted more snugly in their 'V' shaped cradles of angled posts helped prevent sudden twisting of the walkway surface, as did small roundwood posts driven obliquely through mortise holes in the planks. Vertical posts acting as props under the plank ends, helped prevent that end depressing and the opposing end flying up when walked on. Such tinkering with the basic design helped to create a useable walkway surface that was little more than the width of a foot wide. It was discovered that two people could pass each other, even on the narrowest planks, if a degree of intimacy was permitted. Perhaps this may have added to the attraction of the original structure?

Figure 2.2: 1997 reconstruction of the Sweet Track in a reedbed in Shapwick Heath NNR. Source: Richard Brunning.

Although the 1997 trackway was not in constant use, the experiment permitted a reasonably reliable estimate of the lifespan of the structural components to be determined. The original raised walkway was supported by pairs of hazel roundwood stakes forming 'V' shaped cradles for the split planks of the walkway surface. After three years significant decay had taken place on the hazel stakes of the reconstruction at the interface between the air and water and after four years they began to break when the trackway was used. If the trackway had been in daily use, all the roundwood stakes would have required replacing after this period of time. Dendrochronological analysis has shown that planks were added to the original trackway in 3800 BC, six years after its creation (Hillam *et al.* 1990). This means that at least one replacement of roundwood posts was required during that period.

Suction prevented the removal of the broken roundwood posts on the reconstruction and this would probably also have been the case with the original, so all the stakes used in the life of the structure should have been visible during the excavations. Examination of the published plans (Coles *et al.* 1973; Coles and Orme 1976, 1979, 1984b) showed enough stakes to support the idea of one wholesale replacement, but not enough for two. This suggests that the trackway had an active life of seven to eight years as any longer period would have required a second replacement. The trackway built in 3806 BC therefore probably underwent wholesale repair in 3803 BC or 3802 BC, had some replacement planks added in 3800 BC and must have gone out of use by 3798 BC.

When left unused, the reconstruction in the reedbed disappeared in less than three months, to the extent that it was almost impossible to find among the reeds, even though its exact location was known. The end of the original structure may have been as rapid. An active use of only eight years may seem to be very short but parallels can be seen in Neolithic settlements on the continent that have similar dendrochronological precision. Hornstaad-Hornle 1A (Bodensee, Germany) for example, was built in 3917 BC, but abandoned by around 3904 BC (Billamboz 2006) and Egolzwil (Wauwilersee, Switzerland) lasted only twelve years, with three of the seven houses being rebuilt after just six years (Coles and Coles 1989, 105).

The famous reconstruction painting of the Sweet Track by Edward Mortlemans (Figure 2.1) shows a group of Neolithic pedestrians separated by a wide space from the reed beds on either side, the reeds having been cut back from the edge. Building the 1997 replica in a similar environment led to the appreciation that, unless frequently cut, over the 2 km length of the track, the reeds would inevitably have grown right up to the track, creating a narrow tunnel that would have risen above head height in summer. This suggests that the theorised use of the trackway for hunting can be discounted, as the only visible targets would have been fleeting glimpses of birds flying overhead. Instead the route would have felt very enclosed, with the only long views being the trackway ahead and behind and the sky above. Even walking the short (30 m) replica felt very strange, especially when the wind was blowing noisily through the reeds.

The reconstruction provides some support to authors who have argued for the spiritual and ritual aspects of the trackway and its associated artefacts (Bond 2004; Van de Noort and O'Sullivan 2006). The large quantity of artefacts found beside the Sweet Track stands in stark contrast to the overwhelming majority of prehistoric wooden paths in the UK that are devoid of any artefactual associations (Brunning 2007, 197-200). This, combined with the high status of some objects such as the jadeite axe and the finer pottery, strongly suggest that ritual deposition was carried out beside the monument.

Canoes

In 1997 a replica Iron Age canoe was made at the Peat Moors Centre near Shapwick in the centre of the Brue valley. The canoe was based on a vessel that had been discovered nearby in 1906 during ditch clearing (Figure 2.3; Godwin 1967). The new version of the Shapwick canoe was made using axes and adzes that were similar in design to Iron Age tools. However, the tools were modern steel rather than iron and the log itself was not a natural English oak but was instead a part Turkey Oak cross. This made the wood very hard to work by hand but had the overwhelming advantage of being a free gift.

As an archaeological experiment, the canoe build had some positive results. The original had a series of small augured holes in its base. The experimental build proved that these holes were vital during the construction for gauging the thickness of the timber as the inside of the vessel was being hollowed out. As work progressed a stick could be poked through the hole to measure the thickness of the remaining timber and ensure that just the right amount was left. Any estimate of the length of time needed to make such a canoe was rendered meaningless by the inexperience of

Figure 2.3: The discovery of the Shapwick canoe in 1906. Source: Richard Brunning.

the modern builders, the complication of the Turkey Oak cross, and the fact that the original tree was not felled by hand. Once completed however, the finished vessel demonstrated that it was perfectly capable of carrying four adults (or ten children) and that one advantage of having two sloping punt-like ends, was that the direction of the canoe could be speedily reversed by the paddlers turning about rather then the whole vessel. This must have been an advantage in the narrow channels that probably existed in the extensive reed beds and salt marshes of the area in the Iron Age. On land it proved relatively easy to move the heavy canoe around over short distance using rollers and levers. Any significant portage would have been a major undertaking however.

The canoe was last used in 2013, sixteen years after its initial construction, and with a few minor repairs it should be serviceable for many more. This demonstrates that even with far from perfect care and maintenance, the considerable effort involved in the initial creation is vastly repaid by the longevity of the finished vessel. Gradual drying out has inevitably opened up some cracks. Many of these can be plugged and if the ones at one end become too troublesome, the end could be cut short and a transom board fitted. Such transoms are a common feature of dugout canoes in the UK but they are usually assumed to be original features, perhaps due to the need to remove an end with irreparable 'shakes' (cracks) from felling at the butt end of the log. The Shapwick canoe replica may eventually suggest that repairs during the life of the vessel could also be a possible reason for transom creation.

Figure 2.4: The original roundhouse at the Peat Moors Centre. Source: Richard Brunning.

Thousands of people saw the canoe during its construction but very few have experienced paddling it. That is probably the greatest failure of the project, as the asset did not achieve its potential for 'experiential archaeology' due to the lack of a suitable water body where it could be routinely used. In 2006 one memorable event was a mass gathering of the descendants of the four people in the photo of the original discovery of the vessel in 1906 (Figure 2.3), who posed for a new photograph beside the replica after the celebration. The replica thus played its part for a group of people reaffirming their intimate connection to a cherished local archaeological discovery.

Roundhouses

A total of three roundhouses have been built at the Peat Moors Centre in Shapwick, all of them based on the foundation plans from Glastonbury Lake Village. The first one was built in 1992 to celebrate the centenary of Bulleid's discovery of the Lake Village in 1892 (Figure 2.4), the second in the following year and the third a few years later. For over twenty years the roundhouses played a vital part in the educational role of the centre, both entrancing the general public with their unfamiliar atmosphere and also forming a backdrop and prop for school visits. Over that period between 200,000 and 250,000 people visited the centre and benefited from seeing, touching, feeling and smelling the roundhouse. They made an impression on many people and numerous requests for overnight stays and weddings had to be politely refused over the years.

In terms of experimental archaeology the roundhouses are perhaps of less value. They were made of similar materials to the original buildings and to the same ground plan, but there was very little archaeological evidence for what was above ground level. The roundhouses followed much of the modern perceived wisdom for replica roundhouses in the British Isles that can probably be traced back to the beginnings of Butser Ancient Farm. In retrospect, more radical design changes could have been experimented with, such as using considerably less thatch or varying the roofing material or installing windows with shutters. The one minor alteration that did appear in the third roundhouse was a smoke vent high above the doorway. This does help to draw smoke out of the building at a higher level than in the previous roundhouses where the top of the door often provided the base level for the smoke. If well seasoned wood had always been available, the smoke problem would have been considerably less and this was probably the case in the Iron Age. The position of the doorway may also have an effect, as the door of the third roundhouse faces into the prevailing westerly wind, which may swirl the smoke around. Unfortunately no consistent experiments were made when all three roundhouses were extant. The second roundhouse felt the lightest because its doorway faced south-west, while the first faced north-east, but again no comparative measurements were made. Lime washing the inside of the second roundhouse definitely gave it a lighter feel.

The first two roundhouses have both been demolished after both staying up for two decades. This may give an impression of how long such structures could last but neither building was consistently lived in and both were left unheated during the closed winter season. This may have substantially reduced the longevity of the structures, as for example, a daily smoking would have helped to prevent the activity of woodworm and would have kept the thatch drier and more resistant to decay.

Reading University have taken some samples from the floor of the initial roundhouse, along with those from many other prehistoric building reconstructions but the results are not yet known. In its death, the first roundhouse has provided an interesting experiment of what would happen if such a building were left to decay. The walls gradually decayed and collapsed, although the semi-collapsed building could safely have been used as a habitation or store. The woven roof was most resistant to decay but is now virtually flat and is rotting rapidly. Around the walls a circle of young growth has surprisingly sprung up and spread inwards, although it is uncertain if this is because the wall posts may have actually have rooted themselves (Figure 2.5). Further decay patterns will be interesting to observe and the roundhouses may prove to be better experiments in death than in life.

Future projects

A series of new archaeological reconstructions are being developed over the next two years as part of the Avalon Marshes Landscape Partnership project, a Heritage Lottery Fund scheme preserving and celebrating that area. Three buildings are being built, representing different periods and based on local archaeological evidence. A roundhouse will be created, following evidence from Glastonbury

Figure 2.5: The original roundhouse at the Peat Moors Centre a year after its collapse began. Source: Richard Brunning.

Lake Village, the dining room of a Romano-British villa is being made, complete with working hypocaust system, and a Saxon hall has been erected based on the first hall at Cheddar Palace (Rahtz 1979).

The three buildings will demonstrate the use of varying materials and building styles and will provide the setting for educational activities. It is intended that each building will be more completely and permanently furnished than was possible at the previous Peat Moors Centre. The thermal dynamics of each building will be examined and contrasted, to incorporate some experimental archaeology into their operation. The new roundhouse will have a much reduced thatch and will incorporate two shuttered windows so that some of the experimentation not incorporated into the first three roundhouses can be made in the fourth one. Smoke, light and heat experiments can then take place with the contrasting third and fourth roundhouses.

In addition to the buildings, two logboats have been made and it is intended that they would be used in occasional voyages across the wetlands of the nearby nature reserves, allowing people to experience what it may have been like to travel to and from Glastonbury Lake Village in the Iron Age. The proposed new Avalon Marshes Centre, which will be the 'home port' of the fleet, will include an area of open water where school groups and the public can have a brief experience of the canoes afloat.

A series of trackways have been built in Shapwick Heath NNR, but the brushwood, hurdle and corduroy ones have been deemed by Natural England to be too unsafe for the public to use without supervision. The public have been allowed to walk on replicas of the Meare Heath and Sweet Track plank walkways. Both these trackways have been specially modified to make them safer for the public and so will not constitute proper archaeological experiments. However, their appearance will be similar to the originals and and it is now possible for the public to walk in the footsteps of their ancestors along a replica of the Sweet Track through a reed bed on exactly the same line as the original structure 5,821 years earlier. A poor experiment, but hopefully a marvellous experience.

Bibliography

Billamboz, A. 2006. Dendroarchäologische Untersuchungen in den neolithischen Ufersiedlungen von Hornstaad-Hörnle. In Stuttgart, R.P. (ed.) *Landesamt für Denkmalpflege (Hrsg.), Siedlungsarchäologie im Alpenvorland IX. Forsch. u. Ber. Vor u. Frühgesch*. Baden Württemberg 98: Stuttgart. pp. 297-359.

Bond, C.J. 2004. The Sweet Track, Somerset: a place mediating culture and spirituality? In T. Insoll (ed.) *Belief in the Past. The Proceedings of the Manchester Conference on Archaeology and Religion*. BAR British Series 212: Oxford. pp. 37-50.

Brunning, R. 2007. *Structural Wood in Prehistoric England and Wales*. Unpublished PhD thesis, University of Exeter.

Bulleid, A. 1933. Ancient trackways in Meare Heath, Somerset. *Proc. Somerset Archaeology and Nat. Hist. Soc.*, 79: 19-29.

Bulleid, A. and Gray, H.St.G. 1911. *The Glastonbury Lake Village Volume 1*. Glastonbury.

Bulleid, A. and Gray, H.St.G. 1917. *The Glastonbury Lake Village Volume 2*. Glastonbury.

Bulleid, A. and Gray, H.St.G. 1948. *The Meare Lake Village Volume 1*. Glastonbury.

Coles, B.J. and Coles, J.M. 1986. *Sweet Track to Glastonbury: The Somerset Levels in Prehistory*. Thames and Hudson. London.

Coles, J.M. 1987. Meare Village East, the excavations of A. Bulleid and H. St. George Gray 1932-1956. *Somerset Levels Papers* 13.

Coles, B. and Brunning, R. 2009. Following the Sweet Track. In G. Cooney, K. Becker, J. Coles, M. Ryan and S. Sievers (eds.). *Relics of Old Decency: archaeological studies in later prehistory*. Wordwell: Dublin. pp. 25-37.

Coles, J.M. and Coles, B.J. 1989. *People of the Wetlands: Bogs, Bodies and Lake-Dwellers*. Thames and Hudson: London.

Coles, J.M., Coles B.J. and Morgan, R.A. 1988. Excavations at the Glastonbury Lake Village 1984. *Somerset Levels Papers* 14: 57-62.

Coles, J.M., Hibbert, F.A. and Orme, B.J. 1973. Prehistoric roads and tracks in Somerset, England 3. The Sweet Track. *Proc. Prehistoric. Soc.* 39: 256-293.

Coles, J.M. and Orme, B.J. 1976. The Sweet Track, Railway Site. *Somerset Levels Papers* 2: 34-65.

Coles, J.M. and Orme, B.J. 1979. The Sweet Track, Drove Site. *Somerset Levels Papers* 5: 43-64.

Coles, J.M. and Orme, B.J. 1984a. A reconstruction of the Sweet Track. *Somerset Levels Papers* 10: 107-109.

Coles, J.M. and Orme, B.J. 1984b. Ten excavations along the Sweet Track (3200 bc). *Somerset Levels Papers* 10: 5-45.

Coles, J.M. and Minnitt, S. 1995. *Industrious and fairly civilised: The Glastonbury lake Village.* Somerset Levels Project and Somerset County Museum Service: Exeter.

Godwin, H. 1960. Prehistoric wooden trackways of the Somerset Levels: their construction, age and relation to climate change. *Proc. Prehistoric Soc.* 26: 1-36.

Godwin, H. 1967. Discoveries in the peat near Shapwick Station, Somerset. *Proc. Somerset Archaeological and Natural History Society* 111: 20-23.

Gray, H.St.G. and Bulleid, A. 1953. *The Meare Lake Village Volume 2.* Glastonbury.

Gray, H.St.G. 1966. *The Meare Lake Village Volume 3.* Glastonbury.

Hillam, J., Groves, C.M., Brown, D.M., Baillie, M.G.L., Coles, J.M. and Coles, B.J. 1990 Dendrochronology of the English Neolithic. *Antiquity* 64: 210-219.

Rahtz, P. 1979. *The Saxon and Medieval palaces at Cheddar.* BAR British Series 56. British Archaeological Papers: Oxford.

Stradling, W. 1849. The turbaries between Glaston and the Sea. *Proc. Somerset Archaeology and Nat. Hist. Soc.* 1, pt ii: 48-62.

Stradling, W. 1854. A young turf-bearer's find in the turbaries. *Proc. Somerset Archaeology and Nat. Hist. Soc.* 5, pt ii: 91-4.

Van de Noort, R. and O'Sullivan, A. 2006. *Rethinking Wetland Archaeology.* Duckworth. London.

"U Pagliaru"

Studies of traditional shepherd's huts and their relevance to a Bronze Age hut-rebuilding project in Sicily

Kati Caruso and Claudia Speciale

Introduction

The study of traditional shepherd's huts is embedded into an ongoing experimental rebuilding project headed by a new association *ArchaeoGreen*. The aim of the project was to reconstruct a Bronze Age hut during September and October 2013. Traditional buildings are an incredible ethnographic source in Southern Italy, especially in Sicily where shepherds practices were, until recently, very developed and conservative (Germanà 1999; Lima 1984, 97-108; Rubino 1921).

The study of vernacular architecture, together with the consultation and practical help of some traditional builders was extremely helpful in the hut rebuilding process. A combination of archaeological and ethnographic studies is commonly used in archaeology and all of these factors were incorporated into the plan and design of a Bronze Age hut. Taking advantage of contemporary ethnographic studies is rare but enables insights into the meaning placed upon plants; the information on the best time of year to collect and use them gives a further dimension to the life cycle approach that cannot be seen archaeologically.

Archaeological evidence

Archaeological investigation in this area has been going on for about five years, which has included excavation and archaeological landscape studies by the Arkeos Cooperative (Giannitrapani & Iannì 2014). The reconstruction is based on the archaeological remains of an early Bronze Age village site at Tornambè (Pietraperzia, Enna), central Sicily, in the Salso Valley. Hut 1 has a round plan with a diameter of 8m and the remains of a low level wall, with a maximum height of about 70 cm, constructed using different shaped dry stones – with no use of mortar. Besides a little inner wall on the Northern side, there are at least three post holes probably necessary to support the roof (Giannitrapani 2012, 50-51). The archaeological remains are similar in construction to modern *pagliaru* (shepherds shelters) that are still being constructed in parts of Sicily today.

Ethnographic evidence

The area of the Madonie mountains was considered as the same kind of buildings are spread in most of the island mountain belts; a little different only in the area of Iblei Mountains, in terms of architectural choices (Barbera *et al.* 2010; Tiralongo 2006). Madonie are a mountain range in Northern-central Sicily; the highest peak is almost 2000 m mean sea level (Figure 3.1). Most of the territory is covered by woods, garrigues (open shrubby vegetation) and pastures and pastoralism is very common (Giacomarra 2006).

The *pagliaru* (or *pagghiaru*) is a shepherd's shelter that can be occupied during some seasons or all year long. Typical features are the plan – usually square or rectangular, but they can also be round, constructed with a drystone wall and a conical thatched roof. Rectangular shaped huts tend to have a gabled roof. The height at the top is between 2.5 and 5 m. The internal spaces could be used differently, but usually there was a *jazzu*, a pallet for at least two people (Giacomarra 2006, 67-68).

The ethnographic research considered three different case studies:

1. An analysis of an abandoned structure – it was not possible to find the builder (Piano Pomieri)

2. A study of a building together with the experience of the known builder (Contrada Colombo)

3. The experience of the twins, two brothers who have been building *pagliari* for a long time (the Nicolosi twins).

Analysis of an abandoned structure

The plan of a *pagliaru* in Piano Pomieri (1425 m. MSL) (Figure 3.2) is an irregular square, almost trapezoidal, and the building is partially recessed into the ground (on the north and west sides). The door is open to the south-east. The wall is more than 70 cm in height, approximately 80-90 cm thick with the total height of the structure being 3.10 m. The door is not exactly in the middle of the side and the thickness of the walls varies. Common sandstones were used and regularly shaped on door sides, less so on inner sides, where sloping wooden poles are wedged into the wall. Probably different species of *Quercus* were used for the posts (3 m long). Long holly branches (*Ilex aquifolium*) and other shrubs easily available in the surroundings were used for the roof, along with reeds (*Phragmites australis* or *Arundo donax*), definitely relevant to lower altitude and wetter conditions. Non-vegetal materials are present too, as in many modern *pagliari*.

What can be said about its life cycle? Unfortunately not much, as the builder was not traceable. Probably this *pagliaru* was used only seasonally (maybe for the transhumance during the summer) and it was most likely that the roof at least would need to be repaired annually.

Figure 3.1: Madonie Mountains, Pizzo Carbonara, Sicily, Italy. Source: Kati Caruso and Claudia Speciale.

Figure 3.2: Pagliaru in Piano Pomieri. Source: Kati Caruso and Claudia Speciale.

A builder's view

The second case study is the *pagliaru* of Contrada Colombo (995 m. MSL) (Figure 3.3), for which there is the personal account by one of the builders (Mariano Anzaldi, 82 years old). The *pagliaru* was built at the beginning of the 80s by 6 men in about 15 days of non-continuous work and used as a temporary shelter. The choice of location and orientation were related to soil morphology and not to winds or sun exposure.

The building is recessed in the ground on the east and south sides; the drystone wall is 1.20 m high and the door is not symmetrical because the two main posts have to support the ridge beam. The total height of the structure is 2.85 m and wall thickness is about 55-60 cm, with the exception of the short side with the door where it is more than 1 m thick.

According to Mariano Anzaldi's report, after soil regularisation, the two main poles were wedged into the wall and then the ridge beam was placed on top, with a fork system; then the sloping poles (10-12 per gable) were put in place. On the rear short side, half tree trunks were used as horizontal elements; finally, the roof was completed by using reeds of different shape and diameter. The builders did not choose very accurately what kind of trees to use however, the local vegetation is composed of trees with good building potential such as oaks, ash, and chestnuts. Nevertheless an important consideration was the timing of the tree felling. Wire or *Rubus ulmifolius* was used to secure the elements – *Rubus* branches can be several

Figure 3.3: Pagliaru in c.da Colombo. Source: Kati Caruso and Claudia Speciale.

metres long. The *jazzu* was used as a seat for 5-6 people – for example in case of rain – or it was a bed for 2 or 4 people.

What can we say about its life cycle? The structure was built about 30 years ago. It was mainly used for the first 10 years with yearly maintenance, after which the *pagliaru* was abandoned at the beginning of the 90s. After 20 years of abandonment, the wall condition is almost perfect on two sides (the ground-recessed ones). On the door side, the stones are partially fallen inside, while on the northern side the stones fell outside, probably associated with the roof falling. The main poles are still standing and the roofing reeds have no evidence of decay thus the vegetal materials are well preserved after 20 years.

The area is quite protected from strong winds, but rain, snow and wet conditions did not affect very much of the *pagliaru*, that could be easily fixed in a few days. According to Mariano Anzaldi's story, it seems that the choice and the time of collecting the materials is the leading requisite in order to obtain a good structure. The third ethnographic study agreed with this and gave more detail.

The Twin's Tale

Carmelo and Micu Nicolosi are 62-years old twins (Figure 3.4) who have been building *pagliari* for other people for years. In their description of the construction of *pagliari* they used very specific vocabulary that was accurately recorded. Carmelo said the choice of the plan changed during the Middle Ages, from round to rectangular or squared because the space inside could be used better and more beds could be put inside. Actually, we considered this explanation unreliable, even if recurrent in traditional para-historical interpretations.

The twins described the whole building process. First, they made the soil preparation. The first step was the excavation of the *travata*, a channel in the soil where the first row of stones was placed. Then they erected the drystone wall that was about 1 m thick; the door was 90 cm wide and about 1.50 m high. Diagonal posts (usually oaks) were then placed on the drystone wall. Brush, reeds and finally thorny brushes (like *Genista* sp.) were layered – this last layer is to prevent animals eating the reeds. The next step was the placement of horizontal wooden beams (usually chestnut or ash tree because of their flexibility). The process was similar but a bit different for a conical roof, where the posts were tied at the top and reeds were collected together into sheaves. The door was always simple, with no hinges. At the end, a little channel was traced around for drawing water.

What kind of other information did they give us? They explained the importance in the choice of the place as this could depend on winds. It was better for the *pagliari* to be built by no more than four people because the space was not very wide – the building process took about 15 days. They always used *Rubus ulmifolius* (blackberry) instead of wire for fixings. *Rubus* was chosen instead of willow because it would last longer; the *rubus* was manipulated to remove the thorns and then twisted to give more strength to the fiber. The use of *rubus* as a building material had not been considered by the authors and therefore was an extremely important discovery. Oak is the most common wood in *pagliari*. The structure got warmer from year to year because, for the yearly maintenance, they put on new layers of reeds.

Figure 3.4: Twins Nicolosi (above); one of them helping in the hut rebuilding project (below). Source: Kati Caruso and Claudia Speciale.

The best period to build is September and for the plant gathering, they said "luna sutta e tramuntana e dura" – "building while the moon is down and north wind is blowing gives strength to the structure". To prolong the wear of vegetal materials, they chose days when the cold north wind (*tramuntana*) was blowing and a moment of the day when the moon was below the skyline. This kind of precaution was for avoiding the attack of the insects (*camula*). Trees were cut down usually during the winter. The most part of the expediencies they suggested, even if not scientific, are related to the life cycle of the plants – for example the sap and its connection to the moon rising.

The ethnographic research that we developed especially thanks to the Workshop (Exeter, May 2013) gave us the possibility to collect a lot of information about traditional structures. The contact with people who make this type of building always using the same techniques, sometimes for hundred years, is the primary

Figure 3.5: Hut rebuilding, Pietraperzia, Enna, Sicily, Italy. Source: Kati Caruso and Claudia Speciale.

approach during the initial phase of the project and complements the analysis of the archaeological and palaeoenvironmental data. The most important point of view they shared with us is definitely the importance of knowing the territory and the weather condition in order to choose the right materials. Then, that knowing the plant properties and skills can help in preserving the structure, even for many years and the choices could affect the longstanding durability of the building, sometimes more than static features. A lot of the advice and the knowledge collected were applied in the hut reconstruction and one of the twins even helped us in the process.

Archaeological reconstruction

One of the three main rebuilding hypotheses was chosen and reproduced in a 1:2 scale (Figure 3.5). In the scale model, ten posts were positioned around the circumference of the structure to support the roof (Giannitrapani 2012, 50-51). The drystone wall was constructed to a height of 60 cm. The upper part of the wall – made by intertwined reeds – is about 40 cm high; the inner side was daubed with a clay, sand and straw mixture; the roof has a wooden structure made by ash rafters and horizontal elements, to which reed bundles were tied; *Ampelodesmos* twisted ropes and long blackberry branches (*Rubus ulmifolius*) were used, employing some specific knotting techniques. After three months, the only deterioration concerns the slipping of some reeds; this did not affect the reliability of the roof nor the waterproofing (Caruso & Speciale in press).

Conclusion

Finally, this paper was a way to keep in contact with a world that is slowly disappearing: today, there is no national or regional law that helps in preserving the personal knowledge and experience, the savoir-faire, the know-how, not even just the buildings, examples of this plenty-of-secrets-and-interest millenary tradition. Will the strength of the *pagliari* be enough to last forever only by passing from father to son?

Bibliography

Barbera, G., Cullotta, S., Rossi-Doria, I., Rühl, J. and Rossi-Doria, B. 2010. *I paesaggi a terrazze in Sicilia: Metodologie per l'analisi, la tutela e la valorizzazione.* ARPA: Sicilia.

Caruso, K. and Speciale, C. in press. Dallo scavo alla ricostruzione di una capanna: archeologia sperimentale a Tornambè (Pietraperzia, Enna) *Proceedings of V Convegno Nazionale dei Giovani Archeologi, Catania 23-26 Maggio.*

Germanà, M.L. 1999. *L'architettura rurale tradizionale in Sicilia: conservazione e recupero.* Publisicula: Palermo.

Giacomarra, M. 2006. *I pastori delle Madonie*, Publisicula: Palermo.

Giannitrapani, E. 2012. *Dalla capanna alla casa. Architettura domestica nella preistoria della Sicilia centrale.* In Bonanno, C. and Valbruzzi, F. (eds.), *Mito e archeologia degli Erei: museo diffuso ennese, itinerari archeologici,* Publisicula: Palermo. pp. 47-53.

Giannitrapani, E. and Iannì, F. 2012. La tarda età del Rame nella Sicilia centrale, *Proceedings of the XLIII Scientific Conference of Istituto Italiano di Preistoria e Protostoria, L'età del Rame in Italia,* pp. 271-278.

Giannitrapani, E. and Iannì, F. 2014. Età del Rame – Sicilia. Tornambè (Pietraperzia, Prov. di Enna): campagne di scavo 2012-2013, in *Notiziario di Preistoria e Protostoria – 1.IV. 2014 ,* pp. 101-102.

Lima, A.J. 1984. *La dimensione sacrale del paesaggio. Ambiente e architettura popolare di Sicilia,* Publisicula: Palermo.

Rubino, R. 1921. Villaggi di capanne nei boschi siciliani, in *La Lettura: Rivista mensile del Corriere della Sera,* 9, pp. 679-681.

Sottile, R. 2002. *Lessico dei pastori delle Madonie,* Centro di studi filologici e linguistici siciliani, Dipartimento di scienze filologiche e linguistiche, Università di Palermo: Palermo.

Tiralongo, P. 2006. *Pietra su pietra. Architettura in pietra a secco degli Iblei,* Edizioni Argo: Ragusa.

Part Two

Thinking through structures

Plant materials, hides and skins as structural components

Perishable material culture and archaeological invisibility

Linda Hurcombe and Theresa Emmerich Kamper

Introduction

Many Archaeological Open-Air Museums (AOAMs) have to speculate on the above-ground aspects of their reconstructions even when the modern building is based on a specific set of archaeological evidence and can be considered a full scale model (FSM). This speculation is often intensely researched and fully reasoned but it is still a challenge and part of the tangible:intangible issue which is both a dilemma and the unique contribution of AOAMs (Hurcombe 2015). The invisibility of perishable material culture has been called the missing majority (Hurcombe 2014).

The archaeological invisibility of structures built from perishable materials is two-fold. Firstly, the perishable components survive only under special conditions. Even where some organic material does survive there may be bias. The larger wooden elements such as timbers may survive, but not thin wooden stakes; and even where the latter survive the stalks and leaves of thinner plant material may not. Preservation conditions may favour structural components made from processed skin over plant materials or the reverse. Secondly, the visibility also relies on the archaeological 'footprint' so that larger post settings comprised of substantial post holes are easier to define archaeologically than smaller post holes or simply stakes pushed into the ground. Structures which prop poles against one another may not disturb the ground at all, though the cultural debris of stone and ceramic artefacts can be recovered, there will be no direct evidence of the structure itself. These two-fold issues of the archaeological invisibility of organic structures can be compounded by modern day access to raw material, technologies and expertise. Within this discussion the issue of perishable material culture is discussed explicitly and some of the parameters are identified in order to help with this reasoning process and to show that there is still a bias in the evidence and biases in the representation of the least visible structures in the totality of the AOAM reconstructions. There are understandable reasons for this but also the issue needs debate in an overt way. This article is a contribution to this discussion.

The focus here is on organic structures from regions with some cold and wet weather as these are more similar to the general climate of many European AOAMs. Hides, skins and plant materials can form a large part of many kinds of shelters, whether permanent or temporary, and, as smaller units, they can contribute a significant component of structures in the form of lashings, doors, and hinges amongst other purposes (see Morgan 1965, Shelter 1973, Laubin and Laubin 1977, Stewart 1984 for a range of ethnographic examples). Structures can also encompass boats where hides and plant materials again form a significant component of the overall structure (see Hurcombe and Cumby this volume). Direct archaeological evidence for hides and plant materials in structures is most often lacking due to natural tendencies to recycle materials in life (see below) and because, overall, very little ancient plant material and hide work survives the post-depositional processes of degradation and destruction. Archaeological Open-Air Museums have to address the missing elements of archaeological material culture in their reconstructed buildings and many rise to the challenge of reconstructing perishable material culture admirably (Hurcombe 2015).

Hides and plant materials form an important part of this challenge and reconstructions make the most of scant archaeological evidence and secondary traces, supplemented by ethnographic data showing the roles of plant materials and hide work in structures in various climates. There are two key caveats. Firstly, the ethnographic data is largely from areas of the world with very different climates than the conditions prevailing in the populated areas which tend to have AOAMs; consequently the direct analogies may be lacking. Secondly, the skills of manufacture and processing in these materials are less evident in the modern world. For example in temperate Europe, the skills of traditional hide tanning and building structures and components from them may be entirely lacking or very limited, while the skills of thatching are now largely confined to one material, *Phragmites*. For wider variation in roof materials see Walker *et al.* (1996) which discusses heather, bracken, various straws and dock amongst other plants. The ethnographic evidence tends to give some well-known ethnographic examples a prominence in reconstructions that may not be justified (not every Palaeolithic hide structure needs to resemble a tipi from the Great Plains), and the skills issue tends to make it difficult to produce reconstructions with materials processed in authentic ways (to use chrome tan leather in place of traditional tanned products is like putting up plywood as a house wall in a reconstruction). The expense of hand processed or rare factory vegetable or fat/oil tan methods make these tanning types expensive materials for AOAMs to use. Ideally the ideas of construction as performance, and the processing of materials as activities undertaken by skilled staff or volunteers on site, not only adds to the actions visitors can see but also provides a source of relevant materials. In general it is easier to source roundwood, grasses, and such materials from plants and trees growing on site or relatively nearby than it is to obtain fresh skins of relevant species in sufficient quantities and then process these using period-appropriate techniques. Even for local plant materials, the raw materials may not be able to be used due to their rarity and because of sustainability issues. For example, taking large sheets of bark off trees means the death of the tree: taking enough sheets to cover a roof would destroy too many trees. However, whatever choices are made the dialogue with science is there in every stage if the material can be sourced and produced locally and preferably as part of visitor-engagement facilities. The selection of materials becomes explicit and part of the debate on authenticity. Furthermore, the repair and durability of the structures can be part of the narrative. In this way the full life cycle approach to building structures can be part of research and visitor experiences alike.

The selection of materials for building structures in the past is a combination of the suitable plants and animals available in the environment, moderated by more cultural and social choices. Though this article includes both plant materials and hides, each has specific issues requiring some separate discussion. For a general overview of plant materials and hides and many other references see Hurcombe (2015) and Emmerich Kamper (2016 forthcoming).

Characteristics and Parameters for Hides and Skins

Skin has many qualities which make it a desirable material for structural components. For a mobile community it is lightweight compared to many plant based alternatives and able to cover a large surface area quickly. These properties are necessary and desirable for a portable shelter. More characteristics which dictate the various purposes for which processed skin is used include; durability, high tensile strength, an inherent wind proof property which woven fabrics struggle to emulate; and, depending on how it is processed, the ability to be folded or rolled up as well as possessing varying degrees of water resistance and opacity.

Perhaps the soundest argument for considering the use of skin in structures is that it is present, being a by-product of animal procurement. While skin as an available by-product is a valid observation, the value of skin as a commodity in its own right should be considered as well. Though most often thought of as a secondary product from hunting, with meat being the primary goal, there is ethnographic documentation of the skin being the primary resource and the nutritional component of the kill being simply a bonus. In some cases, much of the meat is left behind (Burch 1972, 362). This is easier to understand when the number of skins a person would need and the regularity with which this would need to be replaced is considered. If in addition to clothing and bedding a group were to use skins as part of, or the entirety of, the shelter system, it becomes apparent that an average family would require a substantial number of skins over the course of the annual cycle (Gramly 1977; Webster 1979). An example from North America estimates that an average Black Foot style tipi cover requires 6-12 bison (*Bison bison*) skins to construct (Bradley 1923) and though if well cared for one of these covers can last for a number of years, hard-wear can mean it needs replacing annually (Laubin and Laubin 1977, 201). Where large animals with suitable skins can be hunted in good number, shelters made with hide coverings are a viable possibility. This is especially true of areas which can employ hunting strategies resulting in multiple kills from large animals such as bison, and reindeer (*Rangifer tarandus*). The research on Roman army skin tents make clear the skins for the cover are a major resource during later periods of European history as well (Driel-Murray 1990 and 1991).

Terminology surrounding skin processing varies by location and time period and can be confusing. Terms which are often used in a generic way actually have definitions which inform a reader about a specific state a skin is in, or a processing method used on it. Table 1 attempts to present some of these terms for ease of comparison in addition to in-text discussion. Terms such as the difference between 'hide' and 'skin' are less problematic, this is a differentiation based on size. Large animals such as cattle, oxen and horses provide hides and smaller species such as sheep, goat and deer are traditionally referred to as skins (Reed 1972). This designation however has little importance in general dialogue as long as the species of origin is mentioned. However, in order for an author to convey their intended meaning, terms such as 'rawhide' are important to use appropriately as it defines a specific process and product. While a similar term, 'raw skin', designates a skin which has been freshly separated from a carcass.

'Tanning' is a term which today is used in a generalised way when talking about making leather using any technology or method. However the term 'tanning' originally referred specifically to the use of tannins in the vegetable tanning process. This strict definition caused some authors to refer to non-vegetable tanned skins as 'untanned' or occasionally 'rawhide'. These terms do not convey the authors' intended meaning of a non-vegetable tanned skin but instead portray past peoples as wearing 'raw skins' which would rot, or 'rawhide' which has the fit and feel of a cardboard box. This unintentionally perpetuates a classic primitive cave man picture of past skin processing technologies, which does not do justice to the level of technological refinement of these simple tanning technologies. As 'tanning' is an entrenched generalized term with which the majority of readers are familiar, a simple solution to this problem is to prefix the term tanning with a more specific technology such as oil-tanned, smoke-tanned, or mineral-tanned. As a replacement term when talking in an overarching or generalised way 'skin processing' is a good way of describing the preservation and manipulation of animal skins to prevent decay and produce a material which is suited to its required task.

Correct terminology is important as the different tanning technologies produce skins with very different characteristics, or strengths and weaknesses. For example hides which are used as floor or door coverings may not need to be softened and hair-on or off rawhide may suffice. However in damp climates the same product used for doors, windows (if not protected from precipitation) or roof coverings would quickly rot. Thus the precise tanning technologies and processing stages for a hide for structural purposes is part of the overall repertoire of hide-work within a community, but the exact choice for treatment will suit the intended purpose.

Characteristics and Parameters for Plant Materials

The category 'plant materials' covers a broader range of materials than 'hides'. The structural strength varies greatly from mature timber to canes, reeds, *Typha* (cattail, reedmace), *Scirpus* also known as *Schoenoplectus* (and commonly called tule or rushes in North America and Europe respectively), sedges, grasses, heather and moss. Structures can be seen as two interacting systems, the loadbearing framework and the covering, which often involve cordage. All of these plant materials can be

Key Terms	Definition	Possible Uses
Raw Skin	A skin as it exists when first removed from the carcass. No reduction processes such as de-fleshing, or de-hairing have been done. It is still a raw skin if it has been salted, frozen or dried.	Sometimes eaten in times of famine.
Rawhide	Raw skin which has undergone some reduction processes. This product is most often defleshed and dehaired then dried. A skin that has been defleshed but the hair left intact is hair-on rawhide.	Windows, rigid doors, lashing, shoe soles, drum covers, bed or floor skins, spark arresters and containers.
Tanned	Originally a term reserved for vegetable tanned skins, but today used as a general term with a meaning synonymous with 'processed skin'.	
Processed Skin	The preservation and manipulation of animal skins to prevent decay and produce a material which is suited to its required task	
Fat/Oil Tan	Skin processed using fat or oil where these ingredients are active tanning agents. When oils/fats of the right type are used the oxidation of these produces aldehydes which are the active tanning agent. The most familiar modern form of this tannage type is 'chamois' sold in the automotive industry for drying cars.	Clothing, furs, lashing, bedding, shoe uppers or soft soles, flexible doors, spark arrestors, and bags
Smoke Tan	Skin processing using smoke. Smoke contains aldehydes and acrolein which are the active tanning agents. Often this technology is used in conjunction with fat or oil tanning to improve this tannage type's ability to withstand repeated wet and dry cycles.	Clothing, furs, lashing, bedding, shoe uppers or soft soles, shelter coverings, flexible doors, spark arrestors,
Vegetable Tan	Skin processed using vegetable matter containing tannins. Tannins are the active tanning agents and bark, leaves, galls, seed pods and roots from various plants which contain appreciable amounts of tannin have all been used historically.	Outer clothing, furs, door or window hinges, belts and straps, bags, flexible doors, spark arrestors, water containers and shelter coverings.
Mineral Tan	Skin processed using minerals such as alum, aluminium, chromium, or zirconium as the active tanning agents. Of these only alum was used prior to the industrial revolution and is referred to in much of the literature as 'alum taw'. Alum taw can't be wetted.	

Table 4.1: Skin processing terminology. Source: Linda Hurcombe and Theresa Emmerich Kamper.

Figure 4.1: The new Mesolithic hut being built at Archeon, November 2015, showing the lattice of poles with reinforcing wicker at the base visible through the doorway. Source: Linda Hurcombe and Theresa Emmerich Kamper.

used as structural elements as well as coverings, but turf tends to be formed into walls, or is used as roofing over another structural element. Whereas, the softer plant materials can only be used as smaller structural elements and often they must be bound into bundles to achieve greater strength (Ochsenchlager 2014, 150-161), (Figure 4.1). In many cases there are multiple combinations acting together to make the structure. For each tree or plant the species may have specific characteristics that affect its use and the plant or tree may give different characteristics according to the age, plant part used or the manner of preparation. Three basic divisions are used here; trees and tree products, plants, and turf or sod where plant and soil combine to form the building material. These definitions are inherently fluid, as something such as willow shoots would fall into the 'plant' category but the same species fifty years later would be considered a tree. The boundaries are difficult to define along the botanical classification lines.

Modern seasoned timber has known strengths as it is tested for the building trade, but sawn timber is not as strong as riven timber of similar size because the wood fibres are intact in the latter. Entire tree trunks or young, thin trees used as poles both benefit from the same intact fibre structure. Bark is known to be important as a covering material. The use of sheets of birch bark is widely documented in colder regions and in warmer climates elm bark can be used for similar purposes (Nabokov and Easton 1989, 22-23, 56-65, 83). Both need to be removed in the spring and laid flat with weights in order to dry flat. The elm and birch bark can be laid over wooden structures and held in place with another set of poles (Figure 4.2). Pieces of birch bark have been found in the archaeological record (e.g. Mason 2005, 83) and covering made from bark can also be overlaid with moss and sod or sod alone. Brushwood can also be used to fill the spaces between a large wood frame-work or if large brush is laid carefully this material can form an entire structure (Heizer and Kroeber 1979, 152).

Figure 4.2: This small birch bark house has been built at Oerlinghausen Museum, Germany. Source: Linda Hurcombe and Theresa Emmerich Kamper.

Shingles split from large timber exist in both the ethnographic and archaeological record. The use of split shingles has been suggested for circum-alpine Bronze Age houses circa 1000 BC (Arnold 1990, Fig. 69). The use of shingles in stone tool using societies should not be discounted, as the technology needed for their production is documented ethnographically in areas such as the American Northwest Coast (Turner 1998, 70-79; Shelter 1973, 61). However, this technology when seen in the light of stone tools is dependent upon the presence of tree species which grow in a reasonably straight-grained manner making splitting an economically viable option. In wood-rich areas, roundwood can be used both as a framework and the first layer of the roofing material (followed by moss and birch bark), and also form the floors. For example the houses at Kierikki Stone Age Centre and Saarijärvi, Finland (Lehtinen 2014, and Murrimäki this volume).

Woody plants such as heather can be used as a fill between the frame elements or as roofing material, often in some combination with other material. Bracken can form a base layer for multi component rooves or it can be used thickly as a covering. Small plants with no structural strength such as moss or bracken, can be used as one layer within rooves or as insulating material pushed between wicker structures, or as the stuffing between logs and planks often referred to as 'chinking'. Materials such as moss and grasses can be used as part of turf or sod construction forming a living roof where their root structure helps bind the material onto the roof. Other stronger plants can be used such as canes, which are important in Southern Europe, notably *Arundo donax*. This can be used either with larger timber or clay to form structures. The mature dry canes have strength but the green growing shoots with leaves have greater flexibility and could be used as covering material.

In many cases the state of the material makes a difference to the ease of the harvest, strength or longevity. Softer plant materials can be used green when they are more flexible, but they shrink as they dry and so materials can become loose. If materials are used green but tightly packed they may not dry out but instead start to rot. This is especially true of rushes or plants with a high sugar content. These and other plants can be dried and at a later date remoistened to soften them. Softer plants such as grasses, reeds and rushes can also be used as mats. These can be produced by twining with string or in the case of *Typha* stalks by drawing the string through the stalk (Nabokov and Easton 1989, 74). The extra effort involved in making mats for covering materials may allow roofing materials to be rolled for ease of transportation, or to be recycled in different layers as the mat degrades (Nabokov and Easton 1989, 21). Mats need to be weighted down with stones or poles but the individual elements may not be as susceptible to windy conditions.

Neolithic societies have made use of the straw from crops in a variety of ways including using it as bedding, chopped up as part of mudbrick and also directly as thatch. A more recent tradition using straw to make ropes and plaits (braids) can be seen on the islands of Orkney off Scotland. These stronger and thicker combinations were used as ropes to hold down thatch and also as a thatching material (Parks 2004). In Ireland cylindrical granaries were made of straw rope with layers of straw and other thatching materials held down by tying straw ropes around the thatch and then weighting these with stones (Hogan 2001, 187-190).

In these ways individual stems are combined to make stronger structural elements. There are also styles of building using grasses and straw which give less well known composite structures. A bentwood frame can have grasses or similar flexible plant material woven into it in a thick layer. Some are horizontally laid, others are vertical. These grass houses can resemble an upside down basket and are covered by sod or other variations (Nabokov and Easton 1989, 21, 144-149, 310). When considering different kinds of roofing, the pitch of the roof is important. Thinner thatch or less regularly laid material may require a steeper pitch for quicker run off. The apex of a curved roof or ridge line is often the most difficult area to achieve a watertight covering.

The effort, tools and technology to use these different plant products is an important element. Archaeologists thinking about stone tool using societies may need to reason through the economics of locally available materials in the past as a complex interplay between the environment, access to knappable stone, and the tool material culture repertoire. The whole is a task, technologies, tools approach, which has been a strong theme within our experimentation in the OpenArch programme and forms an ongoing collaboration with several AOAMs.

Perishable material components and archaeological invisibility

A short review of the types of structures which may incorporate skin and plant material components shows the breadth of the possibilities outlined by ethnographic information. Temporary structures, built with either the intention of moving the majority of the parts from one site to another or built to fulfil a short term need for shelter such as lean-to, brush or debris shelters, windbreaks and even fire reflectors, leave very little in the way of an archaeological foot print. These types of structures were important, and in many areas still comprise the main living space for a variety of groups.

Even permanent structures still fall within the realm of archaeological invisibility, for while a more massive superstructure of logs or planks may provide a more obvious foot print, the components made from skin or thinner plant materials are still found only in rare instances of exceptional preservation. This class of structure, while sharing some common skin and plant material components with temporary and semi-permanent shelters such as lashing, is unlikely to include hides on the same scale as more mobile shelters. Instead of being an integral part of the superstructure skin is incorporated into more interior elements. Rawhide when tightly stretched, and left to dry without being manipulated becomes transparent, with thinner skins being more transparent than thicker skins. This characteristic has led to a long history of rawhide used as window panes and door coverings, as long as they fall under an eave or overhang to keep off the majority of precipitation (Figure 4.3). Skin used in this way is quite durable. Hinges for doors and unfixed windows can also be made from skin and have been used into historical times in log cabins in the western USA. A more traditional view of a skin door has it hanging from the superstructure of the shelter. This type of door skin would require a level of pliability not inherent in rawhide and would need to be made

Figure 4.3: Daylight shining through a window made from rawhide in one of Archeon's Stone Age houses (Netherlands). Source: Linda Hurcombe and Theresa Emmerich Kamper.

from skin processed using a different technology such as fat, mineral or vegetable tanning. These technologies can provide the level of flexibility necessary for a hanging style door to function well. Floors can also be made of skin or made more comfortable by its addition. In Sami winter homes floors made of boughs were often covered with reindeer furs. The furs and boughs function as a unit giving the effect of a sprung floor and provided much needed insulation from the ground in a traditional Sami gamme (Norsk Folk Museum n.d.).

> *'Two bent posts are joined at one end creating a smooth arch. This arched pair is joined to another by a long pole at the top of the arch, and by another pole along each side of the arch. Poles are then placed vertically against this framework and are covered by a layer of birch bark followed by a layer of sod. A gamme could last up to 30 years. … … The ground was covered by birch branches and reindeer skins.* (Norsk Folk Museum n.d.).

Indoor fires, while providing warmth and a convenient cooking proximity, bring with them a host of problems. An apparent immediate danger is that of sparks and hot floating ash within a structure composed of flammable materials. One solution is to have a high ceiling, which, while reducing the risk of lighting the roof on fire means much of the heat is far above where it is most desirable. Spark arresters made from a non-flammable material such as skin can reduce the risk of sparks making their way into the roof structure. Skin is less flammable than plant materials such as rush and reed which are often used as roofing material. A skin or a few skins sewn together and hung above the fire to stop errant sparks from drifting upward may also be of use in directing smoke toward an outlet or even changing the height of the smoke ceiling. An interior ceiling hung below the actual ceiling can help reduce the tendency for smoke to cycle back toward the ground as it cools. It instead sits on the interior ceiling as it makes its way out of the structure, leaving the living space nearer to the ground clearer (Christensen and Ryhl-Svendsen, 2014). Even in a permanent structure smoke flaps above a mid-roof opening or at the ends of the roof within the gables are one possible solution to manipulating air flow (Figure 4.4). They can be used to create a drawing effect which pulls the smoke from the interior of the structure. The smoke flaps are a distinctive aspect of many hide structures used in North America. Excessive interior smoke is more

Figure 4.4: A gable end with an adjustable smoke flap made from skin in Archeon's Stone Age area. Source: Linda Hurcombe and Theresa Emmerich Kamper.

than an inconvenience; it can cause long term health concerns or more acutely death by carbon monoxide poisoning. It seems likely that smoke was a major factor influencing how structures were built and governing how interior elements were used to direct it (See Christensen this volume).

Interior partitions are another item for which hide and plant materials would have been well suited. Partitions can serve multiple purposes. Functional duties such as maintaining more heat in one area of the structure than another or blocking smoke from sleeping quarters are a few. Other uses could include serving as privacy screens for multi-family homes or for separating areas restricted by social attitudes.

One of the least visible elements of a structure is cordage. Cordage can be used to tie bentwood frames or poles together making resilient composite frameworks. Coverings can be tied on with cordage or held down by poles which will need to be wedged tightly or tied down. Some forms of thatch can be packed or stuffed into a frame, or formed into knotted bundles with the knot placed inside and held in place by the next row of knotted bundles. A thatching needle (these can be made of wood and be over 30 cm in length) can be used to sew the thatch onto the roof. For this technique to work relatively smooth cordage is essential. Rawhide would work but would behave differently than the plant thatch material and in a damp environment degrade quickly, otherwise twisted plant fibres plyed into a thicker string might be used. Even a roof of hides will need sewing together and weighting down or hides can be individually tied onto the roof, though the irregular shape of skins means that this method comes with its own set of challenges. Cordage can be made from bark strips removed from saplings and can be used without further processing or, it can be retted bark materials: a variety of preparation including drying before processing into individual elements or plying can all be used. Roots of trees such as spruce (*Picea*) also make strong cordage and ties. Straight roots growing in easily dug soil are the easiest to exploit (Stewart 1984). In the houses at Saarijärvi open air museum in Finland, 2 kilometres of spruce root were used in the construction (Murrimäki reported in Lehtinen 2014). A temporary structure might make expedient use of materials, nonetheless, cordage is an essential element of most structures in one way or another.

Life Cycles

As with many organic objects used in daily life, an item's original intended purpose is seldom its last or only use. Skin and plant material used in structures are no exception, and over the course of its life cycle the same piece may have many incarnations which make up its object biography. There is no set cycle of use, but some general characteristics of skin mean that a piece which has served certain purposes will be better suited to another use than an unused or fresh skin would be. The sticky viscous substance within the fibre matrix of the skin is composed of mucopolysaccharide (also know as glycosaminoglycans), which are commonly referred to as 'ground substance'. This breaks down with age. Varying amounts of the ground substance is removed depending on the type of tanning technology used to process the skin. Therefore, skins which have spent the first part of their use life as hair on rawhide used as bed padding or suspended from the rafters as an interior ceiling will be easier to work into a soft state than fresh skins. Any skin which has been exposed to smoke for an extended period of time will also be easier to soften with the added benefit of being more resistant to putrefaction and subsequently less appealing to insect pests and camp dogs. The attributes acquired from exposure to smoke make old smoke flaps, interior ceilings and even doors and windows in need of replacing ideal material for cutting into thong for lashing. Though it might seem a waste to cut an entire skin into thong it becomes more understandable when one considers the amount of work which goes into gathering, processing, and spinning the vegetable or animal fibres which are the other options for cordage making. Rawhide thong for lashing can also be a by-product of scraping or softening skins using a frame. There is always an area around the outside of the hide where the lacing or stakes are placed that doesn't soften and can be considered a waste product. It is however, perfectly suitable as lashing material. Bed skins which over time lose their hair or fur can be re-scraped and used for clothing. Old clothing as it wears out may become patches for less worn clothing or turned into bags or thin thong for sewing.

In general, plant materials are less durable, but they are also likely to change roles slightly over time. Fresh new mats may be made annually and placed under older mats on a roof in a continuous cycle (Napokov and Easton 1989, 21, 75). Plant materials used for floor coverings or bedding can be topped up with fresh material rather than being replaced. At Sibudu in S. Africa 77,000 years ago there is evidence for layers of plant materials being used for bedding (Wadley *et al.* 2011). Furthermore, some of the species selected also have insect repellent qualities.

Modern reconstruction concerns

The AOAMs use a lot of perishable elements in their FSMs or generalised reconstructions. Many of these elements are best estimates with essential compromises over the availability and cost of materials today, and yet, they are still providing useful information for research. The key is to capture some observations and make these accessible for research purposes and to inform the decisions made when planning new FSMs. In each case future work can be better designed by building on these observation and experiences. We present here some observations drawn from the OpenArch project to outline the value of these structures. Both authors and a number of Exeter postgraduates, and other OpenArch partners were privileged to be part of an experimental programme in front of the public at AÖZA (Germany), in the summer of 2015. A mosaic of different researchers, museum interpreters and crafts people interacted in the 'Living Mesolithic Project'. The two houses at the museum became lived in 'homes'. The short report (Pfeifer 2014) on the construction of the houses provided useful insights to mesh with these experiences. The report on the building of two huts in the Mesolithic area of AÖZA, is well illustrated and covers both the experience of building the huts and also reflections on the first year of their use. The extracts below show the value of even a short reflective report.

Large hut:

We found, that the relatively much drier environment and the smoke prevented any moulding in the inner. We had mould on the part where reed and ground touched. As the ground floor stayed moist in parts of the inside, we added a shallow trench under the roof line. In combination with moving the roof ground wall to the inside of the hut, we could observe that the ground floor became dry. Once moved, the ground wall inside the hut created a very welcoming sitting bench. Sparks of the fire don't ignite the reed at all, so there was never a need to create a raw hide spark catch... ...The birch poles became very dry (and brittle) by end of this first season, and three of them cracked where they bend most. We think that the weight of the thatching is a bit too much here. We replaced these poles with fresh ones and added wooden pillars to support the poles... ...The common reed thatching is water proof.

The small hut:

The roof is completely made from common reed. We moved the ground wall under the thatching into the inside of the hut as well, as the roof started getting mouldy too... ...As the entrance faces the main wind direction, the wind stirs up the smoke of a fire inside in such a way, that we never use the hut with a fire inside. The birch poles did not crack in this hut. The roof angle is steeper than in the big hut, so the poles are not bent so strong.

(Extracts from Pfeifer 2014: *slightly rewritten for English and to shorten the text.*)

The conclusion mentions the importance of the pitch of the roof, and suggests 20 cm of reed thatch is sufficient and assesses the living environment of warmth, dryness, light, smoke movement and direction of prevailing wind as affected by design features and material choices. The report clearly shows not just the building of the structure but also offers insights into a more object biography approach to structures. The images of the construction phase suggest the means by which the frame can become a temporary half-dome shelter whist the other half is thatched, or how a few skins or mats could be laid over the framework (Pfeifer 2014, fig. 3). Pfeifer fig. 6 shows the original pole-based structure with horizontal cross poles and his figure 13 shows the projecting opening in side view. This lets in a lot more light and the overlapping shell-like roof shape allows light to come in and also draws the smoke out effectively. However, the report goes on to state that some supports were replaced as they had begun to crack and extra supports were added. There are now also arching poles going across diagonals to help brace the structure against the weight of the thatch.

The two huts were in use continuously for six weeks in 2015 as the main dwelling spaces for the participants in the 'Mesolithic Living Project'. As a participant, the huts were experienced as comfortable spaces. Inside the hut, the top-most thatch was observed to be well smoked, which was not surprising as during the Mesolithic Living project we had been using the same roof space to smoke hides using just the normal domestic fire. Many OpenArch discussions have centred on rooves and the weight and thinness of thatch. We had speculated at a project workshop in 2013 on the way a thinner thatch might become 'smoked thatch' and how this might become more waterproof. The observations we made in Summer 2015 after two summers of use suggests that this smoking effect builds up quickly. AÖZA shuts for the winter season, but during the main season fires are lit daily and during the Mesolithic Living Project in 2015 the fire was fairly constant for six weeks and will be so again during the planned project in 2016. Since, to our knowledge, no other hut of this type has seen greater realistic 'in-life' usage and, as it is unlikely that somebody today would wish to live all-year round in such a hut, the AÖZA hut can be seen as the closest proxy for understanding such issues. Further observations in the coming years ensures that these 'Mesolithic huts' will continue to provide much-needed information on the performance of a different kind of roof.

In a similar way another OpenArch partner, Archeon (Netherlands), is contributing to knowledge about different styles of thatch by using the same plant material in a different way. The small oval houses in their Mesolithic area have presented visitors with a 'comfortable' impression of an unfamiliar house-type. In the summer of 2015 they have, with visitors help, pulled down the older of the two huts and have now started to build a new one. Figure 4.1. shows the structure is formed from bent green poles forming a crossing lattice with a wicker-style woven base. This framework is gradually being covered by *Phragmites* reed harvested just off-site and added in bent over layers as the building progresses (see also van Gijn and Pomstra this volume). The stalks and leaves are being used together unlike the same plant's usage as a traditional thatching material where it is harvested in the winter when the stem is bare. Archeon are pinning the thatch down using other horizontal poles which saves on cordage. Though the thickness of the covering can be clearly seen and will act to keep rain and wind out, the material will also act as insulation. Short reports on this experience will also provide relevant information on the life cycle of this kind of building and thatch style although these huts will not be lived in.

The authors also visited the Freilichtmuseum Oerlinghausen (Germany) in the summer of 2015. There are a range of buildings representing different periods and with rooves of traditional thatch and shingle as well as much smaller houses presenting different building styles of much earlier periods. Multiple reconstructions give multiple possibilities making clear to the public that the same archaeological data can be interpreted in different ways. An example of this type of approach exists in Oerlinghausen where three varieties of structures based on a roughly circular or oval footprints have been built using very different coverings of hide, birch bark and *Phragmites* reeds. The museum planned a rolling replacement of these accepting that they had a quicker life cycle but also that they were smaller construction tasks because of their size. Even so the birch bark and hides are more expensive elements and of the three houses the birch bark, which has natural preservative qualities, has withstood the elements better than the hides which have grown mould.

The reconstructed buildings at Calafell (Spain) have stone and clay walls with rooves made from *Arundo donax* canes closely spaced and capped with clay. The flow of water across these flatter rooves is part of ongoing observations at Calafell and one outbuilding with a hole in the roof has been left untouched to observe the way the roof behaves as it deteriorates (see p. 22 fig. 1.6).

During the OpenArch project we have made three visits to Luke Winter and the team at the Ancient Technology Centre, Cranborne Chase (UK). They are situated a short drive from Stonehenge and were chosen to construct the Stonehenge Visitor Centre houses. During the 2nd Exeter Dialogue with Science workshop in 2013 Luke showed participants around the temporary experimentation area. Here a mosaic of different walling, roof framework and thatch materials and styles were explained prior to choosing the system that would be used for the buildings at the Visitor Centre (Figure 4.5). In November 2015 we made a return visit as Luke and the team were repairing one of the experimental buildings. The diversity of sizes and styles are all based on direct evidence from the excavations

Figure 4.5: A section of roof from one of the ATC's temporary Neolithic hut structures where a mosaic of different materials were selected and tested. Source: Ancient Technology Centre.

at nearby Durrington Walls (UK), but the diversity also offers visitors multiple possibilities. The volunteers acting as interpreters were given information by Luke and in some cases they participated in helping to construct the houses. The FSMs are unfortunately not permitted to have lit fires which, as often remarked in OpenArch discussions, has hastened some issues of decay. One effect of smoke is that it discourages mice nesting in the thatch. Their work has explored the cordage issue *e.g.* using willow bark ties or withy ties and a simple self-knot technique for attaching bundles of thatch. The ongoing discussions showed that Luke Winter and the ATC team are gaining interesting insights from the experience and there are good records from his staff on amounts of coppice and other materials used, which will form an important publication. There are implications in this research for many phases within the life cycle of the structures and with a clear sense of experimenting with different forms of thatch and organic materials.

Conclusions

Missing data is always a problem but knowing the parameters of what might be missing allows fewer mistakes to be made. In many generalised reconstructions and specific FSMs compromises have to be made. Those most often made include using readily available commercial thatch, using readily available commercial string, using mechanised tools to rough out large scale timbers, or modern steel tools to make the entirety of the product with a final tidy up to remove obvious modern tool marks.

There is a focus on houses at the expense of other structures. Where buildings have been lived in, the importance of other structures providing outdoor 'working spaces' suggests windbreaks or open shelters providing dryer or shadier places to work on projects would be very useful. Dry storage for materials and firewood has also been important under living conditions. Even simple drying racks can add to the structures around a house. There exists some bias toward round houses or Bronze Age or Neolithic at the expense of earlier structures. This is in part because roundhouses are a more manageable size from a construction standpoint than structures such as a Roman Villa. Roundhouses are also big enough to house a class, whereas some of the earlier prehistoric buildings are not. Small scale house structures can be erected quickly but may not be able to cope with visitor numbers.

The size and species of timber may need to be compromised due to availability. In most cases the large timber is a substantial part of the costs of the materials and the project as a whole.

Hide structures generally suffer from lack of relevant expertise. Hide tents or coverings can be seen as a dialogue with research and as a discussion point with visitors. In the same way that an expert thatcher is used so other experts such as traditional tanners might be able to improve the iterations of hide structures. If AOAMs are planning new structures and want to include different kinds of plant materials or hide materials we would be happy to offer advice or possibly collaborate, because we know the potential and see ongoing discussions and experimentation as part of a mutual dialogue with science.

The tangible/intangible evidence constraints are inevitable but these can be both the research dimension and add to the visitor experience. Taking on the issues of the lifecycle of structures makes the building part of a dynamic debate. The object biography of individual structures and variations across a continuum again shows the richness of the experience and its relevance to research. The Dialogue with Science around authenticity can be a part of the discussions on evidence, reasoning, research on the possibilities, and draw researchers and visitors alike into a more engaging experience overall. As this short review has shown there is the potential to explore the invisibility of much of the perishable components of structures in an overt way. Researchers and museums can work together benefitting both parties.

Bibliography

Arnold, B. 1990. *Cortaillod-Est et les villages du lac de Neuchâtel au Bronze final: Archéologie Neuchâteloise 6*, Ed. du Ruau: Sainte Blaise.

Bradley, James H. 1923. Characteristics, Habits and Customs of the Blackfoot Indians *Montana Historical Society Contributions*, Vol. IX.

Burch, E.S., Jr. 1972. The Caribou/Wild Reindeer as a Human Resource. *American Antiquity,* 37, 339-368.

Christensen, J.M. and Ryhl-Svendsen, M. 2014. Household air pollution from wood burning in two reconstructed houses from the Danish Viking Age. *Indoor air*, *25*(3), pp. 329-340.

Driel-Murray, C van. 1990. New light on old tents. *Journal of roman military equipment studies* 1: 109-137.

Driel-Murray, C van. 1991. 'A roman tent: Vindolanda tent. In V. A. Maxfield and M. J. Dobson (eds.) *Roman frontier studies 1989: proceedings of the XVth International Congress of Roman Frontier Studies*. University of Exeter Press: Exeter. pp. 367-372.

Emmerich Kamper, T. 2016 (forthcoming). *Determining Traditional Tanning Technologies, the macroscopic and microscopic characteristics of experimental samples and archaeologicalfinds*. Exeter University PhD Thesis.

Gramly, R.M. 1977. Deerskins and Hunting Territories: Competition for a Scarce Resource of the Northeastern Woodlands. *American Antiquity,* 42, 601-605.

Heizer, R.F. and Kroeber, T. (eds.) 1979. *Ishi the Last Yahi: A documentary history*. University of California Press Ltd: California.

Hogan, J. 2001. *Basketmaking in Ireland*. Wordwell Ltd: Wicklow.

Hurcombe, L. 2014. *Perishable Material Culture in Prehistory: Investigating the Missing Majority*. Routledge: London.

Hurcombe, L. 2015. Tangible and Intangible knowledge: the unique contribution of archaeological open-air museum. *Exarc Journal Digest 2:* 34-36.

Laubin, R. and Laubin, G. 1977. *The Indian Tipi: its history, construction, and use* (2nd Edition). University of Oklahoma: Norman.

Mason, S. 2005. Other plant remains. In Price, T.D. and Gebauer, A.B. (eds.) *Smakkerup Huse: A late Mesolithic coastal site in Northwest Zealand, Denmark.* Aarhus University Press: Aarhus. pp. 80-83.

Morgan, L.H. 1965. *Houses and House-life of the American Aborigines.* Phoenix Books and University of Chicago Press: Chicago.

Nabokov, P. and Easton, R. 1989. *Native American Architecture.* Oxford University Press: Oxford.

Norsk Folk Museum n.d. *The Sami Site,* http://www.norskfolkemuseum.no/en/Exhibits/The-Open-Air-Museum/The-Countyrside/The-Sami-Settlement-/.

Parks, J. 2004. *Simmans, Sookans and Straw Backed Chairs.* The Orcadian: Kirkwall.

Pfeifer, W. 2014. *Experience with building Mesolithic huts in the Stone Age Park, Dithmarschen.* stohttp://openarchaeology.info/issue-2015-4/at/experience-building-mesolithic-huts-stone-age-park-dithmarschen-2014.

Ochsenschlager, E.L. 2014. *Iraq's Marsh Arabs in the Garden of Eden.* University of Pennsylvania Press: Philadelphia.

Reed, R. 1972. *Ancient skins, parchments and leathers.* Seminar Press Ltd: London.

Shelter Publications. 1973. *Shelter.* Shelter Publications: California.

Stewart, H. 1984. *Cedar: Tree of Life to the northwest coast Indians.* Douglas and McIntyre, University of British Columbia: Vancouver.

Turner, N.J. 1998. *Plant technology of first peoples in British Columbia.* University of British Columbia Press: Vancouver.

Wadley, L., Sievers, C., Bamford, M., Goldberg, P., Berna, F. and Miller, C. 2011. Middle Stone Age Bedding Construction and Settlement Patterns at Sibudu, South Africa, *Science* 334: 1388-1391.

Webster, G.S. 1979. Deer Hides and Tribal Confederacies: An Appraisal of Gramly's Hypothesis. *American Antiquity,* 44, 816-820.

Saving it for later
Gathering, processing and food storage structures

Penny Cunningham

Introduction

One of the main aims of archaeological open-air museums (AOAMs) is to present archaeological reconstructions to the public and as such, they have a strong educational remit and engage with the presentation of the past in multiple ways. Some of the house reconstructions are archaeological experiments highlighting to the public that archaeology is about interpretation and that experimental archaeology is a method that aids interpretation (Crothers 2008, 41).

The focus of experimentation at AOAMs is mainly on the construction and maintenance of reconstructed buildings often including a host of internal secondary structures such as looms, hearths, ovens and partitioning walls to enable an understanding of how the buildings may have been used in the past. However, there are a host of secondary external structures such as kilns, storage facilities, banks and ditches, and animal pens that are equally important in understanding how people not only interacted with the house, but also how they lived in the past. Despite many secondary structures leaving little trace in the archaeological record most would have been fundamental to the success of a community.

One such important type of secondary structures are food storage facilities. Food storage is fundamental to the success of any community, not only as a risk buffering method to cover periods of predictable and/or unpredictable food shortages, but as a meaningful act that on one hand enables food to be consumed at a later date whilst also having important social implications (Cunningham 2011a; Cheeson & Goodale 2014). Storage is not an isolated activity but one that is embedded within a series of activities including gathering/hunting, preparing food for storage and the creation of storage facilities; such actions are largely invisible archaeologically but all contribute to the success of a community.

Through the use of experimental pilot studies, including the gathering, processing and storage of hazelnuts and acorns, this paper takes a life cycle approach to consider some of the nuances associated with storage in prehistoric Northern Europe. This paper does not discuss specific storage structures but factors that influence their design and use. Storage is an act that requires several strands of action including the gathering and preparation of plants to be stored, along with the collection of materials required for the storage structures, and their subsequent ongoing maintenance and repair needs. Additionally, these factors demonstrate that storage structures can also be used as part of a reconstruction where they would help to give meaning to the structures whilst also being a means in which to actively engage the public with the past.

Gathering of nuts for storage

It is likely that the construction or repair of storage facilities would occur once the quantity to be stored is known. Gathering successfully requires knowledge of the production patterns of plants: when and how often they bear fruit, the local environment including position of the trees within woodlands and the timing of gathering: without this knowledge successful storage is difficult and unpredictable.

Throughout the summer of 2004, several small woodlands in Devon (UK) with hazel and oak were monitored to determine the best time and location to gather hazelnuts and acorns. The position of the hazel bushes within the woodland had a huge impact on their capability to produce nuts and upon our ability to gather them. The trees positioned in full sunlight were more likely to have a heavy crop than those within dark woodland. Hazel growing in direct sunlight tended to be short with dense foliage; it was easier to pick the nuts straight from the branches leaving their husks behind, but sometimes the dense undergrowth beneath the bushes hindered gathering by preventing access to hazel bushes. Hazel growing within the woodland grew very tall and the canopy was too high to estimate the quantity of nuts. The tree canopy created a lot of shade and thus restricted the growth of understory plants making it much easier to gather the hazelnuts from the ground (Cunningham 2008).

When gathering the weather also played a significant role. Gathering on damp days made it very difficult to remove the husks efficiently and thus some husk residue remained on the shell causing the nutshells to develop mould; these nuts were removed during the drying phase.

It only took two gathering sessions, in two oak dominated woods in south Devon, to collect enough acorns for some storage experiments. The sheer quantity of acorns on the trees indicated that 2004 was a good acorn mast year for the majority of oaks. In contrast, Devon suffered from a shortage of hazelnuts and acorns in the autumn of 2005.

During the Mesolithic and Neolithic the gathering of nuts would be just one of many activities taking place during the early autumn, an important time of the year for the procurement and processing of food in preparation for the coming winter and early spring. During this period, people would have had to make specific choices surrounding which resources to gather (including the resources to construct storage facilities and other secondary structures). Most of the environmental evidence indicates that nut species came from within walking distance of the majority of Mesolithic and Neolithic sites. Nevertheless, there are exceptions.

During the Mesolithic, people moved regularly around the southern Hebridian islands (UK), but settlement sites appear mainly on the island of Islay. This regular movement meant that people would have explored all the islands and knew exactly which resources were available and more importantly, when the most appropriate time was to gather/hunt certain resources. Throughout this period the island of Colonsay was covered in hazel and it is on this island, at the Mesolithic site of

Staosnaig, that a pit containing the largest deposit of charred hazelnut shells (c. 300, 000) in northern Europe was found This large deposit of charred hazelnut shells, alongside smaller possible nut roasting pits, suggests that hazelnut processing was the main activity at this site (Mithen 2000). Furthermore, we could suggest that a group of Mesolithic hunter-gatherers arrived at Staosnaig, by boat, set up a temporary camp knowing that it was a good year to gather and process hazelnuts and other autumnal fruits.

At the Neolithic site of Aartswoud (Netherlands), the acorns and hazelnuts (and other fruits) most likely came from the nearest deciduous woodland which was approximately 20 km away (Pals 1984, 320). We could suggest that at this site, perhaps due to poor cereal harvests, people travelled some distance to gather wild plants in order to ensure that they had enough food to see them through the lean period. Transporting the gathered resources would have required the use of containers, possibly made out of basketry, animal skin, wood, or bark. If the nuts were collected from a second deciduous wood located 30 km away from Aartswoud, the gathering of nuts may have included the use of a boat and the establishment of temporary camps (Pals 1984).

Distance travelled by both the Mesolithic groups of the southern Hebrides and the Neolithic peoples of Aartswoud indicate the length people travelled to collect certain resources. The questions we need to consider are did they collect their resources and take them back to their more permanent settlements to consume or store, or did they leave them at the gathering site in storage to collect at a later time? The evidence form Staosnaig suggests that they processed (roasted) the hazelnuts (Mithen 2000; Score and Mithen 2000) but did they then store them on the island or did they transport them back to Islay?

On a practical level, gathering requires knowledge of the trees and bushes that are likely to produce the most nuts in any given year enabling the collection of large quantities of nuts in the least possible time. As natural and human produced woodland clearings would increase the production of nuts and, possibly, the number of foraging animals, they may have been favoured areas in which to gather and hunt. No matter the gathering strategy, once gathered, decisions had to be made regarding whether the nuts were for immediate consumption or storage. If for storage do they need to be dried to increase their storage potential and are the nuts to be transported back to the settlement or stored at the gathering site?

Nuts are very versatile, they can be boiled, baked, roasted, ground to a flour and eaten raw (except acorns) but before storing the nuts whole they need to be 'dried' to extend their storability.

In 2004, the drying period for the nuts became quite extensive because the weather became increasingly damp, consequently the hazelnuts were dried for 5-7 weeks prior to storage. The issue here is that in a temperate climate, such as experienced during autumn in most of northern Europe, nut drying naturally in the sun may not actually be possible. However, nuts can be dried using a variety of methods including in baskets and bags hung from rafters within a structure or on a rack placed over a heat source (Saunders 1920; Quinn 1955; Mason 1992) none of which would leave a clearly identifiable trace in the archaeological record. A quick and efficient method of 'drying' the nuts for storage especially in a damp climate is to roast them.

Nut Roasting

Nutritional data indicates that there are some advantages to using heat to process carbohydrate and fat enriched food such as nuts. Hazelnuts are edible without roasting, but roasting improves their flavour, digestibility and prevents them becoming rancid during storage, especially when storing for an extended period (i.e. over 6 months). Acorns cannot be eaten without processing, and roasting is just one of many processing methods that will rid them of their tannins making them more digestible (Leopald and Ardrey 1972; Stahl 1989; Wandsnider 1997). Acorns need to roast slowly and do not need a high temperature, this matches the nutritional data that suggests that food high in starches, such as acorns, benefit from slow cooking (Smith *et al.* 2001, 180). The high fat content of hazelnuts also benefits from dry roasting and slow cooking (Wandsnider 1997).

Archaeological evidence of stone lined pits at Staosnaig (UK) and the double pits at Timmerås (Sweden) hint at two possible nut roasting methods. At Staosnaig the pits were lined with sandstone suggesting that perhaps the stones were used as insulators, as once heated they would retain heat for a long period, and used to line the pits (Mithen 2000) enabling the nuts to be roasted slowly and reducing contact with direct heat (i.e. a fire). The mixing of hazelnuts with hot charcoal and stones in a shallow pit next to a hearth at Timmerås indicates another and probably quicker method of nut roasting (Hernek 2003) and informed one of the methods used in pilot nut roasting experiments.

Roasting nuts was not just limited to the Mesolithic, there are Neolithic and Bronze Age sites with evidence of possible roasting pits. At the Neolithic site at Puddlehill, England, Pit 3 contained roasted hazelnut shells, fire cracked sandstone and charcoal, which is very similar to the evidence of pit roasting from the Mesolithic sites of Ageröd V (Sweden) and Duvensee W.6 and W.8 (Germany) (Bokelmann 1981; Field *et al.* 1963; Larsson 1983). The evidence from Pit 3 suggests a roasting method avoiding the hazelnuts having direct contact with a heat source (fire) using hot stones in deep cylindrical shaped pit (Figure 5.1).

Pilot Roasting experiments

Previous hazelnut roasting experiments by Bokelmann (1981), Larsson (1983), Groenendijk (1987) McComb (1996), and Score and Mithen's (2000) focused on evidence of possible nut roasting from Mesolithic sites in Europe and other

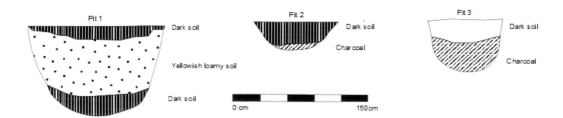

Figure 5.1: Three pits from Puddlehill. Note the difference in size, shape and fill of the pits from which we can suggest that they potentially represent different activities. For example, the lack of charcoal in Pit 1 suggests that it might be a storage pit (after Field et al. 1963, 361).

Pit Roasting Method	Nut Species	Pit dimensions	Bark lining	Protective layer material	Percentage of roasted nuts
1	Hazelnuts	Depth 30 cm Dia. 35 cm	None	Soil and ash	41%
2	Hazelnuts/acorns	Depth 13 cm Dia. 70 cm	N/A	Soil and ash	36%
3	Acorns	Depth 27 cm Dia 39 cm	Yes	Dry grass	97%

Table 5.1: Roasting experiments: July and Nov-Dec 2006 (Methods 1 and 3: pits were lined with bark (pine) and the hazelnuts protected from direct contact with heat by a thin layer of soil & ash or dry grass: Method 2 no lining but the hazelnuts were protected by a thin layer of soil & ash).

experiments by O'Kelly (1954), Wood (2000), Smith and McNees (1999), and Smith *et al.* (2001) explore roasting of a variety of foods. All these experiments highlight different pit roasting methods and how the methods are devised to suit the food that is being cooked.

Throughout the pilot roasting experiments the most significant variables were the moisture levels in the atmosphere, wood and soil, as well as the wind speed and the type of wood used to construct the fires. The wood used was largely pine, but the weather between and during the experiments may have changed the moisture content of the wood and soil. All these variables would have some effect on the experiment methodology and results (Cunningham 2008) (Figures 5.2 & 5.3).

The experiments were adapted and changed due to the different times of the year, the environment and the availability of resources. For example, in July 2004 (method 3) soil and ash was used as both a protective and insulating layer between the hot stones and the nuts but in the experiments conducted the following November and December, the soil and ash was too damp and cold to use and was replaced with dry grass (growing near the roasting site).

The change in material highlights the important role that the climate and environment play in the design of the roasting methodology. The considerably colder, damper ground and air temperature during the second series of experiments hindered the ability of method 2 to roast the hazelnuts however, using grass as a protective layer enabled enough sufficient heat to roast the acorns (Table 5.1, Figure 5.4).

Preparing for storage

While the plants/nuts are being prepared for storage decisions need to be made regarding how the food is to be stored. One way of viewing this is whether the food will be required intermittently over a given period or required at a specific time, perhaps when other food is running low, or as a surplus for trade or reciprocation or even for a specific event/celebration. The quantity is another issue: is there too much to take back to a settlement thus requiring storage at the gathering site. Do special storage facilities need to be made or repaired? Are the stored resources for communal use or for a family unit? What resources need to be collected and made to ensure that the stored foods are kept in the right conditions to enable successful storage?

Figure 5.2: Roasting method 1: Hot rocks placed on top of hazelnuts (Photo: Penny Cunningham).

Figure 5.3: Roasting method 2: Hazelnuts in a shallow pit (Photo: Penny Cunningham).

Figure 5.4: Roasted acorns in shallow storage pit (Photo: Penny Cunningham).

Discussion

Although storage is difficult to identify in the archaeological record especially in the Mesolithic. There is evidence of small caches of hazelnuts at the temporary Mesolithic site of Lough Boora (Ireland) (Ryan 1980; McComb and Simpson 1999). We can also suggest that some of the pits at Staosnaig (UK), Mount Sandel (UK) and Verrebroek 'Dok 1' (Belgium) were used as storage pits (Ryan 1980; Woodman 1985; Mithen 2000; Sergant *et al.* 2006). All of which suggest very simple storage methods where hazelnuts were simply placed in the pits. At Mount Sandel small holes in the sides of a possible storage pit, located within a structure, suggest that perhaps wicker lining was used. A number of storage pits from Jomon sites (Japan) demonstrate a variety of different pit storage methods including the use of basketry lining and baskets, the storage of more than one type of plant and multiple pits in one location (Woodman 1985; Miyaji 1999; Habu 2004).

Storage pits from Neolithic sites at Winterbourne Dauntsey and Boscombe Down East (UK) have stake holes around the edges indicating some sort of capping structure (Field *et al.* 1964). Evidence from pits at Balfarg (UK), also hints at a possible capping method: a number of storage pits had a layer of stones at the top of the pit (Barclay and Russell-White 1993) and at Hurst Fen (UK), some of the storage pits contained a single pot of grain (Clark *et al.* 1960). Even with a very simple way of storing food – a pit – the archaeological evidence indicates a variety of different methods and locations i.e. within and outside of a structure, at a temporary camp and/or within a settlement.

A number of experiments have tested the suitability of below ground storage in small pits and have focused on the storage of hazelnuts and acorns (McComb 1996; Cunningham 2005, 2008, 2011b). These experiments explored some of the visible and invisible aspects of pit storage including the capping, lining, and the use of containers (i.e. baskets, clay pots) with varying degrees of success (McComb1996, Cunningham 2005, 2008, and 2011b).

With above ground storage facilities, whether they are external granaries or internal clay bins, issues of maintenance, repair and reuse must be considered and perhaps this happens once the quantity and type of food to be stored is known.

Archaeological evidence of above ground storage facilities include four-sided clay bins for storing grain within houses in the early-mid Neolithic of the central Balkans and central Anatolia. In addition, concentration of grain and other plant food found on the floor possibly indicates the use of organic containers for storage which have not survived. Basket impressions from clay bins in Çatalhöyük indicate that plants were stored in containers within the bins in addition ceramic vessels were also used for storage for both dry foods (cereals) and liquids. The bins were sealed to prevent rodents eating the stored resources and sometimes ceramic vessels were also used to store food in pits (Bogaard *et al.* 2009; Tripković 2011).

In addition to finding the stored resources within containers, we also find nuts mixed with grain in large pits and silos that are situated within larger settlements or stored separately during the Bronze Age including charred acorns in pits at the Iron Age sites of Evergem-Ralingen and Boezinge (Belgium) (de Ceunynck 1991, 290-292; Deforce *et al.* 2009). The Alpine region, has a number of sites with acorns in pottery vessels (Sakellaridis 1979) and at Fiavé (Italy) acorns were stored alongside cereals, but each food type had their own location within the structures (Jones and Rowley-Conwy 1984) very similar to the evidence of storage in Anatolia (Bogaard *et al.* 2009). Ethnogrpahic studies from the Morocco indicate that storage containers can be made out of variety of locally made materials including dung, clay, pottery, plant fibres, cork, canes and straw (Peña-Chacarro *et al.* 2015).

Many Iron Age sites have evidence of both pit storage and granaries for the storage of grain (Cunliffe 2004). To explore how successful Iron Age storage pits are at storing grain Reynolds (1974) undertook a number of grain pit storage experiments using several methods including sealing pits with a layer of clay to create anaerobic conditions and using a basketry lining. He found that grain stored best in sealed pits but once opened, the grain will begin to deteriorate and sprout suggesting that pit storage would have been used to store grain for planting not consumption. An argument supported by Cunliffe (2004) who also divides above and below ground storage of grain into two distinct functions: grain for consumption stored in the granaries as access is easy and seed grain in pits – left until needed for planting.

However, Marshall's (2011) grain storage experiments indicate that grain can be successfully stored in pits and retrieved intermittently. Marshall (2011) explored the storage potential of sealed and unsealed rock-cut pits (or silos, approx. >5m^3) that were covered with waterproof 'roofs' (based on archaeological evidence) which proved to be a more successful method than unlined sealed pit and pits lined with straw and then sealed. A notable additional advantage was that the grain was accessible when required. The results are in contrast to Reynolds (1974) experiments, however, this is not surprising considering the different environmental conditions in which the experiments were conducted. Which may also account for the opening of silos every 3-4 weeks in some parts of Morocco whereas in other regions the silos were opened and emptied in one go (Peña-Chacarro *et al.* 2015).

The results from Reynolds (1974) and Marshalls (2011) experiments along with those conducted by McComb (1996) and Cunningham (2005, 2008, 2011b) clearly demonstrate how the local environment (i.e. soil conditions and climate) impact on the storage methodology and the value of using experiments to understand this important food strategy.

As we can see from the archaeological evidence there is a whole array of different food storage methods both above ground and below. The archaeological evidence for granaries and clay bins for grain storage is little more obvious than those used for the storage of wild plants. Furthermore a whole variety of plants and not just for consumption but also for medicinal and craft purposes would need to be stored. Ethnographic and ethnohistorical data indicates that in California the location and methodology of acorn granaries was determined by the use of the acorns after storage; those required for continual use were stored in granaries (Mason 1992). The granaries came in a variety of sizes between 3-5ft diameter and 8-13ft high depending on the quantity of nuts stored and located within the settlement area or at the gathering sites (Kidder 2004).

The ethnographic data indicates that there was not a universal method of storing acorns although certain criteria had to be met; the use of a variety of different materials and design indicates that local environment was an important factor and so was the use of readily available materials. In addition, there is the issue of gathering and collecting materials to create the above ground storage facilities which may also have to be processed/stored.

Furthermore, what happens to the storage facilities once the resources have been moved? Are they discarded, dismantled, refilled, repaired or reused? When considering the life cycle of storage we have to consider that pits can be used and reused without necessarily leaving any trace that they were ever used for storage let alone repeated storage (or used for roasting then storing). Is it reused immediately or is there a period when the pit is not needed, in which case, is it backfilled it or left open and exposed? If backfilled and closed, is it possible to identify the location when it is required again for storage?

Reynolds (1974) argued that pits could be used indefinitely for as many times as needed, as long as they received proper maintenance. After being used for storage some pits would have to be cleaned and this would alter the size and shape. This may account for the shape (narrower at the top) of many Iron Age grain storage pits, and may also account for the multiple pits found at some Jomon sites (Japan) and many Iron Age sites in the UK.

Conclusion

Taking a life cycle approach to storage emphasises that storage is one part of a process that helps to ensure the continued success of a community. The pilot experiments (gathering and roasting) highlight that storage cannot be viewed as an isolated act but part of a process. Storage begins with the monitoring of potential stored resources (i.e. quantity and type that will be available), the gathering of materials to be used for storage facilities and the creation or repair of the storage facilities/containers. All of which will be partly determined by the local environment, cultural tradition, type of food to be stored and the duration of storage. Thus storage facilities are designed or redesigned or even go in and out of use based on a variety of factors which may be related to the cultural and social identity of a community and/or individuals, and perhaps, account for the multiple storage facilities identified in the archaeological record and ethnographically.

Storage structures are therefore an important aspect of prehistoric life ways and to ensure successful storage requires planning, awareness of plant fruiting cycles, the most appropriate storage materials and methods to ensure a successful outcome. Storage is more complex than simply 'saving it for later' and is an integral part of the life cycle of prehistoric structures and communities. Storage demonstrates that individuals have an intimate relationship with plants in a variety of ways and it is this relationship that enables communities to be successful.

Furthermore the inclusion of storage facilities as part of reconstructions at AOAMs not only offers a huge amount of research potential, but also interesting engagement opportunities for visitors relating to spatial organisation, participation through archaeological experiments, understanding of the local environment and of the past beyond the house reconstruction.

Bibliography

Barclay, G.J. and Russell-White, C.J. 1993. Excavations at the ceremonial complex of the fourth millennium BC at Balfarg/Balbirnie, Glenrothes, Fife. *Proceedings of the Society of Antiquaries of Scotland* 123: 43-211.

Bogaard, A., Charles, M., Twiss, K.C., Fairbairn, A., Yalman, N., Filipović, D., Demirergi, A.G., Ertug, F., Russell, N. and Henecke, J. 2009. Private pantries and celebrated surplus: storing and sharing food at Neolithic Çatalhöyük, Central Anatolia. *Antiquity* 83: 649-668.

Bokelmann, K. 1981. Eine neue borealzeitliche fundstelle in Schleswig-Holstein. *Kölner Jahubuch* 15: 181-188.

Chession, M.S. and Goodale, N. 2014. Population aggregation, residential storage and socioeconomic inequality at Early Bronze Age Numayra, Jordan. *Journal of Anthropological Archaeology* 35: 117-134.

Clark, J.C.D. 1960. Excavations at the Neolithic site at Hurst Fen, Mildenhall, Suffolk (1954, 1957 and 1958). *Proceedings of the Prehistoric Society* 11: 202-245.

Crothers, M.E. 2008. Experimental archaeology within the heritage industry: publicity and the public at West Stow Anglo-Saxon Village. In Cunningham, P., Heeb, J. and Paardekooper, R. (eds.) *Experiencing archaeology by experiment.* Oxbow: Oxford. pp. 22-37.

Cunliffe, B. 2004. *Iron Age Communities in Britain (4th edition extensively revised).* London: Routledge.

Cunningham, P. 2005. Assumptive holes and how to fill them. *EuroREA* 2: 55-66.

Cunningham, P. 2008. Food for thought: nut exploitation in prehistoric Europe. Unpublished PhD thesis. University of Exeter, Exeter.

Cunningham, P. 2011a. Caching your savings: the use of small-scale storage in European prehistory. *Journal of Anthropological Archaeology* 30: 135-144.

Cunningham, P. 2011b. Cache or carry: food storage in prehistoric Europe. In Millson, D.C.E. (ed.) *Experimentation and interpretation: the use of experimental archaeology in the study of the past,* pp. 7-28. Oxford: Oxbow Book.

DeBoer, W.R. 1988. Subterranean storage and the organization of surplus: the view from Eastern North America. *Southeastern Archaeology* 7 (1):1-20.

de Ceunynck, R. 1991. A find of charred acorns in Evergem-Ralingen near Ghent (Belgian Iron Age). In Renfrew, J. (ed.) *New Light on Early Farming: recent developments in Palaeoethnobotany.* Edinburgh University Press: Edinburgh. pp. 257-76.

Deforce, K., Bastiaens, J., Van Calster, H. & Vanhoutte, S. 2009. Iron Age acorns from Boezinge (Belgium): the role of acorn consumption in prehistory, *Archäologisches Korrespondenzblatt* 39: 381-392.

Dunham, S. 2000. Cache pits: ethnohistory, archaeology and the continuity of tradition. In Nassaney, M.S. and Johnson, E.S. (eds.), Interpretations of native North American life: material cultural studies to ethnohistory. Gainsville: Society of Historical Archaeology and University of Florida: pp. 225-260.

Field, N.H., Matthews, C.L. and Smith, I.F. 1964. New Neolithic sites in Dorset and Bedfordshire, with a note on the distribution of Neolithic storage-pits in Britain. *Proceedings of the Prehistoric Society* 15:352-381.

Groenendijk, H.A. 1987. Mesolithic hearth-pits in the Veenkoloniën (Prov. Groningen, The Netherlands), defining a specific use of fire in the Mesolithic. *Palaeohistoria* 29: 85-103.

Habu, J. 2004. *Ancient Jomon of Japan*. Cambridge: Cambridge University Press.

Hernek, R. 2003. A Mesolithic winter site within a sunken dwelling from the Swedish west coast. In Larsson, L., Kindgren, H., Kratsson, K., Loeffer, D. and Åkerlund, A. (eds.) *Mesolithic on the Move*. Oxbow Book: Oxford. pp. 222-29.

Howes, F.N. 1948. *Nuts: Their production and everyday uses*. Faber and Faber Ltd. London.

Jones, G. and Rowley-Conwy. 1984. Plant remains from the north Italian lake dwelling of Fiavé (1400-1200 b.c.) *Patrimonio Storico e Artistico del Trentino* 8:323-355.

Kidder, N. 2004. Acorn Granaries of California. *The Bulletin of Primitive Technology 2004*: 28. http://www.primitiveways.com/acorn%20granary.html.

Larsson, L. 1983. Ageröd V. an Atlantic bog site in central Scania. *Acta Archaeologica Lindensia* 8(12).

Leopald, A.C. and Ardrey, R. 1972. Toxic substance in plans and the food habits of early man. *Science* 176: 512-14.

Loewenfeld, C. 1957. *Britain's wild larder: nuts*. Faber and Faber: London.

Marshall, A. 2011. *Experimental Archaeology: 1. Early Bronze Age cremation pyres. 2. Iron Age grain storage*. BAR British Series 530: Oxford.

Mason, S.L.R. 1992. *Acorns in human subsistence*. Unpublished PhD thesis. Institute of Archaeology, University College London: London.

Mithen, S. 2000. Islay and Colonsay: an introduction to the field work. In Mithen, S. (ed.) *Hunter-gatherer landscape archaeology: The Southern Hebrides Mesolithic Project 1988-98 Vol 1*. McDonald Institute for Archaeological Research: Cambridge. pp. 39-51.

Miyaji, A. 1999. Storage pits and the developments of plant food management in Japan during the Jomon period. In Coles, B., Coles, J. and Schu-Jørgensen, M. (eds.) *Bog Bodies, Sacred Sites and Wetland Archaeology*. WARP Occasional Paper 12. University of Exeter: Exeter. pp. 165-170.

Morgan, C. 2012. Modelling modes of hunter-gatherer food storage. *American Antiquity* 77(4): 714-736.

McComb, A.M.G. 1996. *The ecology of hazel nuts in prehistoric Ireland*. Unpublished BSc dissertation. The Queens University Ireland. Belfast.

McComb, A.M.G. and Simpson, D. 1999. The wild bunch. Exploitation of the hazel in prehistoric Ireland. *Ulster Journal of Archaeology* 58: 1-15.

O'Kelly, M. 1954. Excavation and experiments in ancient Irish cooking-places. *The Journal of the Royal Society of Antiquaries of Ireland*. 84: 105-155.

Pals, J.P. 1984. Plants remains from Aartswoud, a Neolithic settlement in the coastal area. In Van Zeist, W. and Caspare, W.A. (eds.) *Plants and Ancient men: Studies in palaoethnobotany*. A.A. Balkema: Rotterdam. pp. 313-21.

Peña-Chacarro, L., Pérez Jordà, G., Morales Mateos, J. and Zapata, L. 2015. Storage in traditional farming communities of the western Mediterranean: ethnographic, historical and archaeological data. *Environmental Archaeology 2015* DOI 10.1179/1749631415Y.0000000004.

Quinn, D.B. (ed) 1955. *The Roanoke Voyages 1548-1590. Volume 1.* Hakluyt Society: London.

Reynolds, P.J. 1974. Experimental Iron Age storage pits: an interim report. *Proceedings of the Prehistoric Society* 40: 118-31.

Ryan, M. 1980. An early Mesolithic sites in the Irish Midlands. *Antiquity* 54: 46-47.

Sakellaridis, M. 1979. *The Mesolithic and Neolithic of the Swiss area.* BAR International Series 67: Oxford.

Saunders, C.F. 1920. *Useful wild plants of the United States and Canada.* Robert. M. McBride and Co: New York.

Sergant, J., Crombé, P, and Perdaen, Y. 2006. The 'invisible' hearths: a contribution to the discernment of Mesolithic non-structure surface hearths. *Journal of Archaeological Science* 33: 999-1007.

Score, D. and Mithen, S. 2000. The experimental roasting of hazelnuts. In Mithen, S. (ed.) *Hunter-gatherer landscape archaeology: The Southern Hebrides Mesolithic Project 1988-98 Vol 2.* McDonald Institute for Archaeological Research: Cambridge. pp. 507-512.

Smith, C.S. and McNees, L.M. 1999. Facilities and hunter-gatherer long-term land use patterns: an example from southwest Wyoming. *American Antiquity* 64(1): 117-136.

Smith, C.S., Martin, W. and Johansen, K.A. 2001. Sego lilies and prehistoric foragers: Return rates, pit ovens, and carbohydrates. *Journal of Archaeological Science* 28: 169-183.

Stahl, A.B. 1989. Plant food processing: implications for dietary quality. Harris, D.R. and Hillman, G.C. (eds.) *Foraging and Farming: the evolution of plant exploitation.* Unwin Hyman: London. pp. 171-194.

Stopp, M.P. 2002. Ethnohistories analogies for storage as an adaptive strategy in northeastern subarctic prehistory. *Journal of Anthropological Archaeology* 21: 301-328.

Tripković, B. 2011. Containers and grains: food storage and symbolism in the Central Balkans (Vinča period). *Documenta Praehistorica* 38: 159-172.

Wandsnider, L. 1997. The roasted and boiled: Food composition and heat treatment with special emphasis on pit hearth cooking. *Journal of Anthropological Archaeology* 16(1): 1-48.

Wood, J. 2000. Food and drink in European prehistory. *European Journal of Archaeology* 3(1): 89-111.

Woodman, P.C. 1985. *Excavations at Mount Sandel 1973-77.* Northern Ireland Archaeological Monographs: No 2: Belfast.

Boats as structures: an overview

Linda Hurcombe and Brian Cumby

Introduction

Boats are structures and are included here because of personal research and practice interests and because they are a successful feature of many Archaeological Open-Air Museums (AOAMs). In much the same way as a house, boats go through a life cycle. They are constructed and then, once brought into use, they may need to be maintained or repaired, they can be reused or elements from them can be replaced or recycled, and they may be catastrophically lost in use, formally deposited or destroyed, or abandoned and allowed to decay slowly. Each category of boat has different possibilities within the type as well as between different ones. Even for a well-understood and simple category such as logboats, built essentially from one large tree trunk, there are also examples which have an end (stern) section formed from a separate piece of wood known as a transom: the categories of hide boats likewise vary in size and precise details of their construction and one cultural group may make several different categories of simple watercraft to suit varied purposes (Andersen 2013; Marsden 2004; Mac Cárthaigh 2008; Nielson & Gebauer 2005; McGrail 1988, 2001; Osgood 1940, 359-382; Petersen 1986; Foteviken Museum). Some hide boats from Greenland are designed to be both a large vessel and also form the roof of shelters. They serve two purposes very effectively not as recycling or re-purposing but as a planned flexibility of function (Petersen 1986 and see also Hurcombe and Emmerich Kamper, this volume). The large Greenland skin boats, umiaks, can carry large numbers of people and goods: they are substantial and long-lived structures which can be inherited in complex ways (Petersen 1986:161-189). In some documented examples, the covering and lashings are known to have been replaced, and also the frame has been repaired, but these changes have enabled the boat to be used by three generations before being kept, unused, by a fourth generation who then sold it to a museum in the 1970s. The museum then restored the boat some 90 years after it was originally built (Petersen 1986, 180-184). This kind of documented complex individual history makes the case for extensive life cycles and for the value of an object biography approach. For boats which are no longer part of active boat building traditions there may be literary and pictorial sources which allow replicas to be built and tested for their performance in use, giving rise to important new understanding and a sense of pride and involvement of the builders and crew (e.g. the classical Trireme, Morrison *et al.* 2000, Shaw 1993; medieval cog, Foteviken museum, and the Jewel of Muscat project, Vosmer *et al.* 2011).

The period of manufacture can be protracted and involve many hands and sets of skills. The authors of this paper first worked together on the AHRC funded project *Cornwall and the Sea in the Bronze Age* a project involving researchers from the universities of Exeter (Robert van de Noort, Linda Hurcombe, Anthony Harding, Andy Wetherelt and Brian Cumby), Oxford Brookes (Paul Inham), and Southampton (Lucy Blue) and staff at the National Maritime Museum Cornwall (Andy Wyke, Jenny Wittamore). Brian Cumby was employed as the experienced shipwright leading a team of volunteers to construct a Bronze Age sewn plank boat as a living display which we termed 'construction as performance' because it took place in the museum workshop on public view in the National Maritime Museum, Cornwall (NMMC), Falmouth (van de Noort *et al.* 2014). This paper is a result of this interaction and then further collaboration between the authors as part of the OpenArch EU funded project involving work with Kierikki Stone Age Centre and a workshop in Exeter as well as OpenArch participation in the project in Falmouth. During the production of this volume Brian sadly died and this book is dedicated to him. This paper begins by outlining the context of boat biographies explored during the workshop in Exeter and Falmouth, before outlining three different case studies of boats as structures, all related to or interacting with the OpenArch project activities.

1. 'Construction as performance' and 'the inverted exhibition': key issues in building *Morgawr*, the Bronze Age sewn plank boat, within a museum setting at the National Maritime Museum, Cornwall (NMMC), Falmouth, UK.

2. 'Paddling as public participation' and 'maintenance as performance': building and repairing small logboats at Kierikki Stone Age Centre, Finland.

3. Boats as choices in a 'tasks, tools, technology' approach: experiments building a variety of simple watercraft within the setting of Kierikki Stone Age Centre, Finland, and the Steinzeit Park, AÖZA, Albersdorf, Germany.

Boats are key archaeological finds because they are rare survivals being made of perishable materials (Hurcombe 2014). Though they are important for transport, they are also important as a means of communication and can serve local communities or enable long distance contacts (see van de Noort 2011). Often they are found in the archaeological record in a deteriorated state and with elements missing or distorted. As boats become more complex, multiple skills may be involved in their production, but the conservative traditions of boat building are a strong theme in archaeological research within nautical archaeology (Burningham and De Jong 1997; van de Noort *et al.* 2014; Crumlin-Pedersen 1995, 1996, 1999, 2006; Crumlin-Pedersen and McGrail 2006; Crumlin-Pedersen Trakadas 2003; Clark 2004 a & b, 2013; Coates *et al.* 1995; Coates 2005; Darragh 2004, 2012; Morrison *et al.* 2000; Nicolaisen & Damgård-Sørensen 1991; Shaw 1993; Vosmer *et al.* 2011). These fit in with more widespread ideas about the transmission of craft skills and communities of practice (Wendrich 2012). Both museums and research projects have commissioned reconstructions of ships and sailed them. The Viking Ship Museum, Roskilde, Denmark, has reconstructed a set of boats, with some undertaking major voyages and some being available for taking out museum visitors (van de Noort *et al.* 2014). They explain the archaeological finds exhibited in the museum, but they also serve as activities for visitors to participate in and watch, as well as being a major draw for museum visitors and a publicity mechanism. The live activities boost visitor numbers.

There are many ways of presenting boats within AOAMs and of using boat building, performance, and maintenance, as opportunities for research. The case studies here offer just some ways of thinking about boats as a dynamic engagement with the life cycle of structures.

'Construction as performance' and 'the inverted exhibition': key issues in building *Morgawr*, the Bronze Age sewn plank boat, using volunteer labour, within a museum setting at the National Maritime Museum, Cornwall (NMMC), UK

The boat Morgawr

Morgawr (named after a Cornish sea serpent) is a reconstruction of a Bronze Age sewn plank boat, reconstructed as part of a project formed by a team of academics, museum curators, and the shipwright (Brian Cumby). It was built as a full scale model (FSM) in the sense outlined in chapter 1 this volume. The process of construction was fully recorded with details available online in a publication and series of videos (van de Noort *et al.* 2014, and see the bibliography for videos of the build as details and time lapse footage, and as sea trials and documentary films). The boat is made from large trunks carved into the shape of the keel plate and cleats, and with side strakes also carved from massive timbers. The whole is joined together by yew (*Taxus baccata*) withies which stitch the components together and onto the frames with a caulking of moss between the joints all drawn from archaeological evidence from the UK (see Figure 6.1 for the completed boat and for the workshop context with surrounding exhibition see Figure 1.1 this volume; Bevan & Jones 2002). The boat was built within the museum by a team of volunteers. Though the construction was within a traditional museum workshop rather than in an open air museum, the project had elements that are relevant to the work of open air museums, there were several visits and interactions with the OpenArch project, and the build was at times augmented by public lectures and children's activities etc. The modern museum is built directly on Falmouth harbour. There were many technical problems to overcome and decisions to be made. Brian Cumby drew on almost 40 years of experience in boat building but was still faced with many distinct and novel challenges. In the modern world the large mature trees were very rare and the wood for the project cost c £20,000 pounds. Once the trunks were chosen, even if flaws were discovered later, the money was committed and there was no money for replacement trees. The bronze axes, adzes and chisels that were used were adapted according to negotiations with Brian Cumby as the person whose body was going to use them for months on end and with what was known in the archaeological record. Debates included the length of handles, whether the project should use chisels because there were none known from that period in Britain (the decision was that small axes were

Figure 6.1: Morgawr on launch day (Photo J. Bennett).

used as chisels) and the number of blades mounted as adzes rather than axes. The tools needed to be provided quickly and as the order was placed for 30 tools to be used by a large number of initially inexperienced tool-users, it was decided to use modern robust hafting and modern replaceable handles.

The whole build, though guided by the archaeological evidence, had to result in a functioning boat: where the archaeological evidence was lacking or unclear, experience was crucial and at times modifications to the original ideas had to be made as work progressed. Brian Cumby built the boat largely 'by eye' with large timbers having to be lifted up and checked for a good fit many times in order to individually shape each major side strake. There were many discussions over the style of organisation in the past and how this might have differed from the team of shipwright plus volunteer builders' in the present. This intellectual debate was integrated closely with the physical work and the combination together with a sociable working atmosphere proved a powerful draw for the long term volunteers. The role of the volunteers was crucial to the project and an investigation on this aspect is reported here as so many AOAMs rely on this source of labour. The evidence is drawn from interviews with volunteers and NMMC staff conducted by Linda Hurcombe towards the end of the project.

The NMMC makes extensive use of volunteers with c 175 working across a variety of tasks organised into teams such as library, gallery, office, curatorial, education, front of house, and general boat work. The volunteers for the Bronze Age boat project formed their own separate group under the project shipwright, Brian Cumby. The specific issues for the boat project lay in building the team by attracting, training, and keeping volunteers. Some of those who joined the project were already involved in the general boat work team and moved across to the new project. New volunteers heard about the project by word of mouth, college/university information, or via publicity generated by the museum across a range of media including Facebook, Twitter and local radio. A number of volunteers saw the project in action and were inspired to join it, including some who were drawn to the sound while walking past the exhibition or past the open outside door. This is a case of the sound within a construction project causing interactions in a different way to the sound experiences usually discussed in a museum context (Sharp 2013).

Some people contributed for short periods but by the end of the project 58 longer term volunteers were regularly contributing to the project with still more (c 100) credited on the final video. The numbers of people who contributed to the build in some way is significantly higher because students (studying a range of subjects such as archaeology, boatbuilding, arts and crafts, and theatre design), college and university staff, and workshop participants from the UK and abroad also participated (including those from the OpenArch project). However, the success of the project relied on the input from the long term volunteer cohort. Twenty-one of the longer term volunteers (i.e. 36% sample) were interviewed towards the end of the project. Their responses showed that their individual work patterns varied from one afternoon a week, to a few hours early every morning, to several days a week. The project ran seven days a week due to the volunteers' availability. The advantage was that both weekend and weekday visitors were able to see live construction. This was seen as a significant advantage by the museum compared to other projects which had used the same space but stopped at weekends just when visitor numbers were highest. However, the work pattern highlighted the need for a future project to plan for two paid staff to share the seven day working week. Tom Monrad Hansen started off as an MA in Experimental Archaeology student at Exeter University who volunteered on the project. Once his course finished he spent more of his time volunteering and eventually became the second employed person supporting the shipwright.

Volunteers ranged from 18-84 years of age with fewer in the middle of this range because this group had to earn a living and had family commitments. The younger volunteers were mostly students, while the older ones were retired. Some out-of-work tradespeople also contributed but left when they had paid work; some people used their holidays to spend blocks of time on the project. Of those that stopped volunteering, most cited other commitments or money as significant reasons and the shipwright also appreciated that some simply found the work too physical or could not accept the ethos of the project. Many volunteers who stayed stressed that they were drawn to the project by the combination of intellectual challenges, practical skills, and the camaraderie which developed within the team. One described it as 'a feast for the soul', another said that they 'went home with their brain buzzing'. They enjoyed the variety of backgrounds (fine arts and crafts, green woodworking and bushcrafts, carpenters, builders, engineers, and many others) and ages which met to achieve a common task. Almost all interviewees stated the importance of the character of the shipwright who had to lead the project but who also required excellent people skills to be able to use volunteers according to their abilities, develop their skills, and encourage them to stay. The interview statements showed the volunteers had a great respect both for the quiet authority of the extensive experience of the shipwright and the leadership skills by which he encouraged people to feel valued. This combination of both boatbuilding experience and people skills is clearly essential for the success of this project and any similar one in the future.

The key volunteer issues for this project followed stages. Firstly, attracting the first set of volunteers was of necessity a slow process as it would have been impossible to cope with an influx of untrained people in one go, and, as with any new volunteering project, the match between methods of work and people had to be right, so some came and left. In this initial phase the work was very slow as the half trunks were squared off by hand and the endpoint of the 'boat' was hard to envisage for potential volunteers and visitors alike. The full scale, FSM, component was an important aspect for researchers, volunteers and visitors and for the eventual launch and trials.

Figure 6.2: Checking the lines and fit of the boat frequently by eye (above). Making major design decisions using a physical visual aid (below) (Photos J. Bennett).

THE LIFE CYCLE OF STRUCTURES IN EXPERIMENTAL ARCHAEOLOGY

Construction as performance

The construction of the sewn plank boat took place seven days a week in full view of the public with an explanatory exhibition all around one third of the gated build space so that visitors could easily watch (see Figure 1.1 this volume). The full scale reconstruction also allowed the public to understand the size and complexity of the vessel. When appointing the shipwright a key question hinged on trust – whose boat would you want to go to sea in? In addition, the shipwright had to run a multi-faceted major experimental archaeology project and the person had to attract volunteers, train them, and then retain them. All these responsibilities then have to come together to build the boat. As work progressed many of the small details and larger design decisions were taking place in front of the public because much of the build was enacting a 'look'. Many times a day Brian would be checking lines and fits visually and actively demonstrating this kind of boatbuilding, his adage was *'if it looks right it's right'*. Sometimes modern materials were used to create this visual impression such as a key design stage when the breadth amidships was being decided (see Figure 6.2). Though this process used battens as the workshop floor was made of concrete, the build team were aware that in building such a boat on a flat estuary shore in prehistory, string lines and willow withies could be used in the same approach. This visual process allowed an important decision to be made to streamline the shape of the boat in order to ensure that paddlers could be positioned effectively rather than work against each other. The harbour and sea trials of *Morgawr* (see online video sources given in the bibliography) show the practical effects of this design decision.

There were also several 'open weekends' where work stopped so that the public could be allowed into the workshop space itself to see, touch and discuss the boat. The visitor comments book that was kept nearby clearly show the role of a multi-sensory approach with smell, touch and sound all appreciated (Hurcombe 2007; Sharp 2013). The same source also recorded that people were making repeat visits to the museum to see the progress. Since the NMMC relies on paying visitors this was particularly significant. The whole project was an exceptional success in terms of publicity for the museum and University researchers. The museum's experience of the volunteers has enabled them to have a living exhibition with 'construction as performance' seven days a week for almost a year and they have also gained a cohort of people who are willing to be drawn into other projects and developments. The volunteer experience has thus been a positive aspect of the current project on which future projects can build.

The inverted exhibition

In most exhibitions the news story is the opening and the publicity coverage then tails off but for *Morgawr*, the publicity and media coverage of the building process increased over the life of the construction project. We have called this opposite situation to normal publicity 'the inverted exhibition'. Social media and press releases were able to use the punctuations of the life cycle to generate news items from the arrival of the large tree trunks, to the finishing off of the keel plate, to laying the last side strake, and finally to the launch day itself. Along with presenting research through experimental archaeology, the life cycle approach and the inverted exhibition principle offered rich opportunities for publicity across a range of media. It created unprecedented opportunities for engagement with local, regional, national and international audiences. During the course of the project in October 2011-March 2013, the live construction was accompanied by:

1. an exhibition focussed on Cornwall in the Bronze Age and on the connections of the UK in that period with continental Europe and Ireland, and which featured the first UK display of the master copy of the Bronze Age Nebra Skydisc (found in Germany in 1999) whose gold and tin content may have come from Cornwall.

2. a programme of lectures and education activities aimed at primary school children in the Falmouth region.

3. the dynamic dissemination of progress in the construction of the sewn-plank boat through social media such as Facebook (the first time a specific exhibition at the museum had its own Facebook page), which has to date received more than 1,289 'likes' (59% from outside the UK including mainland Europe, Egypt, Australia and the Americas), and up to 21,621 views for the most popular individual post.

4. the posting of monthly time-lapse videos on YouTube with over 20,000 views to date.

The project has been reported in 59 separate international, national and regional printed press reports (e.g. *The Times, The Sunday Times ,The Daily Mail, The Guardian, The Independent, Current Archaeology, British Archaeology* and a full page feature in BBC History Magazine), and 66 individual online media sites across the world (e.g. *www.springer.de*). The University of Exeter's own web stories were viewed 3,100 times. The project, and the successful launch of the boat in April 2013, were reported by the BBC and ITV in extended reports on national and local television and radio. The interest generated is reflected in the filming that has taken place for a series of documentaries including the Discovery Channel's 'Stonehenge Boat', BBC's 'Stonehenge Connections', BBC Coast 2014 series, and Time Team Special on Bronze Age seafaring.

During the project, 131,835 visitors witnessed the building of the boat in person, over 500 individuals attended one or more of the public lectures, over 1,000 children took part in one of the specially designed education programmes, and over 100 volunteers gave at least one full day to the project. During the exhibition there were 18,000 additional visitors compared to the previous year, and during an Archaeology Week in June 2012 there were 7,500 visitors (compared to 4,500 in the same period in 2011). Qualitatively, the project was highly rated by visitors leaving feedback, and the project gained consistently positive feedback in questionnaires and surveys undertaken by the NMMC. The success of the project to build *Morgawr* has allowed the NMMC to undertake construction of another traditional boat in their workshop.

The publicity arising from the building process and the stages within this has thus been a major outcome for the museum and the dynamic profile of 'the inverted exhibition' is a key learning point for other museums undertaking construction projects.

'paddling as public participation' and 'maintenance as performance': building and repairing small logboats at Kierikki Stone Age Centre, Finland

Logboats have proved to be a very successful addition to many AOAMs especially where it is possible for visitors to try them out for themselves (for example, Sagnlandet Lejre, Denmark; Kierikki, Finland; and Archeon, Netherlands). Logboats are robust compared to other simple watercrafts and also unusual enough in the modern world to form a distinctive part of the AOAM experience for visitors so it is not surprising that they are a popular choice for offering public activities (see Brunning this volume; Nielsen & Gebauer 2005). In some cases there are local logboat finds (e.g. see Knight 2013; Smith 2013 for an online account of the 8 logboats found in one site in the UK) which form a direct basis for the full scale models (FSMs) but many logboats are generic forms providing tangible and plausible reminders of possible boats for which there is no direct evidence nearby. The logboats provide an experience for visitors but they also provide information on performance issues and longevity. Their mere presence can start a dynamic discussion with visitors over transportation and the use of river and marine resources. Logboats are just one form of simple watercraft and flotation aids and it is noted that there is very early evidence for sea travel for which there are no surviving boats so the form of these is unknown (e.g. Simmons and DiBenedetto 2014). The OpenArch collaborative project work by Exeter Univeristy with staff at Kierikki and AÖZA intended to explore these simple boats as part of planned and ongoing experiments. It was in this generic and exploratory experimental framework that the Exeter University team cooperated with Kierikki on a logboat project over two summers. Linda Hurcombe, Brian Cumby, shipwright, and Bruce Bradley, Theresa Emmerich Kamper, and Tom Monrad Hansen travelled to Kierikki to work alongside colleagues at Kierikki and take part in logboat- related activities as part of the Stone Age Market in July 2013 and again in 2014 when Penny Cunningham also participated in the project. The team worked to maintain existing logboats and build a new one using a variety of tools and methods, and all in the public eye.

The aims were:

1. repair and offer maintenance advice on their existing logboats,

2. build a new logboat using timber provided by Kierikki,

3. explore the effectiveness of different tool types, including flaked stone, polished stone, antler and bronze on seasoned and unseasoned wood using charred and uncharred methods.

The experiments with relevant tool edges formed part of a wider use wear experimental programme related to a 'task, tool, technology' oriented approach to understanding the choices made by prehistoric communities in building simple water craft.

The shipwright Brian Cumby looked over the existing logboats at Kierikki. Two of the three were leaking, and taking on water. During the project the brother of the man who had made some of the logboats visited and offered additional information on the existing logboats stating that two of the boats were built in 2008 so some were 5 years old. He stated that the trees for these boats were from c 10 km away. The trees were not easy to obtain as either the tree trunk was broad but a major branch occurred shortly up the trunk, or other tree trunks were longer with no branches but not as broad. Thus most of Kierikki's logboats are suitable for children and narrow hipped adults who can sit down in them. Note though that Mikka Vanhapiha can be seen paddling one of the repaired logboats in the film 'The Sunstone' (Markkula 2012), showing that more experienced paddlers can use even narrow logboats very effectively. Following Brian Cumby's advice the leaking logboats were submerged in water for 24 hours using heavy stones. When emptied and bailed out, they proved to be perfectly tight (i.e. did not leak). As an extra precaution the Exeter and Kierikki team caulked (filled) obvious cracks and splits with locally available moss. This proved very successful and by the end of seven days the boats were floating with no sign of leakage. The maintenance took place in front of visitors who were interested in the work and engaged with the 'dialogue with science' aspects of primary evidence and the longevity issues of these boats. The use of the boats by the public was presented as part of a life cycle and paddling as a public participation in this. The life cycle issues of use and maintenance were an active asset to the visitor experience.

Brian Cumby offered further advice that if, in the future, the moss alone does not work, then substances such as animal fats and or pitch/tar could be painted over the bottom of the boats to ensure no ingress (letting in) of water. Discussions on whether such materials might have been used to help maintain logboats in the past were held and form part of the ongoing problem of deciding how much reasoned guesswork can be used when the direct archaeological evidence is lacking. Likewise, discussions also centred on whether the logboats in museums were under distinct disadvantages because of their museum role. Most AOAMs want to get the best use from their boats and Brian Cumby was able to offer advice on maintenance and storage.

It was clear that the leaks were partly due to the wood getting too dry as the logboats were spending a lot of time on the bank drawn up out of the water. The key advice is, if logboats are afloat and the weather is hot and dry ensure the boats are kept wet. This could be as simple as putting a bucket of water in them overnight when the weather is hot. Many museums close during the winter requiring the logboats to be stored. Brian Cumby recommended that if boats were hauled out for the winter period, they should be stored on substantial timbers to allow a good air flow under and around each hull. To protect them from frost and severe weather, the boats can be covered with straw and then tarpaulins. Ideally it would be good to store them inside a timber framed shelter to keep off snow and ice. The same shelter could also be a useful extra workshop space to repair

Figure 6.3: Experiments at Kierikki created a functional logboat (left) 'and tested tools of antler, flaked stone, polished stone, and bronze (right). Source: Linda Hurcombe.

and build boats and other items in the winter. Although the logboats are heavy, a simple set of logs used as rollers allow them to be moved easily. Once the boat is seasoned, with good care, there is no reason a boat will not last for many years. If the logboat was intended as an example from a later period it might be appropriate to plan an annual overhaul to include an oil or wax application.

In many museums old logboats serve other purposes. They can be upturned as benches or storage places. They can serve as large containers for soaking materials either submerged in water or on the bank filled with liquid. Their size can make them effective containers for large-scale cooking related to feasting or for rendering materials such as oils from fish. The old logboats can sit alongside the usable ones, and those under construction, so that different aspects of the life cycle can form part of the narrative with visitors.

The team also built a new logboat for Kierikki, *Kuikka* (Figure 6.3). Following the Stone Age ethos of the park it was not possible to name or mark the boat in any way, but following the modern ethos it was seen as important to choose a name for the logboat. The boat was named *Kiukka* after a sea bird, a black throated loon or arctic diver, *Gavia artica*. The work was undertaken using a mixture of modern tools and timed experiments with a variety of ancient woodworking tools drawn from different time periods. The controlled experiments allowed the team to estimate that two people working for 5 days could have finished it using traditional tools but in practice, the boat was actively constructed in only 3.5 days, as filming and public interaction and controlled experiments all had to be fitted into the work. If the museum was very busy, the time spent talking to the public could account for half of the time spent depending on the numbers of visitors coming past. Thus if 'construction as performance' was one of the aims of the project then one person working for a month could make a good finely-finished logboat and also have time to engage the public in discussing the construction process. The size of the logboat meant that it was not safe to have more than two people working on the boat for most of the work. If a museum was planning logboat building in

0	**Impossible**; completely ineffective
1	**Almost impossible**; almost ineffective
2	**Problematic**; very small amounts of wood removed so possible; edge effectiveness compromised easily
3	**Problematic but possible**, only small amounts of wood removed but possible to use; edge stable if extremely careful
4	**Slightly problematic**, small amounts of wood removed so slow; some care needed with edge
5	**Ok**, steady removal possible; care needed with edge
6	**Fair**, steady removal possible; some care needed with edge
7	**Fairly Good** rapid removal; no problems with tool edge at all with moderate care
8	**Good**, rapid removal; edge effective with a little care
9	**Very good**, fast and effective removal; edge is sharp, and with a little care durable
10	**Excellent**, fast and effective removal: extremely durable sharp edge (like high quality steel)

Table 6.1: The scoring system for the user to provide a qualitative assessment of each tool's effectiveness for the task of removing wood.

front of the public then the work could easily take place over the main opening season as part of changing displays. Repeat visits could then be planned with the museum stating a launch and trial date as part of a special event day. The boat itself will need to be tried out on the water and adjustments made. For example, Kuikka was first launched in 2013 and it was apparent that the boat was stern heavy. This was because, due to time constraints, more wood was left in the stern. To improve the lie of the boat in the water it was planned to remove 5 cms of wood from the inside of the stern of the boat taking care not to take too much off of the bottom. This would reduce the weight overall and the boat would sit better in the water. It would also be possible to safely remove wood from the outside of the boat both front and back. This would improve the shape and performance overall as well as reducing the weight. In 2014 this extra shaping was undertaken and Kuikka was re-launched. The advantage of logboat construction is that it is possible to make these adjustments, even over different opening seasons.

In the Kierikki case study the research experiment was an investigation to record the effectiveness of different kinds of tools in their use on seasoned and unseasoned wood, using charred versus uncharred techniques and to retain the experimental tools for usewear analysis. The work was undertaken partly via timed trials and with a variety of experienced tool-users so that evaluations could take account of experiences across different users. Two large trunks, one seasoned, the other still fresh and green, were made available to us at Kierikki. Each tool-user was asked to work with each tool at a pace which could be maintained for a day and in a manner which preserved the edge rather than destroyed it. After a phase of use to extract material from a section of tree trunk (usually involving between 20-30 minutes of use) each person was asked to offer a qualitative and reflective assessment and score the tool by its effectiveness and the ease by which it removed wood whilst retaining the edge and pace using the scale provided (Table 1). Each person used each tool but the tools then had the collective wear traces from all five users for that contact material.

Person	tooltype	green charred	green fire dried	green fresh	preference
A	Antler edgeflaked by time used	8	6	4	1st
A	polished stone	9	7	6	2nd
A	chipped stone	9	5	6	3rd
A	bronze	10	9	9	1st
A's preference for wood state		**1st**	**2nd/3rd**	**2nd/3rd**	
B	antler	10	7	6	3rd
B	polished stone	9	5	6	4th
B	chipped stone	10	6	7	2nd
B	bronze	10	8	8	1st
B's preference for wood state		**1st**	**2nd/3rd**	**2nd/3rd**	
C	Antler edge flaked by time used	8	6	3	4th
C	polished stone	8	6	5	3rd
C	chipped stone	9	7	6	2nd
C	bronze	10	9	9	1st
C's preference for wood state		**1st**	**2nd**	**3rd**	
D	antler	4	3	2	4th
D	polished stone	4	2	2	3rd
D	chipped stone	6	4	2	2nd
D	bronze	10	9	9	1st
D's preference for wood state		**1st**	**2nd/3rd**	**2nd/3rd**	
E	antler	10	7	6	2nd
E	polished stone	10	5	6	3rd
E	chipped stone	10	4	6	4th
E	bronze	10	9	9	1st
E's preference for wood state		**1st**	**2nd/3rd**	**2nd/3rd**	

Table 6.2: A summary of the five participants evaluation of the effectiveness of tools of different material on green (unseasoned) fresh wood, green charred wood, and the layer of 'fire dried wood' 2-4 cms immediately underneath the charred material.

The performance of the tools in this simple set of experiments on charred and uncharred, seasoned and fresh wood was designed to explore the choices prehistoric people might be faced with. In prehistoric Kierikki, the geology meant that knappable materials were not as easily available as elsewhere in Europe. The issues being explored were thus about possible choices and the parameters which might affect the material of the tool – the experiments used tools of antler, flaked stone, polished stone, and bronze (see Figure 6.3)- and the decision to use a charring technique or not. The parameters explored were:

- Does charring save time working the wood (seasoned or fresh)?
- Does charring allow 'readily available' tools to be used rather than 'difficult to obtain' tools?
- Rate of need to resharpen versus ease of resharpening for different tool materials?
- Rate of need to rehaft versus ease of rehafting for different tool materials?

The seasoned trunk was very well seasoned and in the uncharred state the wood was very tough to remove for almost all the tools and in the charred state it was more difficult to control the burn, but all the tools proved equally effective in removing the well-fired charred material. The experiment on tool effectiveness was thus established as charring might make an effective choice for working fresh wood but was harder to use effectively for very well-seasoned wood, where the choice of tool material was almost immaterial and the burn rate was more difficult to control.

The results worth a more detailed report here are the experiments with the unseasoned wood where the different tools working green unseasoned wood and charred green wood (Table 6.2) had more variation in their effectiveness. All agreed that, with the charring method, all the tools of whatever material were effective, including the antler tool. The group also discussed other tools made from organic material and agreed that the charred wood could be removed with even more materials, for example, shell or a wooden tool. Charring was thus a method that reduced the absolute advantage of one kind of tool over another, and at the same time reduced the consumption of the more brittle or softer tools. In regions with good access to softer, light woods, which were more easily worked, (e.g. lime, a frequent choice for such boats in temperate Europe) charring might not save as much time and might increase the risk of burning the trunk too deeply in places. It was noted that once some unevenness in the surface and depth of a burning event occurred it was hard to put this right by getting the next charring to progress more evenly. In Finland the evergreen tree species available such as pine and spruce have pockets of wood with high levels of resin. The team found that it was these areas which were hardest to control in the charring process even if areas were protected by clay, wet mud and similar materials.

During the experiments a further category of 'fire dried' was added to the fresh wood and charred wood categories. The experimenters noted that just underneath the charred wood, the heat had changed the material qualities of the underlying wood making it more resilient than green wood as a material, but a little easier to remove as it came out of the trunk in larger slivers of material and could be prised off in a different way. This 'fire dried' wood was a layer c 2-4 cms deep underneath the charred wood. This feature has not previously been identified to our knowledge.

There were tool mark distinctions visible in the final 'fresh green' surface between the four different tool types no matter which of the five people were responsible for the section of work. The polished stone axe 'pounded' the wood and was characterised by a very fibrous surface; the chipped stone toolmarks had a series of almost perpendicular chop marks across the grain breaking up the surface in a vaguely brickwork pattern; the bronze had a relatively smooth woodworking set of marks and the antler tool, when the tool edge was fresh, was able to chop a small section of surface and then the material came away in a splinter or sliver which left behind a set of surface marks which were fluted along the wood fibres and were more akin to riven wood surfaces. This 'dried wood' layer was not so resilient but was still distinguishable when charring the well-seasoned wood. The detailed results of the tool usewear analyses are ongoing and will form part of a future paper.

Verbal discussions amongst the participants showed that those most used to stone tools found all these tools easy to use because they had already adjusted their body actions to cope with the different edge qualities and were more prepared to see the tools as effective. In areas with poor access to stone and without metal knowledge, antler makes an effective tool. All agreed that the advantage of the metal lay not just in its edge but in the longevity of the tool when handled by experienced users and the ease with which it could be resharpened. Hafting formed part of a separate set of discussions around how quickly a haft could be replaced, and how quickly a blade could be replaced within the same haft: a well-made haft was seen as a distinct advantage and often the most long-lived element of the composite tool.

Boats as choices in a 'tasks, tools, technology' approach: experiments building a variety of simple watercraft within the setting of Kierikki Stone Age Centre, Finland, and the Steinzeit Park, AÖZA, Albersdorf, Germany

Aims

The aim of building small watercraft in Kierikki and at AÖZA was to explore the resources used against the performance of simple watercraft. The research was framed very broadly as although there is evidence for dugout boats and also birchbark canoes in the European Mesolithic and early prehistory there are many ways in which different materials might be used and yet would leave few traces (see broad discussions on simple boats in Andersen 2013, McGrail 2001, Nielsen and Gebauer 2005, Simmons and DiBenedetto 2014 and Castro 2014, 18, fig. 4 for an image of a boat based on inflated sea lion skins, and Wheat 1967, 40-46 for the manufacture of a Paiute tule bundle boat and Skamby Madsen and Hansen 1992 for a discussion of bundle boats). The aim was to explore the complex factors affecting the watercraft choices available to early prehistoric people in temperate Europe focussing especially on boats which would be the most unlikely to survive in the archaeological record. Furthermore, the project also wanted to incorporate flotation aids, diving platforms, platforms to take gear to set out, and other buoyant, but not necessarily dry, aids to the exploitation of subsistence and craft resources in waterscapes in prehistory. The project, with the help and cooperation of the staff at Kierikki and AÖZA, built two types of bundle boat, a hide and withy canoe, and a dugout (built by the Exeter team at Kierikki but with Jake Newport's lime dugout in use in AÖZA). There are very many different kinds of simple watercrafts. Hurcombe has also undertaken birch bark removal experiments at Kierikki using stone tools but it was not possible to build a whole birchbark canoe. Nor was it possible to build other types of boat that were considered, an inflated skin raft style boat (see Castro 2014, 18-19), and a split hazel frame with skin coverings (the skins for the latter were prepared but the design of the wood for the frame proved unsuitable). Time and resources were at a premium. Experiments were of necessity 'distributed' across locations and people. Hurcombe, Kamper, and La Porta worked with professional basketmaker, Linda Lemieux, to harvest *Scirpus*

Figure 6.4: Experiments at AÖZA involved cutting the rush in the UK (above), preparing hides and constructing three small watercraft, two bundle boats of Phragmites and Scirpus lacustris and one from withies and cowskins (below). Source: Linda Hurcombe.

lacustris at Lemieux's rushbeds in the the UK (see Figure 6.4 top). Commercially available bundles of *Phragmites* were provided by AÖZA for us to use in Germany, but Hurcombe undertook experiments harvesting *Phragmites* on local sites in the UK. This allowed the effectiveness of stone tools for harvesting to be assessed (as both time and practical constraints such as the sorting and drying of materials) and for the stone tools to form part of the reference collections of wear traces. It also allowed the ethical sourcing of the plants. The hides for the boats were domestic cattle skins provided by AÖZA: seals and larger ungulates were all of a suitable size but the ethics and accessibility of the materials made domestic cattle skins the best choice. The team tested the simple watercraft in a shallow pond, then in the river Elbe, a slow flowing local river, and the logboat and hide boat were also tested in the Baltic Sea. Figure 6.4 shows the bundle boats and hide and withy boat on the river Elbe. This short overview records some of the experiments as qualitative accounts with supporting quantitative elements in order to draw out the differences between the boats as part of the 'choices' made by prehistoric boatbuilders.

The withy and hide boat

It took Kamper, Kutschera, Hurcombe and Vanhapiha (with some help from other project members) several days each to deflesh and then dehair the four cow skins, using the slipping technique for dehairing. (The boat described here used two skins and the other two were for another version of a hide and wood boat that it was not possible to build). Hurcombe and Kamper have undertaken stone tool experiments on similar hides on other occasions so here modern tools were used alongside some stone age ones. These two estimate rates of one or two days of defleshing per hide. This could take one fit person one very long day of extremely hard work or two people taking it in turns to work the hide for a day. The heavy hide was manoeuvred over a tree trunk and blunt-edged tools were used to dehair them but not remove the grain. The hair was allowed to slip (i.e. partially rot and then came out with a blunt scraping action or plucking action). Removing the hair took another three days per hide, so a team of two for 1.5 days but cutting the hair would be quicker and make the skin more water tight as the hair follicle is still occupied by the hair root. Based on experiments by Hurcombe this could halve the time for dehairing. See chapter 8 for an explanation of terms and note that the hair will tend to hold moisture and make the boat heavier when wet, and make it harder for the boat to dry out quickly. Sewing two skins together took another two days by Kamper, Hofeditz and Pfeiffer. Commercial sinew was used but again, previous experiments extracting and processing sinew can be used to give estimates of a few hours for this preparatory task but with much of this likely to be embedded in other activities. The withies used were black dogwood and willow and most were not thicker than a thumb. All the withies were assembled and woven into shape, in a frame first technique where the major pairs (17 pairs across the width of the boat) were pushed into soft ground and the whole tied in with a three rod wale (a basketry technique using three sets of weavers used as a strengthening weave). The elements of the base were pricked slightly and bent into shape, with lashings to tie the elements together. In general the technique was similar to coracle construction (see O'Gibne website reference) and the skins were added and attached by lashing to the frame by Pfeiffer. The difference was that two hides had to be sewn together. The sewing was a waterproof seam technique where the sewing hole was only through partial thickness of the hide and a double seam was constructed with an overlap of c 5 cm. There were 254 withy rod ends so 127 used in total on the frame with other rods added later to protect the bottom of the boat once the skins had been sewn on. Four extra poles were lashed onto the sides as additional side bracings. The black dogwood was left with the bark on but the willow elements were stripped of bark and the arrangement is clearly visible in Figure 6.4 (lower). Removal of bark was seen as optional.

Significantly, it was possible to build the withy and hide boat with stone blades and scrapers alone, and for the sewing, tools such as an awl and potentially a bone or horn needle. A Mesolithic style flake axe might have felled the shoots and saplings in one blow if it was sharp but these are springy young growth and dull edges simply bounce off them. Unhafted blades used by experienced flint tool users (Hurcombe and Kamper) on similar sized tree shoots in woodlands near Exeter took only 1.5-2 minutes for the 1.5 cm diameter pieces and a little more perhaps for slightly thicker pieces. The tools retained their edge for over an hour. The rods did not need much trimming of side branches but the tops were removed as the frame was built and all the ends were trimmed off once the whole of the wicker frame was complete, giving perhaps another three cutting operations maximum and only the last trimming of the ends needed to be done with care to ensure the hide was not placed against a sharp edge. Thus in the collection and preparation of materials, the hide element rather than the wood element was by far the most time-consuming aspect of this boat. The hide covering was attached and allowed to dry under shelters and needed some care to ensure the shrinking hides did not distort the frame. Large beach stones weighted down areas and tensioning strings were attached across the frame as necessary. As the skin dried out the stitching came under a lot of tension and the seam stretched around the stitches. It was decided to apply birch tar to the seam as a precaution. In use it was important to ensure the loading was correct and that load was not stressing the hide seams but the boat was able to be carried easily by two people. All untreated hide boats need to be pulled out of the water after a few days and allowed to dry as they become waterlogged. The team discussed the nature of a dressing for such hide boats and this boat was lifted into the roof area of the 'mesolithic house' at AÖZA to be smoked. This craft performed exceptionally well as it was able to carry two people (200 kg) easily and at one stage five people were in it (total weight c 403 kg). The boat was still able to function but the stress on the seams was a concern. More withies across the base of the boat would carry the stress across weak points. Two experienced canoeists were able to get back into this boat from the water, and it was possible to paddle it standing up. It turned easily and the smooth exterior gave much less drag than the bundle boats. The hide and wicker vessel performed very well and was able to be carried by two people.

The Bundle boats

The bundle boats were assembled by Hurcombe, Fawcett, Newport, Hofeditz and other project members under some time constraints due to an overrun of the time spent preparing the skins. The buoyancy of plant bundles and the materials to wrap the bundle boats together were tested in the pond at AÖZA for a week to assess which materials would work best. For the bundle boat construction a commercial rope was used for reasons of time, but again Hurcombe and Kamper have conducted a range of cordage experiments with different materials to inform these discussions. Hurcombe tested some commercial and hand-made cords.

Hemp, *Scirpus*, and lime bast were plyed (two ply) by hand and assessed alongside commercially available sea grass, water hyacinth, sisal, and processed hemp. Other materials that could have been used include willow bast and nettle. Each cord was tied around a bundle of *Phragmites* and a bundle of *Scirpus* and the bundles were placed in the pond at AÖZA. They were still floating well after two days and there was little change in the tightness of the ties (it was thought that the plants might have swelled), and so each bundle was then submerged and thoroughly wetted and left in the pond for a further five days. After a week in the pond the bundles were pulled out and the ties were assessed. There was no appreciable difference between the ties on each of the plant bundles. The cords were assessed as follows: Both *Scirpus* and lime bast ply well and have both strength and flexibility. The hemp has long fibres which create problems for making up the two ply cord in one go. It was thought better for this cord to make a single string and then ply this separately:

Lime bast plies well and has both strength and flexibility. It performed well after a week in the pond which tallies with its known rot resistant properties. The *Scirpus* cord worked very well dry, but even after one week it was evident that it was loosening and when pulled slightly one of the elements broke. The commercial cordage of sisal and water-hyacinth both performed well but one commercial cord described as 'white hemp' was too loosely plied and was in a poor condition after even one week. For the boat contruction the tree bast fibres seemed to offer the best traditional cordage, but for reasons of time the team needed to use commercial cordage and used the readily available sisal cordage.

Typical *Phragmites* commercial bolts (the name given to a thatcher's bundle) were 5.7-6.6 kg (average 6.175 kg) when dry. The boat was assembled with nine and a half bundles (four in each side and a central short bundle of the remainder). The overall weight was estimated at 57.7 kg when dry. When wet the boat was much heavier and although it could be moved/dragged by two people, it was easier to manage with three or four people. Cutting *Phragmites* is hard work as the silica-rich stems are very tough on tools and hands. Based on experiments in Exeter a handheld flint tool might cut the equivalent of one thatchers bundle per hour of work cutting dry reed in winter, in summer the stem is a little softer and the task is slightly easier but note van Gijn's comments (this volume) that cutting reed was the least popular task. A hafted arrangement of flint edges would make this quicker but the stems are still tough. Further work on cutting green reed with a hafted flint tool is planned for 2016. The contrast between the two plants, dry and waterlogged is marked: a dry *Phragmites* bolt can easily be lifted with one hand, when waterlogged, with effort, one arm, and the whole bolt remains stiff: a dry *Scirpus* bolt can be lifted with one finger and when wet can be lifted by one hand but the rush will bend around either side of the lifting point.

The time to assemble the plants into boats is estimated at two people working together for one day. In contrast to the other boats, the bundle boats sagged once waterlogged. It was clear that we should have built the *Phragmites* boat with more material, but for lighter individuals (e.g. 55kg), it performed well, and could be used as a diving platform and was easy to get back onto from the water. It could be used to hold materials such as nets or traps though with time it came lower in the water. Once well wetted it was very heavy to lift in and out of the water, but it could be dried provided it could be lifted off the ground slightly.

The *Scirpus* rush was harvested with Linda Lemieux at her rush beds in the UK with a mixture of flint tools and modern tools and with the rush loaded into her coracle. Lemieux also discussed with us the parameters of building her coracle which are factored into the discussion below. An unhafted flint blade used while standing in the river (see Figure 6.4) was very effective and a team of three could easily have harvested the rush for the project in a day and slightly less if the material was simply laid out on the river bank and dried there rather than carried a short distance away for drying. The *Scirpus* was robust when fresh but as it dried (over several weeks) it became much softer and more difficult to bundle tightly. The *Scirpus* bundle boat initially performed well but although three light willow poles had been inserted as a slight stiffening, as the material wetted the shape quickly sagged in the centre and trying this boat with people of different weights showed it worked best with 55kg or less. More material would have assisted the initial buoyancy but the sagging needed more framework poles and tighter bindings on the whole, in order to make the boat perform better. However, with tighter bindings the boat would have had more problems when it was taken out of the water: Attempts to dry out this boat were not successful as the material rotted quickly and tighter bindings would not have stopped the outer layers from rotting.

The log boat and the skin boat both had less drag in the water than the bundle boats. Ethnographic accounts of bundle boats vary in size, design and longevity. There are some accounts where green rush is used, and the whole seems to be built in a day using cordage from *Typha* plants growing in the same area (see Wheat 1967). This account states that the boat is more for holding the gear and food collected such as fish or bird eggs from marshes/lagoon areas with the hunter swimming or wading alongside and where the boat is pulled out to dry after a day of use. This kind of boat is not expected to last more than one season. Further experiments with green reed and rush and with bindings are planned for 2016.

A 'tasks, tools, technologies' approach

The four boats thus covered several different styles of watercraft, plant bundle boats, withy and skin, and dugouts. The 'tasks, tools, and technologies' approach was taken and an evaluation of the effectiveness, performance and durability of the tools was made. The key issues are the resources needed in terms of direct raw materials, time and skill, and the tools required (and consumed) and the time and skill to make these tools. The location of some of the activities in terms of time and space were also considered *e.g.* kinds of environments, storage or dry weather needs, season, logistics of the numbers of people likely to be needed to work together all played a part. Evaluating the relative tools required is a new concept which can be termed 'tool economics'.

The logboat is the largest consumer of tools, though not necessarily of time. Any of the tools tested in Kierikki could have been used to shape the wood. If shaping the wood using the antler or flake tools these would have needed sharpening or replacement more frequently than the polished stone tool, but this tool worked well at a slow and steady pace. The charring technique might help extend the life of the tools and thus might result in an overall saving of time. The wood species also makes a difference. Lime and oak are used in preference in temperate Europe. Oak would have to be worked unseasoned with such tools (Cumby says even steel tools struggle with seasoned oak) and lime is a light wood easy to work with stone/antler tools, (Jake Newport confirmed that his logboat of lime had been easy to work) but this depends on the environment as large lime or oak trees were not available in northern Europe where pine and spruce might take their place. Much depends on the tree species in the environment and the toolkit of the period. As explained above Kierikki is not a site with ready access to large amounts of suitable flint for tool making. Rushes and reeds were available locally and a future experiment at Kierikki with these materials might be useful.

The rush was able to be cut with one hand held flint tool as the rush did not wear the tool edge down when used by experienced flint-tool users but, since a team does the work best, each person might have their own tool. The *Phragmites* would be most effectively harvested by a hafted tool and would take a lot more harvesting time but the resulting bundle boat would be likely to perform better if the bundles are constructed from dried materials. This might change with material used green and the expediency of the need for a boat and the style of the environment might affect the choice. The hide and withy boat was light and relatively durable. The performance of this boat over time will be monitored. The main difference between the dugout boat and the hide and withy one is that the wooden boat would be more robust in areas where there are stones in the riverbed or shorelines. The logboat need not consume more tools (and charring might extend the lives of the tools that were used), though the material for these might vary. This boat needs some form of heavy duty shaping tools but the hide and withy boat needs only blades and scrapers, and, if the boat is to be larger than the largest skins available then a sewing kit of an awl at least, if not an awl and needle, is essential. A coracle or 'bull boat' in the past was covered with one large animal skin. The canoe shape and length achieved by the hide and withy boat needed more than one skin but the trade-off is that the shape allows it to be paddled very effectively. For the logboats versus hide and withy boats the precise qualities of wood vary for different species and these might need to be considered as well as the size of suitable trees for a logboat, whereas the size of the skins available from animals in the environment and the availability of easily cut small saplings and shoots would need to be taken into account for the hide and withy boat.

Conclusions: Life cycle and object biography approaches to boats as structures

These three sets of experiments are in different layers. They bring together research and public aspects of experiments in a series of intersecting interests with different broad and specific questions in cooperation with a traditional museum, an AOAM based around one site, and an AOAM representing multiple periods and sites. The scientific aspects of the work took place in front of the public and formed part of the dialogue with science held with them by the participants and by the staff at the AOAMs. Preparing materials, constructing the boats, making design decisions, launching, repairing, and maintaining boats spark other conversations on the use of tools, the evidence that survives, communication and transport in the past, and skills and difficulties past and present. Kierikki gained from Brian Cumby's advice on the maintenance and storage of their existing logboats and also benefitted from the new logboat which was finished off with modern tools. AÖZA benefitted from the activities of making the craft and from the durable hide and withy boat which intrigued the public. The bundle boats were envisaged as more temporary craft but more will be built in the future to test out some green plants and their effectiveness over a season. The experimental tools used in all the three projects reported here are also part of a scientific project assessing task-focussed wear traces in a 'tasks, tools, technology' approach which will enable a better understanding of archaeological wear traces, and the ongoing usewear analyses will form a separate article in the future. The scientific aspects of the projects all benefitted from a better understanding of the constraints of materials and skills, and the consideration of the possibilities for labour organisation, performance under different conditions, maintenance and durability. The object biography approach was able to create this mosaic of different interests and benefits for researchers and the museums as well as the visitors themselves.

Acknowledgements

The authors would like to thanks Prof Robert van de Noort, Dr Lucy Blue, and Andy Wykes, Jenny Wittamore and the whole team of volunteers at the National Maritime Museum Cornwall, UK, and the Arts and Humanities Research Council, UK for the research project to build *Morgawr*, and Jon Bennett for allowing us to use his images of *Morgawr*. For all the support for the building of the logboat we especially thank Leena Lehtinen and her staff at the Stone Age Centre, Kierikki, Finland, and the team who worked on the boat and the tools and techniques experiments Theresa Emmerich Kamper, Tom Monrad Hansen and Prof Bruce Bradley. In the UK Linda Lemieux kindly allowed Hurcombe, Kamper and Alice La Porta to cut rush in her rush beds. At the Steinzeitpark, AÖZA, Germany, special thanks are due to Dr Rüdiger Kelm, Anka Schroeder, and the active 'friends of the park' for all their support. Some of the participants in the Mesolithic Living Project donated much time, skill and thought to building and testing the small watercraft despite all having other projects of their own: many thanks to Emily Fawcett, Simone Hofeditz, Theresa Emmerich Kamper, Morton Kutschera, Werner Pfeifer, Marco Claussen, Jake Newport, Miika Vanhapiha, Marco Wolff. Mark Hylkema kindly offered some advice on building a bundle boat based on his Californian experience.

Bibliography

Andersen, S.H. 2013. *Tybrind Vig: Submerged Mesolithic settlements in Denmark*. Jutland Archaeological Society Publications and Moesgård Museum: Højbjerg.

Castro, V. 2014. Pre-hispanic cultures in the Atacama Desert: a Pacific coast overview. Sanz, N., Arriaza, B.T. and Standen, V.G. (eds.) *The Chinchorro Culture: A comparative perspective*. The archaeology of the earliest mummification. Arica: Mexico. pp. 11-34.

Bevan-Jones, R. 2002. *The Ancient Yew, a History of Taxus baccata*. Windgather Macclesfield.

Burningham, N. and De Jong, A. 1997. The Duyfken Project: an Age of Discovery ship reconstruction as experimental archaeology. *International Journal of Nautical Archaeology* 26: 277-292.

Clark, P. (ed.). 2004a. *The Dover Bronze Age Boat*. English Heritage: Swindon.

Clark, P. 2004b. The Dover Boat ten years after its discovery. In P. Clark (ed.), *The Dover Bronze Age Boat*. English Heritage: Swindon. pp. 1-12.

Coates, J. 2005. The Bronze Age Ferriby Boats: seagoing ships or estuary ferry boats? *International Journal of Nautical Archaeology* 35 (1), 38-42.

Coates, J., McGrail, S., Brown, D., Gifford, E., Grainge, G., Greenhill, B., Marsden, P., Rankov, B., Tipping, C. and Wright, E.V. 1995. Experimental Boat and Ship Archaeology: Principles and Methods. *International Journal of Nautical Archaeology* 24 (4): 293-301.

Crumlin-Pedersen, O. 1995. Experimental archaeology and ships–bridging the arts and the sciences. *International Journal of Nautical Archaeology* 24(4):303-306.

Crumlin-Pedersen, O. 1996. Problems of Reconstruction and the Estimation of Performance, in R. Gardiner (ed.), *The Earliest Ships. The Evolution of Boats in Ship*. Conway History of the Ship. Conway Maritime Press: London. pp. 111-119.

Crumlin-Pedersen, O. 1999. Experimental ship archaeology in Denmark. Harding, A.F. (ed.) *Experiment and desgin: archaeological studies in Honour of John Cole*s. Oxbow Books: Oxford. pp. 139-147.

Crumlin-Pedersen, O. 2006a. The Dover Boat–a Reconstruction Case-Study. *International Journal of Nautical Archaeology* 35 (1): 58-71.

Crumlin-Pedersen, O. 2006b. Experimental archaeology and ships–principles, problems and examples, in Blue, L., Hocker, F. and Englert, A. (eds.) *Connected by the Sea; Proceedings of the Tenth International Symposium on Boat and Ship Archaeology, Roskilde 2003*. 1-7. Oxbow: Oxford. pp. 1-7.

Crumlin-Pedersen, O. and McGrail, S. 2006. Some principles for the reconstruction of ancient boat structures. *International Journal of Nautical Archaeology* 35(1): 53-57.

Crumlin-Pedersen, O. and Trakadas, A. 2003. *Hjortspring: a pre-Roman Iron-Age warship in context*. Viking Ship Museum. Roskilde.

Darrah, R. 2004. The reconstruction experiment, in P. Clark (ed.), *The Dover Bronze Age Boat*. English Heritage: Swindon. pp. 163-188.

Darrah, R. 2012. The reconstruction of the Dover Boat, in A. Lehoërff (ed.), *Beyond the Horizon; Societies of the Channel and North Sea 3,500 years ago.* Somogy Art Publishers: Paris. pp. 44-49.

Hurcombe, L.M. 2007. A sense of materials and sensory perception in concepts of materiality, *World Archaeology* 39(4): 532-545.

Knight, M. 2012. *Must Read* (an account of the Must farm archaeology including the logboats) available to download at pdf http://www.mustfarm.com/wp/wp-content/uploads/MustRead-June2012.pdf.

Marsden, P. 2004. Reconstructing the Dover boat. In Clarke, P. (ed.) *The Dover Bronze Age Boat in Context: Society and water transport in prehistoric Europe.* Oxbow Books: Oxford. pp. 17-19.

Morrison, J.S., Coates, J.F., Rankov, N.B. and Rankov, B. 2000. *The Athenian trireme: the history and reconstruction of an ancient Greek warship.* Cambridge University Press: Cambridge.

Mac Cárthaigh, C. (ed.) 2008. *Traditional boats of Ireland: history, folklore and construction.* The Collins Press: Cork.

McGrail, S. 1988. Assessing the performance of an ancient boat–The Hasholme Logboat. *Oxford Journal of Archaeology* 7(1): 35-46.

McGrail, S. 2001. *Boats of the world: from the Stone Age to medieval times.* Oxford University Press: Oxford.

Nicolaisen, I. and Damgård-Sørensen, T. 1991. *Building a longboat: an essay on the culture and history of a Bornean people.* The Viking Ship Museum, Roskilde: Roskilde.

Nielsen, J. and Gebauer, A.B. 2005. Dugout canoes. In Price, T.D. and Gebauer, A.B. (eds.) *Smakkerup Huse: A late Mesolithic coastal site in Northwest Zealand, Denmark.* Aarhus University Press: Aarhus. pp. 83-84.

Osgood, C. 1940. *Ingalik Material Culture.* Yale University Press: New Haven.

Petersen, H.C. 1986. *Skinboats of Greenland.* The National Museum of Denmark, The Museum of Greenland and The Viking Ship Museum in Roskilde: Roskilde.

Sharp, R. 2013. Sound advice; using sound in exhibitions is a great way to engage visitors, *Museums Journal* January 2013; pp. 24-29.

Shaw, J.T. (ed.) 1993. *The Trireme Project: Operational Experience, 1987-90: Lessons Learnt* (No. 31). Oxbow Books: Oxford.

Shaw-Smith, D. 2003. *Traditional crafts of Ireland.* Thames & Hudson: London.

Simmons, A.H. and DiBenedetto, K. 2014. *Stone Age Sailors: Palaeolithic Seafaring in the Mediterranean*, Left Coast Press: Walnut Creek.

Skamby Madsen, J. and Hansen, K. 1992 Sivbåde. The Viking Ship Museum: Roskilde.

Smith, L. 2013. *Eight sleek Bronze Age log boats that would fit right in at the Boat Race emerge from a silted up river thousands of years after they were sunk.* Http://www.dailymail.co.uk/sciencetech/article-2335273/Eight-Bronze-Age-log-boats-important-Mary-Rose-emerge-silted-river-thousands-years-left-rot.html.

Van de Noort, R. 2011. *North Sea Archaeologies: A maritime biography, 10,000 BC – AD 1500.* Oxford University Press: Oxford.

Van de Noort, R., Cumby, B., Blue, L., Harding, A., Hurcombe, L., Hansen, T.M., Wetherelt, A., Wittamore, J. and Wyke, A. 2014. Morgawr: an experimental Bronze Age-type sewn-plank craft based on the Ferriby boats. *International Journal of Nautical Archaeology*, 43 (2): 292-313.

Vosmer, T. 2000. The reconstruction of the Magan boat. *Prehistoria* 1 (the official journal of the UISPP). pp. 169-173.

Vosmer, T., Belfioretti, L., Staples, E. and Ghidoni, A. 2011. January. The "Jewel of Muscat" Project: reconstructing an early ninth-century CE shipwreck. In *Proceedings of the Seminar for Arabian Studies* 41. Archaeopress: Oxford. pp. 411-424.

Wendrich. W. (ed.) 2012. *Archaeology and Apprenticeship: body knowledge, identity, and communities of practice*. The University of Arizona Press: Tucson.

Wheat, M. 1967. Survival arts of the primitive Paiutes. Nevada University Press: Reno, Nevada.

Videos and social media for *Morgawr*

National Maritime Museum Cornwall Facebook page for the Bronze Age boat reconstruction: http://www.facebook.com/ 2012BCBronzeAgeBoat#!/2012BCBronzeAgeBoat.

Example of YouTube time-lapse video: http://www.youtube.com/watch?v=SOl8rHHJFmE

Example of international press coverage of boat launch at NMMC:http://www.spiegel. de/wissenschaft/mensch/ausgegraben-archaeologe-baut-boot-aus-der-bronzezeit-nach-a-903045.html.

Example of UK TV coverage: http://www.bbc.co.uk/news/uk-england-17775009.

The last yew withy stitch: https://www.youtube.com/watch?v=1NQv-AOD_GQ.

Second sea trial: https://www.youtube.com/watch?v=xG_b5Ghfmy0.

Building the Bronze Age Boat Falmouth: Episode 1 https://www.youtube.com/watch?v=22chM3wYrk0.

Building the Bronze Age Boat Falmouth: Episode 2 https://www.youtube.com/watch?v=3u22j34g85Q.

Building the Bronze Age Boat Falmouth: Episode 3 https://www.youtube.com/watch?v=-ZrhjaDEkiw.

Building the Bronze Age Boat Falmouth: Episode 4 https://www.youtube.com/watch?v=6bQUTBv1kgI.

Building the Bronze Age Boat Falmouth: Episode 5 https://www.youtube.com/watch?v=sWL9XmJhYf4.

Building the Bronze Age Boat Falmouth: Episode 6 https://www.youtube.com/watch?v=P2VFGkj7Spc.

Building the Bronze Age Boat Falmouth: Episode 7 https://www.youtube.com/watch?v=SOl8rHHJFmE.

Maiden voyage: http://taivideotube.com/videos/morgawrs-maiden-voyage-l6v53676a4t585i5n4j6v4.html.

Programme on Stonehenge which has a section on *Morgawr* after 45 minutes https://www.youtube.com/watch?v=1E3OsnT8E2w.

Morgawr (2013) a film produced by Paul Inman and Directed by Mark Jenkin https://vimeo.com/76346352.

Other videos

Fotevikens Museum: How to build a copy of a medieval cog ship https://www.youtube.com/watch?v=gCyUKJV8_WI.

Markkula, P. 2012. *Sun Stone / Aurinkokivi. One year survival in difficult Stone Age conditions.* DVD 16 minutes. Oulu: Kierikki Stone Age Centre.

O'Gibne, Cliadhbh makes hide and wicker coracles and larger boats. http://www.boynecurrach.com/newgrange-currach-project.html.

Tåi video Log Boat or Dugout Building in Finland in 1936 – Kansanperinnenet http://taivideotube.com/videos/log-boat-or-dugout-building-in-finland-in-1936-7645g445p5o505l5q5w5h5.html.

Steven Stolper, Building a tule boat http://www.natureoutside.com/building-a-tule-boat-part-1-the-california-boat/.

Experiments on possible Stone Age glue types

Werner Pfeifer and Marco Claußen

Introduction

There is tangible evidence of birch tar used from early prehistory in Europe (Aveling & Heron 1999; Piotrowski, 1999; Johann *et al.* 2001; Mazza *et al.* 2006; Groom *et al.* 2014; Bleicher *et al.* 2015). This paper considers the production of different kinds of adhesive materials including tar, pitch and glue. In particular, it deals with aceramic birch tar distillation. There are finds of the tar and yet there are no tangible remains of the birch bark reduction process. In a volume on structures, there are many different kinds to explore, some of which leave no trace; instead the evidence is tangible but indirect. The individual experiments presented here provide a possible means of producing this important substance. The methods give reliable results and allow the exploration of the potential archaeological traces to be considered. If the proceeding set of experiments can be brought to the attention of archaeological features; for instance, the remains of a small fire with traces of birch charcoal, amongst other forms of charcoal – and the presence of a thin baked clay layer, may both indicate the remains of birch tar distillation structures. Some of the glue types considered here require no structure, yet the birch bark tar distillation must have some way of restricting air; which then makes seemingly insignificant or enigmatic archaeological features take on greater importance. Although there is direct archaeological evidence for the use of birch bark tar adhesive during the Stone Age, no clear evidence yet exists for the structures that may have distilled the adhesive in question. The glue types produced by the experiments consider a range of possibilities.

Experiments

Making and testing of several possible glue types which might have been used in the hunter and gatherer period of the European Stone Age (without the aid of ceramics).

Glue types produced in this experiment are:

1. Birch bark tar and pitch
2. Pine wood tar and pitch
3. Pine resin / wax glue
4. Pine resin / wax / charcoal glue
5. Hide glue
6. Blue Bell glue

Tar and pitch

Raw materials used for the distillation of tar and pitch are birch bark and pine wood, respectively. The terms tar and pitch have been used interchangeably in the discourse relating to adhesives, thus causing confusion. According to modern terminology in recent publications (Hirzel 2008; Todtenhaupt *et al.* 2007) as well as the commonly understood *e.g.* Wikipedia (https://en.wikipedia.org/wiki/Pitch_%28resin%29), tar is considered as a fluid, watery form, and pitch a more solid form of a very complex chemical composition. This simple definition is useful for archaeologists.

Birch bark tar and pitch

The methods used to reconstruct the possibilities of tar/pitch production were implemented without ceramics to better understand such extraction in eras pre-dating ceramic technology. Two different types of distillation were used, the 'open distillation' -where a pipe leads the gas/steam/tar mixture out during the firing process – and the 'closed distillation' in which the distilled substances collect in a relatively cooler vessel below the 'oven'.

Description of the 'open distillation' experiments

by Werner Pfeifer

The set up for the 'open distillation' is shown in Figures 7.1 & 7.2. A hollowed-out stick from elder (*Sambucus nigra*) leads from the bottom of the 'oven' through the ground whereas the other opening ends above a vessel. The base of the 'oven', as well as the birch bark are covered by a sealing layer consisting of a mixture made of mud, sand and clay and in which the fine grain part of the clay is highly reduced. The mixture should not only hold the layer together, but it should retain its integrity while fired. The layer is only 2 to 3 cm thick, in order to let the heat enter the inner 'oven' area easily. The layer around the bark is then smeared well with watery fingers to close all holes, so that the bark is completely sealed. A ring of stones support the structure (Figure 7.1).

A thick pack of dry grass covers the 'oven' to create a layer of ash around it to possibly fill little cracks that might appear while firing; and then a fire was laid around the structure. Then the oven was fired immediately for two to three hours to reach as high temperature as possible. The wood for the experiments was gathered and stacked beforehand so that the fire could be sustained continuously for this period.

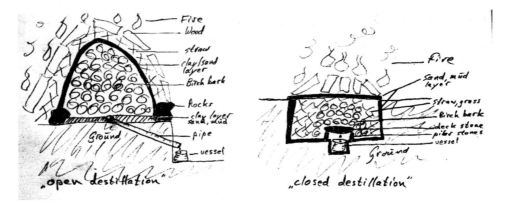

Figure 7.1: Diagrams to show the 'open' distillation and 'closed' distillation arrangements.
Source: Werner Pfeifer and Marco Plaussen.

Observations

In general there was first 'smoke'-which is a mixture of gas and steam – and after about 10 minutes the smoke continued until the firing stopped. After about 20 minutes from the start of the firing, a somewhat clear watery liquid was recognised (wood acid, according to Wikipedia). It was at this stage, that occasional dark brown drops – the tar – began dripping out of the pipe. After the fire burnt down to ashes, the oven was allowed to cool down for half an hour. When breaking open the oven the birch bark had transformed to charcoal. The vessel was then put close by or above either a fire or hot ambers so that the fluid liquid evaporated and left a little bit of black, sticky pitch. The firing process in general consumed a full wheel barrel load of wood for each experiment, sometimes a bit more, when there was a good wind.

With one experiment, the mud/sand/clay sealing layer around the bark cracked slightly during firing and smoke was observed coming out of these cracks. It had contained a higher concentration of fine pottery clay than the other experiments. Filling the cracks with fine sand during firing did not close them properly. In this case it happened in a late stage, so that most of the tar was already extracted and it did not really seem to effect the distillation process.

For comparative purposes we made one distillation firing experiment with a raw (unfired clay pot) and one with a metal pot. The clay pot turned red during the distillation firing process and after cooling down, it was observed to be well-fired. When tapping it with a fingertip it gave a high tone, which indicates a well-fired clay pot and high temperatures during firing. Interestingly, the colour of the pot outside is reddish to light brownish, but inside it was completely black, indicating a burning process without oxygen (Figure 7.2).

Conclusions

All these experiments yielded only a very little pitch but our control distillations with the clay and the metal pot gave very similar results. Thus, it is likely that the birch bark used was not of good quality. It was very, very thin and harvested from young birch trees. There was still a lot of wood on it too and the pieces were small, so it was not possible to pack them in a high density. However, as we still received some

a.

b.

c.

d.

e.

f.

g.

h.

Figure 7.2: The 'open distillation' method. Source: Werner Pfeifer and Marco Plaussen.

pitch each time, the method of construction worked well. The same method was demonstrated a few weeks later in Kierikki, Finland, with thick good quality birch bark was available, and it produced a lot of pitch. These later results strengthened our conclusions regarding the role played by the quality of birch bark.

The sealing layer around the birch bark needs to consist of a high percentage of mud and sand and just a very little bit of fine clay. It must also be very thin (2-3 cm only) in order to let the heat enter the centre of the structure. A previous experiment a year earlier used a thick layer of about 8-10 cm of mud fired for several hours: The experiment was unsuccessful as the bark inside was not burned at all proving that a thick layer prevents the production of tar.

The remains of the clay/mud/sand sealing layer after the firing process are quite soft and brittle, especially when taken in the hand and squeezed a bit. This means, that the remains of the oven will have disappeared within a year or two. It will look just like any normal fire place. Thus as such, recognizing a pitch distillation feature in an archaeological context after thousands of years will be extremely difficult, if not impossible. There might be some remaining microscopic tar traces in the sand, but there needs to be some more investigations done in this matter. We did one experiment without any pipe or pot under the oven; instead we placed a 3 cm thick layer of sand on the base – where the pipe or pot *would have* been – to test if the tar will be visible in the sand afterwards, but we could not find any visual traces of tar at the end. The comparative experiment without the unbaked clay vessel showed that some fragments of fired clay might remain, but identification of such remains might be problematic in the archaeological record if they are off site.

As we needed a lot of wood for gaining very little tar, it is suggested that the pitch distilleries in the Stone Age might not have been in the settlements but rather in the woods where all raw material was in-situ and no extra labour was needed to carry everything into the settlements; except, of course, for the pitch at the end. Thus, finding these places will be very difficult nowadays. This might be a reason why no Stone Age pitch distilleries have ever been found.

The main result from the clay pot distillery experiment was that the pot was black inside but did not smell at all of tar or pitch! It was filled with water after cooling down and there were no indications of oily or other substances on the water surface. The water tasted clear as well. This indicates, that all tar had been removed during distillation, or some might have entered the clay itself, but leaving no visible traces.

A colleague, Mrs Erika Drews in Albersdorf (Germany) had made a small clay pot distillery, which yielded no tar or pith in her experiment, but she claimed that after the experiment her clay pot was waterproof, which is normally not the case with this type of clay. So it might be, that the tar entered the clay during firing and sealed it. This means for archaeologists to look for traces of tar in the clay of late Stone Age vessels itself, especially when they are black inside (Erika Drews pers. comm).

Description of the 'closed distillation' experiments

by Marco Claußen

For the 'closed distillation' experiments, a shallow pit (approximately 30 cm deep and 60 cm in diameter) was dug. A little groove was dug in the centre of the pit in which to place a vessel – either a little clay pot, a metal can or in one case a cut-open part of a deer skull, to collect the tar. As clay pots and cans were not likely invented during most of the hunter-gatherer periods, a deer skull was used to test whether it would prove to be a useful receptacle for collecting tar and producing pitch. The bottom and the sides of the pit were smeared with wet clay to prevent tar from disappearing into the ground

To enable the tar to reach the vessel, a series of small pillar stones (3 cm high) were placed around the vessel and then capped with a deck stone. The deepest point of the deck stone pointed toward the centre of the vessel to enable the tar drip into it. There was a space of about 3-4 cm between the stone pillars for the tar to drip into the relatively cooler space below the deck stone during the firing process.

A thick layer of birch bark was placed around and on top of the deck stone. To stabilize the bark, the space between the bark and the sides of the pit were filled with dry grass and little twigs. The birch bark layer was covered with a layer of dry grass and twigs, filling the entire pit up to ground level followed by a thin layer of sand and then about 2 cm thick sealing layer of clay, mud and sand mixture to seal the whole pit completely. A fire burned on top of the structure for 2-3 hours. Once the fire had burned down the pit was left to cool for least an hour to prevent the heat inside creating a fire when coming in contact with oxygen (Figure 7.1).

Observations

In general, the birch bark had turned into charcoal, especially in the upper layers. The vessel contained quite a lot of liquid and some tar, slightly more than we had in the 'open distillation' experiments.

However, the experiment required a lot of wood (about one to one and a half full wheelbarrow loads). In an attempt to reduce the wood consumption, the depth of the pit was increased in one experiment to 60 cm deep. The increased pit-depth limited the impact from the wind, and it was thought that the depth would slow the wood burning and intensify the heat.

The results demonstrate that due to less oxygen in the deep pit, the fire did not produce the intense heat required for the distillation process.

Building a clay/sand/mud layer over the bark, similar to the technique used in the open distillation experiment, also failed because the isolation layer was too thick. The thick layer was about 3-4 cm of sand covering the bark and a 3-4 cm thick layer of mud/clay prevented the temperature inside becoming hot enough to produce tar. The results produced a watery liquid in the vessel and the bark was not burned at all (Figure 7.3).

In order to have data to which we could compare our results, a controlled experiment was conducted using a metal pot. The quantity of liquid and tar produced in both experiments were similar.

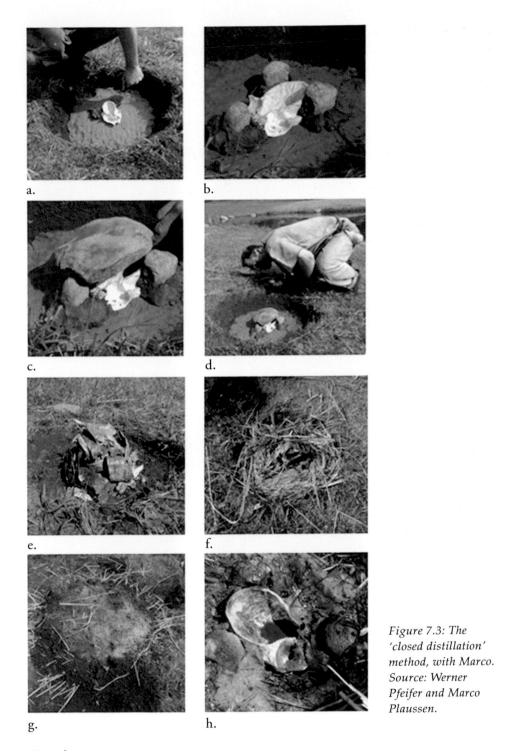

a.

b.

c.

d.

e.

f.

g.

h.

Figure 7.3: The 'closed distillation' method, with Marco. Source: Werner Pfeifer and Marco Plaussen.

Conclusions

As evaporation is prevented in the closed system, the 'closed distillation' yielded slightly more tar than the 'open' method: The 'closed distillation' method is an appropriate method for making tar. It needs just as much wood as the 'open' distillation method suggesting that Stone Age people would probably have done this in the woods, not in the settlements, to reduce labour.

The fire needs lots of oxygen, so firing is best on ground level rather than inside a deep pit. The isolation layer between the fire and the bark needs to be thin for the heat to reach the centre of the structure. Layers of up to 4 cm seem to work well – anything thicker prevents heat reaching the birch bark.

As no real fine clay is needed for the structure, the remains of this distillation method will leave little trace in the ground and the trace is similar to those left be a 'normal' cooking fire after several years. The sand/clay/mud sealing layer used to cover the bottom and sides of the shallow pit and becomes very brittle after firing and after a short time disintegrates.

Turning tar to pitch without pots

To turn tar into pitch, the deer skull used to collect the tar in the 'closed distillation' experiment was hung over a low fire/burning embers over a grill made out of fresh willow branches gently heated. The heat was hot enough to let the liquids evaporate leaving behind a fine pitch. The deer skull proved to be a suitable vessel for this experiment (Figure 7.4). Other vessels that still need to be tested using this method are birch bark containers, hooves, horn and wooden bowls.

Pine wood tar and pitch

The 'open distillation' method as described above, was used to produce pine wood tar. Pine wood was chopped into small finger sized pieces and placed into a metal container. Since the method mentioned above demonstrated the possibility of making tar without using pots we felt it was not necessary to do the same with pine wood. Once the tar had been extracted it was heated to become pitch. The resulting pitch smells slightly different to the birch bark pitch, but looks similar. Future experiments will show if it can be used in as similar way as birch bark pitch. The wood turned into fine charcoal, which was used to 'boil' tar into pitch (Figure 7.5).

Figure 7.4: Turning tar to pitch without pots. Source: Werner Pfeifer and Marco Plaussen.

Figure 7.5: The wood turned into fine charcoal (a & b) and used to boil tar into pitch (c). Source: Werner Pfeifer and Marco Plaussen.

a.

b.

c.

Pine resin and bee wax mix glue

To make the glue, pine resin and bees wax (ratio of 3:1) were heated until they had melted together and became a yellowish creamy liquid. After cooling down the mixture becomes a hard but not brittle glue. In earlier experiments, the resulting glue were tested on flint hafted tools (including arrowheads, spear heads and knife shafts), that had first been bound with string and then covered with the glue. The glue worked very well; it was so much easier and quicker to make; and could be made in much higher quantities than the tar and pitch. As the components – resin from conifers and bees wax – were available during the Stone Age in Europe, the likelihood of making and using this glue is very high; however, there is a lack of archaeological evidence in Europe. The glue recipe comes from Robert Berg who uses it on Atlatl spears made for hunting wild boar (http://www.thunderbirdatlatl.com/).

Pine resin, bee wax and charcoal mix glue

This glue requires mixing pine resin, bees wax and charcoal (or wood ash from a fire place) together (ratio 3:1:1). The mix has to be stirred until a black liquid forms: the resulting glue is very hard. It seems that adding the charcoal creates an even stronger glue than the resin and bees wax. This glue has also been used on hafted arrow heads and works well. As this glue is black and as hard birch bark pitch, some archaeological findings claimed to be birch bark pitch, could be this resin mix glue, especially as it is so much easier to make than any pitch (McNutt 2010).

Hide glue (collagen glue)

Two experiments using raw animal hide were conducted. The first of which used raw hide from a pig, and was unable to produce any glue due to the high fat content. The experiment with raw cow hide worked well. Raw hide pieces were boiled in water until soft. When the water level dropped, the heat was reduced and boiled slowly, thus reducing the hide to a slimy liquid; the resulting glue appeared to be very strong. The glue was used in bow making for gluing layers of wood together and/or gluing raw hides on the bow back. The glue proved to be very strong and flexible but lost its gluing effect when it became wet, which reduces its usefulness in the moist environments of Europe. Furthermore, there seem to be no archaeological records of this glue from European Stone Age, but as the material was regularly available, it might be possible that it was used.

Additional glue types are fish hide glue and, hoof and bone glue. For the glues to be affective they need to be freed from fat and minerals (filtering), watered and heated not higher than 60°C. It is best to heat them in a separate ceramic container placed in hot water. Metal containers are said to interact in a negative way with the glue. Further experiments that need to be conducted to test whether mixing collagen glues with casein, makes the glue waterproof.

Figure 7.6: Bluebells (WARNING: contain toxic glycosides and humans can be poisoned if the bulbs are mistaken for spring onions and eaten. http://www.kew.org/science-conservation/ plants-fungi/hyacinthoides-non-scripta-bluebell). Source: Werner Pfeifer and Marco Plaussen.

Blue Bell glue

The Blue Bell (*Hyacinthoides non scripta*) is a beautiful little plant, growing in some parts of Western Europe. It has a little underground bulb, which if squeezed, produces a sticky liquid. This liquid was used in former times in England for fletching feathers to arrows. The glue is applied directly onto the feather shaft and then stuck onto the arrow shaft (McNutt 2010). This needs to be tested further with some experiments (Figure 7.6).

Other glue types

Wild cherry sap

Fresh sap of wild cherry wood can be used as a glue. By applying the sap as it comes out of the wood no processing necessary (Bruce Bradley pers. comm.).

Pine resin sand glue

In the Kasachstan Region of Russia the people mix very, very fine sand with pine resin and charcoal and used to glue flint arrow heads on to shafts. The reasons for adding sand to the mixture is uncertain but could be related to volume (Ajdar pers comm.).

Gluten glue

Since the Neolithic farmers have had access to starch. By pouring hot water over wheat powder a light sticky glue is produced which might have been used for some purposes where height strength is not necessary, such as, filling little cracks in all kinds of pots and bowls.

Honey glue

Honey is sticky too, but there are doubts that this high valued food will have been used as glue.

Casein-glue

By mixing casein (curd) with calcium hydroxide until it reaches a sticky consistency producing a very strong and waterproof glue used on wood and leather but yet to be tested on projectile points.

Conclusion

Experiments on distillation are ongoing and with each experiment there are different conditions since all of these experiments are actualistic with the weather and fire wood varying. The experiments presented here show two potential methods using structures, which leave few archaeological traces. With each experiment different ideas for the next experiment come to mind with a view to improving success rate of the methods and achieving a better understanding of the key elements of your success.

Bibliography

Aveling, E.M. and Heron, C. 1999. Chewing tar in the early Holocene: an archaeological and ethnographic evaluation.' *Antiquity Oxford* 73: 579-584.

Berg, R. *Thunderbird Altatl.* http://www.thunderbirdatlatl.com/.

Bleicher, N., Kelstrup, C., Olsen, J.V. and Cappellini, E. 2015. Molecular evidence of use of hide glue in 4th millennium BC Europe.' *Journal of Archaeological Science* 63: 65-71.

Groom, P., Schenk, T. and Moéll Pedersen, G. 2013. Experimental explorations into the aceramic dry distillation of *Betula pubescens* (downy birch) bark tar. *Archaeological and Anthropological Science* 7: 47-58.

Helwig, K., Monahan, V., Poulin, J. and Andrews, T.D. 2014. Ancient projectile weapons from ice patches in northwestern Canada: identification of resin and compound resin-ochre hafting adhesives.' *Journal of Archaeological Science* 41: 655-665.

Hirzel, J. 2008. Herstellung von Birkenpech ohne Spuren an gebrannten Tongefäßen. *Experimentelle Archäologie in Europa Bilanz* 7: 67-73.

Hyacinthoides non-scripta (bluebell): Kew Royal Botanic Gardens. http://www.kew.org/science-conservation/plants-fungi/hyacinthoides-non-scripta-bluebell (Accessed 16th June 2015).

Johann, K., Baumer, U., and Mania, D. 2001. High-tech in the Middle Palaeolithic: Neanderthal-manufactured pitch identified.' *European Journal of Archaeology* 4.3: 385-397.

Mazza, P.P.A., Martini, F., Sala, B., Magi, M., Colombini, M.P., Giachi, G., Landucci, F., Lemorini, C., Modugno, F. and Ribechini, E. 2006. A new Palaeolithic discovery: tar-hafted stone tools in a European Mid-Pleistocene bone-bearing bed.' *Journal of Archaeological Science* 33.9: 1310-1318.

McNutt. B. 2010. *Woodsmoke: Bushcraft and Wilderness Surviva*l. http://www.woodsmoke.uk.com/about-us/ben-mcnutt/.

Osipowicz, G. 2005. A method of wood tar production without the use of ceramics. *EuroREA* 2: 11-17.

Palmer, F. 2007. Die Entstehung von Birkenpech in einer Feuerstelle unter paläolithischen Bedingungen. *Mitteilungen der Gesellschaft für Urgeschichte* 16: 75-83.

Piotrowski, W. 1999. Wood-tar and pitch experimnets at Biskupin Museum. Harding, A.F. (ed.) Experiment and desgin: archaeological studies in Honour of John Coles. Oxbow Books: Oxford.

Reynolds, P.J. 1999. The nature of experiment in archaeology Harding, A.F. (ed.) *Experiment and design: archaeological studies in Honour of John Coles.* Oxbow Books: Oxford. pp. 156-162.

Todtenhaupt, D., Elsweiler, F. and Baumer, U. 2007. Das Pech des Neandertalers- eine Möglichkeit der Herstellung. *Experimentelle Archäologie in Europa Bilanz* 6: 145-154.

Zipkin, A.M., Wagner, M., McGrath, K., Brooks, A.S. and Lucas, P.W. 2014. An Experimental Study of Hafting Adhesives and the Implications for Compound Tool Technology.: e112560. http://journals.plos.org/plosone/article?id=10.1371/journal.pone.0112560.

Wikipedia *Pitch (resin)* https://en.wikipedia.org/wiki/Pitch_%28resin%29.

Part Three

Construction

Experiences of thatching at Kierikki Stone Age Village, Finland

Inga Nieminen

Introduction

Kierikki Stone Age village was established in 1997. The first house constructions were covered with birch bark and turf. After a decade some renovations were needed and some of the old houses were replaced by constructions with thatched roofs.

Kierikki Stone Age village is located in Yli-Ii, Northern Osthrobothnia about 40 km northeast from the city of Oulu, on the rivershore of the Iijoki River. Approximately 5000 years ago this area was at the mouth of the river at the shore of the Baltic Sea. After the last Ice Age the postglacial land uplift in the Osthrobothnian area was very rapid. Since then the mouth of the river has moved approximately 30 km westwards (Eilola and Lehtinen 2001, 3). In the Kierikki area the Stone Age people seemed to live a very wealthy life. The local economy was presumably based on seal hunting and trading of the seal skins and train oil. During the warmer periods of the era the seals presumably had conditions to procreate only in the northernmost parts of the Baltic Sea where the ice cover formed on a yearly basis. People in the area lived on the seashore and moved along the receding shoreline. Because of this, a series of Stone Age dwelling sites, dating to back to 5000-3000 B.C. have been found on the river shores (Eilola and Lehtinen, 2001, 10, 14).

Archaeological excavations in the Kierikki area started in 1960 as a result of the harnessing of the river Iijoki for hydroelectric power. Since then archaeological mapping and excavations have been carried out in the area by many different researchers (Eilola & Lehtinen, 2001, 3; Viljanmaa 2014, 8-9).

In the Kierikki area some of the dwelling depressions are in straight lines and these are interpreted as 'row houses'. They can consist of up to seven subsequent rooms, joined by corridors, almost three meters wide (Eilola and Lehtinen 2001, 14, 20).

Today in Kierikki there is a Stone Age Centre with an exhibition introducing the Stone Age in Finland in general. This museum exhibition is accompanied by a set of reconstructions nearby. The Stone Age village is set in authentic surroundings on the bank of the river Iijoki with house constructions representing the villages which existed in the area 5000 years ago and a trapline path presenting traditional ways of hunting (Eilola and Lehtinen 2001, 7; Vaara 2000, 3).

The first Stone Age house constructions in Kierikki

In Finland the soil is acidic and due to this the organic material preserves in the ground only in exceptional circumstances, in most cases in the bogs or at the bottoms of the lakes in anoxic conditions (Huurre 2001a, 17, 42). What we know of the Stone Age dwellings for sure are the shape and dimensions of the floor and sometimes locations of the fireplace and doorways. The materials of the walls and roofs have to be guessed in most cases (Huurre 2001b, 85-86). In house constructions the roofs are usually influenced and modelled on the dwellings of historical arctic peoples (Vaara 2000, 4). In traditional house building the main idea is to use the materials which can be found near the building site (Suna 2007, 31) which can be used as a guideline when considering different possible material options. During the millennia, the Stone Age people undoubtedly used various materials and structures as shelters depending on the needs and availabilities at each time. The time of the year and the purpose of the dwelling unquestionably affected the materials and structures used in the dwellings.

Constructions representing Stone Age houses in Finland are based on both archaeological evidence and information gained from circumpolar indigenous peoples. Archaeological evidence can be interpreted in many ways and house constructions are always interpretations of some sort, not copies of the houses which existed millenniums ago. If the tools and methods used in building work are as stone age like as possible the results of the building work can also be expected to be as close to the stone age house building as we can get. Also the building process itself and the user experience give valuable information about the probability of the different materials, structures and methods used (Muurimäki 2004).

Figure 8.1: Older Stone Age house constructions in Kierikki (Photo: S. Viljanmaa).

In 1997 the first construction for Kierikki Stone Age village was made on the bank of the river Iijoki. The construction was designed by archaeology student Sami Kesti. It was partly based on the Yli-Ii's Korvala and Kuuselankangas excavations, partly on dwellings of ethnic people and influenced by structures in Saarijärvi Stone Age village in Central Finland and Vuollerim Stone Age houses in Jokkmokk, Swedish Lapland. The groundwork was made of logs surrounded by a soil embankment. The vertical wooden frames were on the embankment lying against the groundwork logs and the ridgepole. The roof was covered with birch bark plates and a layer of turf (Figure 8.1). Also the ridgepole was covered except the central part on top of the fireplace where the hole for the smoke was left open. The slope of the roof was only approximately 30 degrees. Because of this the roofing materials stayed well put but the smoke from the fireplace couldn't find its way out (Nieminen and Viljanmaa 2014, 5 & 7).

In 1998-1999 five more constructions were designed and constructed by Rauno Vaara. These houses were based on archaeological excavations held in the Yli-Ii area and completed with the help derived from ethnographic material. One of the buildings had a log foundation, the other four had posts of vertical wooden frames rising straight from the ground (Vaara 2000, 2, 7-9). Some supplements and changes to the buildings were made in 2002 but the structures and appearance stayed mainly the same (Nieminen and Viljanmaa 2014, 6).

The problem with smoke in the first house construction was fixed in the further constructions by lifting the slope of the roof more steeply but due to this the roofing materials started to flow down. Birch bark pieces were not attached to each other nor to the framing of the house. Birch bark pieces can be seen from the inside of the buildings so the material used in attaching them should have been primitive. Roots of trees could have been used but the collecting of the roots and sewing the birch bark pieces to the structure with them would have taken so much time and effort that it was not possible to do so. Birch bark pieces were instead overlapped on the structure and covered with layer of turf (Nieminen and Viljanmaa 2014, 7). The roofing materials of each house slipped down from both slopes of the roof approximately 20 cm each year and needed to be fixed on a yearly basis (Åqvist. pers.comm.).

According to the instructions given by Rauno Vaara (1999) the ridge of the roofs should have been covered with a layer of birch bark and turf after the snow of the first winter had pressed down the structures a bit. This was never done and rainwater and snow had access to the houses. Rain and melting waters of the snow also ran down along the roof and brought moisture to the foundation of the house. In the course of time the log foundations and bases of the wooden frames started to decay (Nieminen and Viljanmaa 2014, 7).

In 2007 some of the houses were in such a bad condition that they needed to be demolished and replaced with new ones (Lehtinen 2007, 3-5). Archaeologist Sami Viljanmaa was hired to design the new houses. When the new constructions were planned, the user experience of the old constructions was considered as a starting point. It was important to choose such structures and materials that as little maintenance work and fixing would be needed as possible. Considering the roofing material options, it was noted that due to quick land rise in the Northern

Ostrobothnia, thick layers of turf probably were not available in the surroundings of the site. Instead it was observed that common reed grows on the coastline of the Baltic even today. In addition, the image of the Stone Age dwellings was deliberately intended to become more diverse (Nieminen and Viljanmaa 2014, 2, 8).

Thatched roofs

Kierikki Stone Age village is a tourist attraction and because of health and safety instructions two doorways were required within the houses. Also enough space for the groups of people was needed. A construction permit was needed and because of this the house could not be built in a depression, similar to the houses made in the Stone Age, but on top of a small mound to avoid the moisture having access to the foundations of the house (Nieminen and Viljanmaa 2014, 8).

Common reed (*Phragmites australis*) grows all around the world. In winter it becomes a hard and hollow tube which forms an extremely good building material with good qualities of sound and thermal insulation (Ikonen 2007, 10). Nowadays the reed used for buildings should be first year growth and one to two meters long. Reeds are cut either from shallow water or from the top of ice cover either by hand or with harvesters. Reeds are dried and packed into bundles according to their size and shape (Sooster 2006, 6-12). When reeds are collected in the early spring the amount of silicic acid in the reeds is large and it works as a flame retardant (Sjöroos 2007, 9). A thatched roof can last up to 100 years if it is properly made (Sooster 2006, 6).

The winter 2007-2008 in Finland was mild and it was not possible to drive the harvesters onto the ice cover of the lakes. Because of the relatively strict timetable it was not possible to cut the reed by hand either. The reed was ordered from Estonia via roofing expert Siim Sooster, who also came to Kierikki to teach the skill of thatching (Nieminen 2010, 9). Later after two roofs had been completed the Stone Age action group Kuttelo tried cutting the reed with a bone tool made according to an ethnographic model (Jasse Tiilikkala pers. comm.). In addition to the author (who made her thesis for arts and crafts school about the topic, Nieminen 2010), there were two British students participating in the roof making through the summer of 2008: Geraldine Sim and Thomas Mann. According to Sooster's estimation the roof making was to take approximately two weeks but there were problems with the availability of twisted birch branches which were used to attach the reed layers to the frame of the house. The summer was very rainy which slowed down the roof making. When Sooster left to go back to Estonia the upper layers of the roof were still unfinished and roof ridge missing. Finally it took six weeks to finish the house. The final result was good and the work itself was very instructive to participants.

After the frame of the house was finished, the roof making began from the lowest layer where short and cone-like reeds were piled up on top of a scaffold. The scaffold was put up to form the right angle for the slope of the roof. The width of the scaffold was approximately 30 cm which was to become also the thickness of the roof. Cone-like reeds were used to lift the eaves high enough. After the bundles were evenly spread along the scaffold a wooden strip was put horizontally on top

Figure 8.2: First layers of the reed were put on a scaffold and attached to the framing of the house with wood strips and twisted birch branches (Photo: I. Nieminen).

of the first reed layer and then tied through the reeds to the wooden framing of the house by using birch branches (Nieminen 2010, 13; Figure 8.2). Branches were first twisted to break the structure and make them more flexible and rope-like. When the twisted branches get dry they tighten and keep the shape in which they were tied.

The next layers of reed were piled on top of the previous ones, attached with wooden strips and birch branches and hit into place to follow the angle of the house frame by using a small serrated board (Figure 8.3). Reeds in the middle of the slope of the roof were laid straight up the slope of the roof and towards the corners the reeds were positioned at a lopsided angle. In the outer corners very long and cone-like reeds were used to make the corners thick enough. In the inner corners the reeds used were straight and thin to get a very thick composition. The inner corners are the spots where the water accumulates and therefore extra attention must be paid when the reeds for the inner corners are chosen. When the layers of reed reached the roof ridge, the reeds of the uppermost layers were bent over the roof top and made to overlap each other (Nieminen 2010, 15).

The roof ridge was covered by a layer of horizontal reeds. Heavy logs were positioned vertically on top of the horizontal reeds and holes were drilled into the upper side of these logs. A wooden strip parallel to the ridgepole was put through the holes to keep the logs in place. The original idea was to leave the logs to hang freely but because it was possible that visitors would want to touch and move the logs it was considered to be safer to attach them to the house frame by using the birch branches (Nieminen 2010, 15; Figure 8.4).

Figure 8.3: The reeds were hit to their final position by using a serrated board, Inga Nieminen in the foreground and Hannele Huumonen in the background (Photo S. Viljanmaa).

Figure 8.4: Walls from the inside. Twisted birch branches holding the wood strips on top of each layer of reed can be seen on the inside (Photo: I. Nieminen).

To the inner side of the house one very thin layer of long and straight reed was added to make the inner wall look more even and to hide all the inflorescence and to stop the reedtops from bending to the inside of the house. The inner side of the house was painted with clay which was also used as a flame retardant (Nieminen 2010, 13, 16). The doorways were covered with hides and the builders experimented with the qualities of a thatched roof house reconstruction as a place to sleep. The fire was kept small but it warmed the house up rapidly. The house was also very quiet despite the birds and construction work outside.

Even though thatched roofs are very long-lasting, the horizontal reed layer covering the roof ridge should be renewed once every decade because it keeps the moisture on itself for much longer periods of time than the vertical reeds in the other parts of the roof (Nieminen 2010, 17).

In 2009 another thatched roof was made with the instructions given by Sooster the previous year and using the small experience gained for the roof making. This time excluding the author, the other roof makers varied through the summer which of course affected the timetable and progress of the work when more guidance and advice was needed. Archaeology student Jasse Tiilikkala, building restoration artisan Hannele Huumonen and Sami Viljanmaa who designed the houses all stayed on the roof making for longer periods of time and were a great help. All together it took seven weeks to finish the second thatched roof (Nieminen 2010, 12-13).

In the first reed house, the horizontal wooden frames of the house structure did not meet each other in the corners and this caused problems when the wooden strips on top of the reed layers did not meet each other either. This was fixed by combining the wooden strips in the corners by using willow branches. This fault of the house frame was fixed in the new house in 2009 but again willows were needed when the wooden strips were so flexible that they did not keep the reed tight enough in the corners (Nieminen 2010, 18).

In 2012 a third thatched roof house was built at Kierikki by archaeology student Antti Palmroos and roofing expert Siim Sooster. Today there are three different reed houses and two houses covered with birch bark and turf. So far the thatched roofs have worked fine and it is likely that they will be more long-lasting than the turf-covered houses have been so far. However the problem with turf roofs has not been the material itself, but some faults in the structure of them.

Winters bring heavy snow to the Kierikki area (Figure 8.5). Stone Age constructions are not normally used and kept warm during the winter months and this undoubtedly affects their life cycle compared to a house that would be in use all year round. During the summer events in Kierikki people often end up sleeping in the Stone Age village and so far reed houses have been more in favour than ones with turf roofing. There were four primitive survival camps held in Kierikki 2010, lead by a French expert Joseph Favré-Felix (Favré-Felix 2014). The participants lived in the first thatched roof house in all seasons.

Figure 8.5: The first two thatched roof houses at Kierikki Stone Age Village (Photo: S. Viljanmaa).

Conclusions

Since the establishment of Kierikki Stone Age village in 1997 five stone age house constructions have been made on the shores of river the Iijoki. First constructions were covered with birch bark and turf but these constructions turned out to need lots of maintenance work. When planning the new buildings for the village in 2007 user experience of the old houses and the paucity of the maintenance work were considered as a starting point.

In 2008 and 2009 the first thatched roof constructions were made in the Stone Age village. Reed was considered as an easily available material in the area also during the Stone Age. The roofs were made by adding layers of reed from bottom to the top of the buildings using materials and methods that were available during the Stone Age. Constructions with thatched roofs have proved to be very water proof and they isolate both warmth and sound very well. When the first thatched roof reconstruction was built six years ago in 2008 the main idea was to build long-lasting constructions with only a little need for maintenance work and also to give visitors a more diverse image of the Stone Age dwellings. So far it seems that those goals were achieved. Nevertheless, the functionality and durability of the houses will remain to be seen in the future.

Bibliography

Unpublished sources

Lehtinen, L. 2007. *Kierikin Kivikauden kylän peruskorjaus.* Hankesuunnitelma ja kustannuslaskelma vuodelle 2008.

Nieminen, I. 2010. *Ruokokattoja kivikauden kylään.* Thesis of Artisan for Arts and Crafts School on Mynämäki. Mynämäki.

Tiilikkala, J. 2014. Personal comment. 1.9.2014.

Vaara, R. 1999. *Kivikauden kylän konstruktioiden huoltotoimista.* Memorandum 29.9.1999. Pohjois-Pohjanmaan ympäristökeskus, Oulu.

Viljanmaa, S. 2014. *Oulu Kierikinkangas. Yleisökaivaus kivikautisella asuinpaikalla* 22.5.-29.8.2013. Excavation report.

Åqvist, S. 2008. Personal comment. 15.8.2009.

Literature

Eilola, M. & Lehtinen, L. (eds.) 2001. *Kierikki Stone Age Centre: exhibition guide.* Oulu.

Huurre, M. 2001a. *9000 vuotta Suomen esihistoriaa.* Otava: Keuruu.

Huurre, M. 2001b. *Kivikauden Suomi.* Otava: Keuruu.

Ikonen, I. 2007. *Rannasta rakennukseen. Ruokorakentaminen Itämeren alueella.* Turun ammattikorkeakoulu: Saarijärvi. pp. 10-13.

Nieminen I. & Viljanmaa S. 2014. Kierikkikeskuksen kivikauden kylän järviruokokattoiset asumuskonstruktiot ja havaintoja kylän aiemmista rakennuksista. *Muinaistutkija* 4.

Sjöroos, S. 2007. Ruokorakentamisen asiantuntemusta. -Hartwig Reuterin haastattelu. *Rannasta rakennukseen. Ruokorakentamista Itämeren alueella.* Turun ammattikorkeakoulu. Saarijärvi. p. 9.

Sooster, S. 2006. *Ruoko- ja olkikattojen valmistusopas.* Oü Rooexpert. Nõmme 8, Käina 92101, Hiiumaa, Eesti.

Suna, E. 2007. Ruokokatot Suomessa. *Rannasta rakennukseen. Ruokorakentaminen Itämeren alueella.* Turun ammattikorkeakoulu. Saarijärvi. pp. 28-32.

Vaara, R. 2000. Yli-Iin Kierikin kivikautinen kylä -asumusrekonstruktiot 1998-1999. *Muinaistutkija* 2: 2-12.

Electronic sources

Favré-Felix, J. 2014. *Primitive Surviving Project.*<https://sites.google.com/site/primitivesurvivingprojectweb/>(Accessed on 18.9.2014).

Muurimäki, E. 2004. *Talojen ennallistaminen.*<http://www.avoinmuseo.fi/kivikaudenkyla/ennallistaminen.sthml>(Accessed on 28.1.2014).

A gateway to the Bronze Age

Experimenting with woodworking methods of the Terramara culture in Montale in Italy

Wolfgang F.A. Lobisser

Introduction

Between 1650 and 1170 B.C. in Northern Italy in the region of the lower reaches of the river Po an extraordinary cultural phenomenon occurred which is these days referred to by researchers as the Terramara culture (Brea, Cardarelli and Cremaschi 1997). It is a regular system of almost square fortified settlements along rivers in lowland areas with inner areas usually in excess of 10,000 m². The inner areas were built mostly in straight rows of houses on piles with raised walkways on wooden platforms clear off the ground. By building this way, we can assume that they wanted to protect themselves from rain and moisture as well as vermin and animals. Between the rows of houses there were streets and paths that allowed access to the various buildings. With the regularity of the structure of the inner areas, one gets the impression that the people of the Middle Bronze Age wanted to get optimal usage from the protected fortified area. The fortifications were several feet high and consisted of rows of log cabin boxes filled with soil and in all probability a palisade or parapet on top. The soil was dug directly in the areas outside the settlements, thereby creating wide water-filled trenches around the settlements which offered additional protection. Access to the settlements was through special gates with earthen or wooden bridges.

In conjunction with the EU project ArchaeoLive and results from local excavations, an archaeological open air museum for the Terramara culture was constructed in 2000 in Montale, a small town south of Modena under the guidance of Andrea Cardarelli and Ilaria Pulini from the Museo Civico Archeologico Etnologico in Modena. Additional partners of this EU project were the Natural History Museum Vienna and the Pfahlbaumuseum Unteruhldingen (Barth, Cardarelli, Lobisser and Schöbel 2003; Cardarelli and Pulini 2004). At the time, I was responsible for the practical construction of the Austrian part of the project at the salt mine Salzberg in Hallstatt (Barth and Lobisser 2002) and that is how I got to know and appreciate our project partners from Italy which resulted in a close and friendly scientific cooperation which continues today.

In the spring of 2006, the experimental group of VIAS – the Vienna Institute for Archaeological Science – was invited by the museum management to construct a portion of the fortification and gateway using experimental archaeological methods (Lobisser 2008). The VIAS accepts such archaeological reconstruction work as scientific research contracts in order to carry out practical studies on researching ancient wooden architecture and craftsmanship for the purpose of experimental archaeology on a wider scale.

Archaeological findings

How can we imagine the layout and construction of such a gateway in detail then? Several archaeological findings can give us clues, of which the most important ones will be presented shortly. The Middle Bronze Age settlement in Montale indicated lengths of about 100 to 120 m on the sides. The outline of the fortification, rounded at the corners, could be clearly detected in the ground. House remains on the inside with preserved woods gave valuable indications on the design of the former building (Brea, Cardarelli and Cremaschi 1997). In another settlement at the Terramara di la Braglia, a gate area could be documented, where they had cut out an approximately 3 to 4 m wide area of the fortification. At a fortification from approximately the same period further south in Coppa Nevigata in Puglia, we know of the preserved stone foundations of a gate where the gateway was about 3.7 m wide and 8.5 m long and additionally, tower-like constructions seem to have flanked the gate area here. There is a revealing find at the Terramara di Castione Marchesi (Pigorini 1882-83) of the wooden structures inside the walls. On a photograph from an excavation from the 19th century, one was able to clearly

Figure 9.1: A photograph from the excavation at Terramara di Castione Marchesi from 1877 clearly shows wooden boxes placed together in a block design (Photo: L. Pigorini).

identify wooden log cabin boxes placed together in a block design (Figure 9.1), joined together in such a way that the protuberances of the boxes in turn formed their own compartments lengthways.

Based on the archaeological evidence mentioned above, a construction of four log cabin boxes with internal dimensions of 3 x 3 m was planned for the reconstruction of the gateway in Montale, of which two 3 m apart, create a gateway with a length of about 9 m that leads into the interior of the settlement. Where two log boxes join on the sides, the protuberances were extended so they form a third compartment together between the boxes with a width of about 150 cm. The gate itself, a double leaf door construction was positioned externally at the end of the first pair of log boxes. A bridge was planned over the gate which would have a palisade the same as the boxes themselves and the whole building would be constructed out of oak.

Replica tools made of bronze

The construction of a section of the fortification with gateway and gate gave us the opportunity to deal intensively with the tools and the wood working methods of the Terramara culture, even if it was clear that we could only perform part of the work with authentic bronze tools. As per original archaeological finds, we made tools out of bronze for our work on site and we added handles made of wood. Our tool kit consisted of large and small flanged axes, chisels of different sizes, bronze daggers, bodkins and awls as well as a wooden divider with bronze tips. The large flanged axes were hafted on to angular beech wood handles, so that the cutting edges were parallel to the handle. The hafts consisted of split and rounded parts of the trunk, the parts for the working blades formed from ingrown branches in the trunk. To achieve a stable connection between the handles and the metal blades, the branch parts were equipped with narrow slots into which the blades could be inserted. These joints were additionally secured using twine lashings. Our small blades were partly also hafted this way.

From the Early and Middle Bronze Age we only know axe blades described as bronze tools. Did they not use any adzes or were they not recognized archeologically as such? We hafted some of the smaller flanged axes perpendicular to the wooden handles to test their suitability as adzes in the experiment. Chisels were usually used in woodworking to produce grooves, slits and openings. Some examples of chisels of the Terramara culture are notable for their particular size. With lengths of 25 cm or more and weighing around 300 grams, they most certainly also represented a significant value. We wanted to use awls for marking wooden joints. We attached two points made of bronze to a wooden divider to be used to mark the log building components. Dagger blades – the common form of knives at that time – could certainly be used in many aspects (Figure 9.2).

Practical questions for the reconstruction

From the outset there were many questions: How can we envisage the construction of a fortification from the Middle Bronze Age? Which wood joining techniques can we prove or assume? How robust are bronze tools when working on solid oak

Figure 9.2: Some of the replicated tools we used made from bronze: flanged axes, adze, dividers, dagger, chisels and awl (Photo: W.F.A. Lobisser).

logs? How much building material was needed? How many working hours were required? Our goal was to achieve a better understanding of the possible physical woodworking methods of the Terramara culture through our practical work in Montale. We wanted to find out what types of tools were particularly suitable for which kind of work, and what their limitations were.

Building material

Since it proved extremely difficult to find suitable straight grown oak in the required quantity in Italy, we purchased the building materials in Austria and transported it over 900 kilometres to Montale. The stems for the log cabin boxes – in total about 50 m³ – were straight for the most part, up to 5 m long and 20-35 cm in diameter. The heaviest logs would have weighed approximately 400 kilos. The diameters of the logs for the palisades were between 15 and 20 cm. This data was important for us because we would forgo using modern tools such as cranes or hoists and wanted to bring all the construction elements in position by hand with the help of levers, pulleys and inclined levels. Experimenting with tree felling in advance for this project, we learned that oak logs 30 cm in diameter could be felled in just under an hour using our flanged bronze axes. By chopping well aimed notch cuts and felling cuts, we were in most cases able to make the tree fall in the desired direction which was an important requirement so no one was injured.

Construction of four log cabin boxes

Before starting the construction, the bark was removed from the trunks. To remove the up to 2 cm thick bark, we successfully carried out this task using bronze axes, where the hafted angular handles provided a good grip as you could use it as a lever. With axes the first four logs were then cut to the right length and positioned, whereby the first two logs were placed on the ground approximately 3 m apart and the other two placed at right angles on top. Since the structure was being built out in the open air, we cut out semi-circular notches at the corners of the log box in the top logs, so that rain water could drain off rather than collecting in the hollowed notches and speed up the weathering process. In order to achieve perfectly fitting joints, the logs were individually customized as they all had different diameters

Figure 9.3: The heavy bronze axes were hafted onto naturally grown angular wood handles and proved to be useful tools for the construction of log cabin boxes (Photo: W.F.A. Lobisser).

and we used our bronze tipped wooden dividers for this. When a log was precisely positioned, the length by which it would need to be lowered was marked with the dividers at both contact points, so that the cuts were exactly equal to the diameter of the underlying log. Then the log was rolled inwards and turned 180 degrees so we could cut out the two grooves with axes. After some practice, we managed this task very well using the bronze axes.

We found out the limits of the bronze tools on the tree knots, which left big nicks in the blades or bent them. The practice was to avoid these as much as possible and if this was not possible, we semi-exposed them and then with precise chops cut on the inside of the logs where these branches are usually very thin. It was actually not a big problem to straighten bent blades again. We had cold forged our blades several times over already anyway before starting work to increase their stability. Nicks and flaws had to be laboriously ground away using the grindstone, however.

To uniformly build up the log boxes, it was very important to place two approximately equally thick logs on top. We also had to alternate placing the thick and thin ends of the logs in position. Beams with similar distortion were sorted beforehand and placed on top of each other in order to ensure an as tight a fit as possible. Logs with more pronounced distortion we placed on the inner sides, where they were later covered with soil. The two front log boxes were raised up to a height of about 320 cm (Figure 9.3) and the two at the rear slightly lower. The remaining gaps and cracks between the joists were sealed with split wooden wedges placed in a radial arrangement before filling the boxes with soil.

What quickly became clear was that the people of the Bronze Age could only build regular log boxes with almost vertical walls, if they had a system to reproduce dimensions and distances. One might consider standardized wooden rods or cords with knots. Additionally they must have had a kind of plumb line to be able to build vertical walls.

Construction of gate and bridge

The construction of the gate with a double leaf door presented a great challenge. The door leaves measured about 250 by 130 cm after all and should be made of approximately 5 cm thick oak planks without using any metal parts. Turnstile doors have been found in several fortifications from the Bronze Age with perforated stone foundations in the relevant places. All structural timbers of the door leaves were worked on laid flat. We used the smaller blades as adzes and they were more than suited for this work. Thus it was possible for us to produce very smooth surfaces, without having to make changes to the "axe blade".

To begin with we squared off two approximately 3 meter long oak logs with diameters of about 25 cm at their thicker ends into rectangular beams using the adzes mentioned. About 14 cm thick round pivots were then carved into both ends of each of these logs. They formed the main beams of the door leaves. In the mid section and about 50 cm from either end, three rectangular mortises were then worked into each timber. We used the large bronze chisels and mallets. Using these chisels we were able to cut out pieces 16 cm long, 5 cm wide and 15 cm deep in about 50 minutes.

Figure 9.4: Five people were needed to position one of our gate leaves with an estimated weight of 150 kg and place it in the notches provided (Photo: W.F.A. Lobisser).

In these cut outs, we then put three cross timbers with the corresponding pivots at each end per beam. Each of these joints was then secured by two solid core wood pegs of oak. The holes for the nails were also chiselled but with smaller chisels. The pegs were cleaved from straight grown wood, so we could be sure that every single wood fibre stretched across the entire length of the peg. At each end we carved heads and they were wedged from the back. The smaller bronze axes proved to be very suitable for making the pegs and the finer carvings were made with bronze daggers. We were then able to secure the boards of the door leaves onto the three cross beams with wooden pegs. Additionally these boards were joined together edgeways with dowels. Overall we were able to achieve a stable join of the wooden components of the gate panels, which ultimately each weighed about 150 kg (Figure 9.4).

But how could we install the door leaves in the whole structure? At the start of constructing our log cabin boxes, we embedded a strong oak trunk with a diameter of about 30 cm in the ground where the gate was to be positioned with only about 8 cm of the top sticking out. Both ends of this tree trunk we incorporated into the joining of the boxes. When the log box was at a height of about 260 cm, another beam was incorporated between the log boxes over the gateway that it formed a kind of gate frame together with this and with the embedded trunk. By adding holes of about 15 cm in diameter at the appropriate points in these two cross beams, it enabled us to mount the gate panels. The top beam together with a second cross beam on the same level behind it formed the support for a bridge about 110 cm wide over the gate area.

The palisades

The palisades were made of half logs with diameters between 15 and 20 cm. We split the logs by driving in wooden wedges and the top ends were pointed using axes. The finished log boxes were first filled with soil to about 1 m below the top edge. The logs of the palisades were then spread at this level on the inside against the walls of log boxes. By now filling the log boxes up to the top with the rest of the soil, the posts of the palisades were wedged between the log walls and soil and thereby very securely fixed. Above the bridge, the vertical posts of the parapet were fastened to the cross beams with wooden dowels and twine lashings.

Summary

Overall, we used about 50 m³ of oak wood for the construction of a gate model of the Terramara culture – approximately 250 logs of different diameters. Our aim was to find out in the course of the work, which types of tools would be particularly suitable for which kind of task. We used the large axes specifically for felling and cutting of timbers, as well as to shape the semi-circular notches at the corners of the log cabin boxes. Finer work could be done with the smaller axes, such as making the wooden pegs and dowels. Overall, large and small bronze blades worked very well on fresh oak. Experiments to work on oak dried for several years have shown us that it was doing more damage to the blades which they most likely wanted to avoid in the Bronze Age.

We also believe we have found the adzes of the Bronze Age: it turned out that it was possible to use normal bronze "axe blades" laterally also as adzes to flatten wood. Our experimental results working with these tools were convincing. Without any problems we were able to hew round logs into square timbers with such adzes. Clearly the so-called axe blades of the Early and Middle Bronze Age were multifunctional and could be used both as axes and adzes. It therefore stands to reason that the use of rectangular formed timbers was common in the Middle Bronze Age to a considerable extent.

All kinds of grooves, slots and openings could be prepared well with bronze chisels. In particular the large specimens of the Terramara culture with lengths up to 30 cm indicate that relatively complex wooden joints from solid and probably four-sided logs were used in the Middle Bronze Age. We successfully used the large chisels to create rectangular openings in approximately 15 cm thick squared timber. The smaller chisels we used to chisel holes for wooden pegs and we used awls and bodkins to mark wood joints. Our bronze tipped wooden dividers lent themselves very well to transmit the dimensions of the logs for the log boxes to the corresponding next one so that perfectly fitting notches could be cut out.

Four log cabin boxes were built with heights up to 320 cm in the course of our reconstruction work. The gate itself was constructed in double leaf door style, each leaf consisting of eight major construction elements that were solely joined

Figure 9.5: In the autumn of 2006, employees of the VIAS – Vienna Institute for Archaeological Science – reconstructed a part of the Bronze Age fortification at the Terramare settlement in Montale in Italy consisting of four log cabin boxes filled with soil. The structure was completed with a gateway, a bridge and a gate on the basis of archaeological data. All working steps were basically carried out with replicas of Bronze Age tools (Photo: W.F.A. Lobisser).

by pivots, wood plugs and pegs. The two gate panels, each weighing about 150 kilograms are relatively easy to move on round pivots embedded in massive cross beams connecting the two pairs of log boxes above and below the gateway. Above the gate is a bridge with a parapet. The log boxes were equipped with a palisade on top and filled up to the top with soil (Figure 9.5). In the already existing wall, we dug a total of about 100 m palisades about 1 m deep to the left and right of the log boxes.

Conclusions

Our architectural model of a Middle Bronze Age gate system was not the first which was built in Montale. As a kind of prelude to the establishment of the archaeological open air museum "Terramara Montale", a first gate had been built in the late 90s of the 20th century. In the planning it already corresponded to the known archaeological specifications but they had used softwood from the region for this construction which was not very resistant to the decaying effects of the soil. This was an important reason to use hard oak wood for the new reconstruction which is very durable due to its high tannin content.

The construction of the new gate system was put into action in the autumn months of 2006. The reconstruction team from VIAS – Vienna Institute for Archaeological Science – consisted of six people. Our construction work was carried out during the opening times of the museum, so that visitors were able to watch our experimental work in practice. Our construction project was included as an integral part of the professional guided tours of the open-air museum. The public showed great interest and many visitors came several times during this autumn to watch our working progress and became museum regulars to a certain extent.

Partly for this reason, we worked to a great extent using reproductions of tools from the Middle Bronze Age in the construction of the gate. Every other weekend we spent on site in Montale's open air museum to explain our tools, our working methods, but also our scientific questions to interested visitors on special tours and crafts presentations. In order to bridge the language barrier between Austrian German and Italian, an interpreter from the museum team was provided by the museum's management.

The archaeological open air museum "Terramara Montale" is certainly one of the best of its kind in Europe (*cf.* Pelillo 2009). Interested visitors are given the opportunity to comprehend the path of archaeological research itself and thereby understand it better. This path begins with prospecting and leads on to the archaeological excavation, the accurate documentation and processing of finds and records, to the analytical evaluation. It also exemplifies how scientists get new answers and new results to answer archaeological questions by using experimental archaeology and are thereby able to recreate scenes of life in the past. One of the greatest strengths of this open-air museum must certainly include the discerning quality of the guided tours and the presented architectural models prepared affectionately down to the smallest detail with good quality replicas of objects, equipment and tools of the Terramara culture.

Bibliography

Barth, F.E., Cardarelli, A., Lobisser, W.F.A. and Schöbel, G. 2003. Il progetto Archeolive. Parchi archeologici della protostoria europea, In P. Bellintani and L. Moser. (eds.) *Archeologie sperimentali, Metodologie ed esperienze fra verifica, riproducione, comunicazione e simulazione.* Litotipografia Alcione: Trento. pp. 129-142.

Barth, F.E. and Lobisser, W.F.A. 2002. Das EU-Projekt Archaeolive und das archäologische Erbe von Hallstatt. *Veröffentlichungen aus dem Naturhistorischen Museum in Wien.* Neue Folge 29. Malek Press: Wien.

Brea, M.B., Cardarelli, A. and Cremaschi, M. (eds.). 1997. *Le Terramare, La più antica civiltà padana, Catalogo delleMostra.* Milano Press : Modena pp. 196-212.

Cardarelli, A. and Pulini, I. 2004. *Parco archeologico e Museo all`apperto della Terramara di Montale.* Nuova Grafica: Carpi.

Lobisser, W.F.A. 2008. Zur Rekonstruktion einer mittelbronzezeitlichen Befestigungsanlage der Terramare-Kultur in Montale, Italien. *Experimentelle Archäologie in Europa Bilanz 2008 Heft 7.* Isensee: Oldenburg. pp. 33-48.

Pigorini, L. 1883. Terramara dell`età del Bronzo situata in Castione dei Marchesi territorio parmigiano, estratto da "Atti Reale Accademia dei Lincei". s.III, VIII (Reprint) In R. Perini and P. Magnani, (eds.) 1996. *Le Terremare.* Litoprint: Reggio Emilia. pp. 301-312.

Pelillo, A. 2009. *AOAM – Guide to the Archaeological Open Air Museums in Europe.* Nuova Grafica: Reggio Emilia.

"From Earth I Rose"

Experimenting with stone box furnaces of the Finnish Early Iron Age

Joni Karjalainen and Juuso Vattulainen

Introduction

This article focuses on the stone box furnaces that were used for iron smelting in Finland, Russian Karelia and eastern and northern Sweden during the Early Iron Age. This paper will discuss the lifecycle of these furnaces, how it can be seen in the archaeological context and the results from experiments based on our interpretation of the originals. The results suggest that the experiments could hint possible ways by which the furnaces were built, used and repaired between smelts. The pre-experiment was undertaken during the OpenArch "Dialogue with Science"-conference in June 2014 and further experiments were conducted as a part of an OpenArch project in Kierikki Stone Age Centre later in the summer of 2014. More detailed description of the experiments can be found in Karjalainen 2016.

According to the current research the iron production came to Finland from the east along the the extensive river networks that reaches from the Karelian Republic all the way to the Bothnian Bay (Buchwald 2005, Figure 74, 195; Mäkivuoti 1983). The radiocarbon dates from the sites suggest that they were used during the Early Iron Age, 500 BC – 400 AD (Kotivuori 2013, 56-57). One indication of the eastern origin is that the stone box furnaces found in Finland are analogous to the ones discovered in the Karelian Republic (Lavento 1999, 76). Furthermore, the furnaces in Finland do not seem to resemble the ones found from most of the southern Scandinavia and Estonia, where clay or stone lined bowl furnaces and shaft furnaces following the western European tradition were most commonly used (Lavento 1999, 76; Lavento 2003, 255-256; Peets 2003). A few stone box furnaces have been found in eastern and northern Sweden as well (Hansson 1989, 131-151; Hjärthner-Holdar 1993, 97-100; Bennerhag 2009) and their origin possibly lies in the East (Buchwald 2005, 203). This paper will solely concentrate on the furnaces found in Finland.

There is no record of experimentation with stone box furnaces before in Finland with proper documentation. Hannu Kotivuori (pers. comm.) ran a small test with a stone box furnace he built in Rovaniemi, but it was not documented or published. Therefore, we wanted to experiment the use of stone box furnaces and plans were made in the spring of 2014, which ultimately lead to the pre-experiment in the "Dialogue with Science"-conference in Kierikki Stone Age Centre in June

2014. The aim was to build the furnace according to our interpretation of the archaeological examples and see how it worked. The results from the pre-experiment led to two follow-up experiments where the characteristics of the furnace type were experimented further.

Theoretical background

The theoretical background for the life cycle of buildings, constructions and objects has been discussed more thoroughly earlier in this publication (see Introduction) and elsewhere, but our approach is defined below. According to Roger Doonan (2013b) an iron smelting furnace of any type can be understood as a structure having a life cycle similar to any other artefact or structure. But instead of concentrating on the smelting processes this paper will have a look at the actions needed to build and maintain the furnace leading to the eventual abandonment and how these aspects appear on the furnace structure and the surroundings after the experiments. Comparing this to the archaeological finds enables an interpretation on how these stone box furnaces were used by the craftsmen in the Early Iron Age and how it can be seen in the archaeological context. Thus, one of the aims is to include the human aspect involved in the iron smelting process as the lack of focus on human involvement has recently been criticized in experimental archaeology (for example Doonan 2013a).

It has to be noted that during the planning phase and the actual experiments the aim was to study iron smelting in a stone box furnace as a technological process, but in this paper it is approached more as a formation process experiment (see Mathieu 2002; Outram 2008 for discussion about experiment types). Iron smelting actually consists of two processes running side by side, the smelting as one and the furnace construction and use as another, of which the latter will be focused on. The approach taken in this paper is to concentrate on the use of stone box furnace as an operational sequence, which can be divided into following phases: obtaining the materials, building the furnace, using it, maintenance, reuse and ultimately abandonment or destruction.

Archaeology of the furnaces

Five definite and one probable stone box furnaces are known from the following sites in Finland (Figure 10.1): Riitakanranta and Kotijänkä (Figure 10.2.) in Rovaniemi (Kotivuori 1995; Kotivuori 1996), Kitulansuo D in Mikkeli (Lavento 1996; 1997), Äkälänniemi in Kajaani (Nieminen 1983), Kilpisaari 1 in Lahti (Poutiainen 2000) and Neitilä 4 in Kemijärvi (Sarvas 1963) (Table 10.1). Outside Finland several stone box furnaces have been found from Närke, Vestmanland and Haparanda in Sweden (Buchwald 2005, 197-202; Hansson 1989, 131-151) and 18 from the Republic of Karelia in Russia (Kosmenko & Manjuhin 1999). These all share the same characteristic of being formed into a rectangular box shape from slate stone slabs built at least partly underground. In most of the cases one of the short sides has been left open or possibly narrowed with smaller stones. Riitakanranta, Kotijänkä and Äkälänniemi furnaces had stones on the short side forming a door-like feature, which had a roughly two centimeter wide gap between

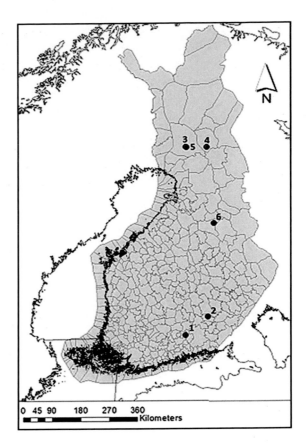

Figure 10.1: Map showing the locations of stone box furnaces in Finland. The numbers indicate the locations of each site from the Table 10.1 (Map: Joni Karjalainen and Juuso Vattulainen).

No.	Location	Outside Dimensions	Slag pit	Roof stone	Clay inlay	Slag
1	Kilpisaari 1, Lahti	77-85 x 43 x c. 23 cm	No	No	Yes	
2	Kitulansuo D, Mikkeli	70 x 50 x 20 cm	No	No	Yes	9 kg
3	Kotijänkä, Rovaniemi	40 x 50 x 25 cm	Yes	Yes	No	170 kg
4	?Neitilä 4, Kemijärvi	Unknown	No	Possibly	Yes	230 kg
5	Riitakanranta, Rovaniemi	65 x 32 x 25 cm	Yes	Yes	No	23 kg
6	Äkälänniemi, Kajaani	70 x 40 x 25 cm	Yes	Possibly	Yes	22,3 kg

Table 10.1: Stone box furnaces.

them (Kotivuori 1996, 109; Nieminen 1983, figures K10. and K11.). The gap between the front stones would have allowed the slag to run out and it is easy to block with clay or turf in order to keep the heat inside. In other cases the door stones were possibly mixed up with the stone debris around the furnaces or the furnaces never had them. In addition to the stones on the edges of the furnace pit, the Riitakanranta furnace also had a lid stone, which had broken into two pieces. The lid was cut on two edges to fit properly on top of the furnace structure (Kotivuori 1995, 20).

Archaeological evidence from Riitakanranta also shows that sand was tempered into the clay (Kotivuori 1995, 19), which did not shrink too much as it dried. This resulted in fewer cracks that could compromise the structure. Still, there was no apparent clay floor or lining for the furnace in Riitakanranta, which seems odd as

Figure 10.2: The furnace from Kotijänkä, Sierijärvi, Rovaniemi, as it is today in the National Museum of Finland reconstructed by Hannu Kotivuori (Photo: Joni Karjalainen).

burned clay was found from the site. On the other hand, the Kitulansuo D and Äkälänniemi furnaces seem to have had clay lining as protection to the walls and possibly to allow slag to run more freely on the furnace floor (Lavento 1997, 12; Nieminen 1983, 8; Figure 10.2).

Furthermore, some furnaces have a slag pit dug in front of them (Kotivuori 1995, 21; Nieminen 1983, 7). Therefore, it is possible that at least some of the furnaces were planned to be run for a longer period of time, in which slag would have to be removed from the furnace. On the other hand, the smelts could have been short enough for slag to stay inside the furnace and in such cases a slag pit or the doorway for the furnace would not have been needed. Nonetheless, it is unknown how or where the slag was tapped or removed, if it ever was, in such cases. The tapping of slag out of the furnace, even with smaller quantities of iron ore, would have allowed the iron bloom to be purer from slag.

The sites with stone box furnaces are always in the immediate proximity of lakes, from which iron ore was harvested for the smelts. The lake and bog iron ores called limonite were used as the main ore types during the Finnish Iron Age and there is no archaeological evidence for the use of mined ore minerals such as hematite and magnetite (Keränen, Itävuori and Kettunen 1991, 2). Therefore, the location of a furnace by a lake is logical as it was more sensible to transfer finished iron instead of extensive amounts of ore. The presence of iron ore today in the lakes with stone box furnaces has not been verified, but Puustinen (2002, Taulukko 1., Kuva 4.) has compiled documentary evidence on 7800 land claims around Finland for sites with lake iron ore in the time period of 1811-2001. The amount of land claims emphasises the abundance of lake iron ore in Finland usable for iron smelting.

Experiments

Planning and building the furnace

The planning process for the experimental furnace included a thorough reading of the excavation reports for the six furnaces found in Finland (Table 10.1). From this information plans were drawn in order to build a furnace in Kierikki. The furnace uses the mean size of the archaeological furnaces being 70 cm long, 40 cm wide and 25 cm tall. Clay lining was used in all the experiments to give better fire resistance to the stones. The only stones without lining were the lid stones.

Stones were collected from a harrowed forest area on two occasions relatively close to Yli-Ii, because they offered good opportunities for finding stones that had already been cut into more manageable sizes by the harrowing machines as a part of forest cultivation. Slate was preferred as it was used in the archaeological examples, but a single piece of granite was used for one of the sides. The second trip was made after the first smelt in order to find more suitable lid stones as the first one broke into pieces in the end of the smelt (see below).

After the first stone gathering trip, the stones were used to start building the furnace to approximately the size of the original furnaces found in Finland. Firstly, a 15 cm deep pit was dug for the stones (Figure 10.3) that were placed roughly into a rectangular form as tightly as possible and the gaps between the stones were filled with the same clay used for the lining. The upper edge of the stones rose to about 18 cm above ground level. Two stones were placed on one of the longer sides and a gap was knapped between them to create a place for a tuyere. There is one possible case of this type of a gap from the archaeological examples (Kotivuori 1995, drawing in Liite 12), but it is sometimes difficult to say if gaps between the stones were done on purpose or as a result of use, decay or a combination of both. For instance, the Äkälänniemi and Kitulansuo D furnaces had several tree roots growing through the structures shifting the stones (Lavento 1997, figure Kuva 16; Nieminen 1983, 6). A small slag pit was dug in front of the door stones following the examples of Riitakanranta, Kotijänkä and Kitulansuo D.

As a preparation for the smelts, the lid stones were heated in a fire for a short while in order to drive out all the water from the possible cracks. In extreme circumstances the stones could have exploded as the water steam expands in the cracks. This was not done for the stones on the sides, because they were lined with clay to protect the stones from extensive heat. Instead, once the stones and the clay were in place, a small fire was burned inside the furnace to drive out the moisture before the experiments.

Experimental setting

In total three smelts were undertaken, and based on the experiences and results from the pre-experiment the placement of iron ore inside the furnace was experimented further. For each experiment ten kilograms of lake iron ore lifted

Figure 10.3: Our furnace with the stones and slag pit in place (Photo: Joni Karjalainen).

			Materials (kg)		Outcome (kg)	
Smelt	Duration (hours)	Ore	Charcoal (pine)	Charcoal (birch)	Iron	Slag
1*	6	10	6	20	c. 0.9	c. 6
2	6	5	7	20	c. 0.6	c. 4
3	8.5	10	7.5	26	1.3	6.5

*Pre-experiment

Table 10.2: The smelting experiments.

from Nerkoonjärvi in Lapinlahti was used. The ore was crushed and roasted in a fire and then the best ore for the smelts was extracted using a magnet and a hand sieve in order to get rid of most of the small stones and sand. This could have been done by sight, but a magnet was faster. The ore used during a smelt was weighed in batches of one kilogram. Due to problems in the second smelt and challenging weather conditions it was not possible to reach the ten cycle limit and as a result only five kilograms was reached.

Charcoal for the smelts came from a local supplier in Ylikiiminki that uses a charcoal kiln based on 18th and 19th century models. Birch charcoal was preferred due to its high temperature efficiency, although pine charcoal was used during the preheating of the furnace because its lower price. Charcoal and ore were added into the furnace simultaneously by lifting the lid stone wearing welder's gloves although thick leather gloves could have been used instead. The amount of charcoal was not measured in similar cycles as ore, because the main concern was to keep the furnace full of charcoal, and not to add ore too quickly. Instead, only the total amount of

Figure 10.4: The furnace during the pre-experiment on Friday 13th in June. The cracks on the lid stone are already easy to see. An infrared thermometer documented 1417°C as the highest temperature reached inside the furnace (Photo: Juuso Vattulainen).

charcoal for each smelt was measured (Table10.2). Air was blown into the furnace using single chamber bellows made of wood and leather.

Using the furnace

During each smelt it soon became apparent that due to the lack of clay lining on the lid stones, they were vulnerable to the high temperatures inside the furnace. The heat damage started as small cracks on the surface of the stones that continued to expand as the smelts proceeded (Figure 10.4). Fortunately there was no need to replace any stones during the smelts. In all experiments the lid lasted to the end of the smelt, but in the last lift it usually broke into pieces and could not be used again as a lid stone. Therefore, after the first smelt we started gathering the pieces of lid stones and other broken stones into a pile near the furnace for possible reuse. For example, the material for new door stones before the second smelt was chosen from this pile. Sometimes the side facing the interior of the furnace was partly fused due to the high temperatures in the furnace, and in the second smelt pieces of lid stone fell into the furnace and were found almost completely fused after the smelt.

The furnace suffered the greatest amount of damage, when the blooms were taken out to be hammered on a tree stump. The lid broke every time at this stage beyond reuse, the clay lining suffered badly due to slag clinging onto it and through vitrification, and the door stones were knocked down in two of the smelts. The reason for knocking down the door stones in the first and third smelts was to get more room to extract the blooms. In both cases they broke and could not be reused. As the second smelt had to be stopped in the last stages due to torrential rain, the door stones survived intact and they were used in the third smelt as well. Recycling and reworking the material led the stone material to breaking into smaller pieces. We decided not to reuse some pieces at all, because they were too cracked or damaged to be reused as raw material for other purposes. In addition to smelting, it was noted that the open furnace could be used as a rather effective forge to heat the bloom again and then forge the slag out of it. We tried to forge the bloom from the second experiment in it, but it fell into pieces due to high slag content as we managed to use only five kilograms of ore for it.

Moreover, in the pre-experiment the clay lining was damaged as the bloom was taken out, because we used a crowbar to sever the bloom from the bottom of the furnace. In the process some lining on the walls cracked and fell off to the bottom of the furnace. In later smelts we used a sharpened iron rod and a hammer to remove the bloom, which proved to be much more gentle to the lining. The clay around the tuyere and the blast zone vitrified obtaining a glassy surface, as the temperature was constantly over 1000 °C in this area. After the first smelt all the vitrified clay was removed and replaced with new lining where needed, but after the second smelt a thin layer of clay was smeared on top of the vitrified layer. Archaeologically it is difficult to say, which method was used. As a result the heat burned holes into the lining exposing the stones on the sides in few places around the tuyere during the third smelt. The tuyeres were also changed after each smelt, because the heat vitrified their nozzles almost completely. Every so often a metal rod was used to poke the tuyeres open as the vitrified clay from the tuyere itself and the lining on the wall blocked it.

Abandoning the furnace

After the third smelt we cleared the furnace of all loose clay, charcoal, slag and stone, because we wanted to document the furnace in its final stage. In the case of archaeological stone box furnaces, once the iron bloom was out and the furnace

Figure 10.5: The smelting area after the three smelts. From left to right you can see the pile of stone and clay debris, small slag heap, parts of the last lid stones, small charcoal pile at the front and the furnace itself (Photo: Antti Palmroos).

was not going to be used anymore, it would have been easier to leave all the debris inside unless the craftsmen wanted to extract every small piece of iron. After the experiments were completed the experimental furnace was abandoned without destroying it any more than what it had suffered during the last smelt. At present, the furnace has stood unused for two years and the intention is to let it be for the moment and observe the decay in order to find out how badly the clay is broken by the freeze-thaw cycles. In only two years the furnace has decayed extensively. The majority of the unburnt or partially burnt lining has started to disintegrate revealing cracks on the stones. Without support from the lining the stones have moved slightly from their original places.

The area surrounding the furnace was also littered with debris from the smelts and working on the raw materials (Figure 10.5). For example, when emptying the furnace before documentation all the loose charcoal was cleared into the slag pit in front of the furnace and surroundings. Similarly, all the loose pieces of burnt and partially burnt clay, stone rubble and slag were placed into their respective piles in the corner of the smelting area. Firstly, a space was cleared around the furnace so that we could work around it more easily without having to worry about the loose debris. Secondly, we especially wanted to have most of the clay in one place so that we could keep ourselves updated how the weather and seasons break it and compare it to the clay inside the furnace.

Interpretation

Evidence that the stone box furnaces could be taken to extremely high temperatures is also evident from the archaeological context. For example, Kotivuori (1995, 23) found some partly fused stone from Riitakanranta and in our pre-experiment the inside part of the lid stone had fused on the surface. Spare stones for repairs are rarely found from the Finnish sites with the exception of Neitilä 4 (Kotivuori 1996, 111; Kehusmaa 1972, 83). The lack of spare stones at other sites could mean that they were used only once and the craftsmen relied that the furnace could take the heat or that the stones were taken away as they could be used as material for another furnace.

One of the clearest indications that the furnace or smelting site was in continuous use is the amount of slag found from the sites, although post-depositional bias has to be kept in mind as slag could have been placed, for instance, into burials (see Shepherd 1997). Between different sites the amounts vary radically and, for instance, at Rovaniemi, where the two nearly identical production sites are located, there is roughly 23 kg of slag from Riitakanranta and 170 kg from Kotijänkä (Kotivuori 1996, 110-111; Kotivuori 1990). In the experiments 10 kg of roasted ore was used, which produced 6-7 kg of slag in the first and third smelt and about 3 kg in the second smelt, when 5 kg of ore was used. The last smelt, which was the most successful, we received a bloom weighing 1.3 kg, thus producing 0.2 kg of iron for each kilogram of slag (compare Kotivuori 1996, 110). The closest parallel to our amount of slag comes from Kitulansuo D, 9 kg of slag (Lavento 1997), and it is possible that it was used once only. Nevertheless, our suspicion is that it is possible to run even longer smelts with the stone box furnace due to the possibility of tapping slag out, although a smelt producing 170 kg, not to mention 230 kg which is the quantity found from Neitilä 4 (Kehusmaa 1972, 80; Sarvas 1963, 6), of slag sounds excessively long and laborious. In the sites of Kotijänkä and Neitilä 4 the most likely explanation is that they were used multiple times with intermediate renovations when necessary. Unfortunately, the excavation report for the furnace in Kotijänkä has not been filed in yet making it difficult for us to research all the aspects we would like to research. On the other hand, the slag could have been taken away from the smelting sites in the cases with less slag, but this seems unlikely.

In our case the abandonment was a rather easy choice, because we wanted to see the effects of decay on the furnace. On the other hand, this raises a question of why the archaeological furnaces were abandoned or only partially destroyed and not completely destroyed or recycled. For example, in Riitakanranta the furnace seems to be in usable condition except for the broken lid, but it was nevertheless abandoned. Was this because of the abundance of stone material, which meant that there was no need to recycle the stones? Another possible explanation could be that the smelting seems to have happened close to the ore resources away from the settlement and thus abandoning the previous work space and moving just the tools to the new one was the easiest option. Obviously there could be a list of practical or even seemingly irrational ritual reasons for the selection of smelting locations, their abandonment and the smelting process itself (see for example Gansum 2004; Shepherd 1997).

Conclusion

After only three smelts it is still really difficult to say anything conclusive about the stone box furnaces and our research on them began in earnest during the same year as the smelts. Thus, a lot remains to be done and some possible future research questions could include, for example, the use of multiple tuyeres, placing the furnace completely underground and using larger quantities of iron ore. Nevertheless, the experiments so far have already given a possible explanation why there is only one lid stone from the six archaeological sites in Finland as they were possibly broken by the heat and then discarded. The absence of door stones could be explained by a similar process or that they were torn off when the iron bloom was taken out. Experiments also show that the clay lining protected the wall stones surprisingly well from damage. In short, the results were more encouraging then we first expected.

Just like a shaft furnace made of clay, these furnaces require careful planning and good resources in the surrounding area starting from the stones and iron ore. Based on the amounts of slag some of them were used only once or twice, while others experienced multiple cycles of use. They were also repaired when necessary in order to keep them functional and ultimately faced abandonment. As a structure the stone box furnace is rather distinctive and it has not reached international attention properly.

Bibliography

Bennerhag, C. 2010. Järnframställning vid Jernbacksmyren under förromerks järnålder. Arkeologisk slutundersökning av Raä 842, Nederalix socken. Luleå. Rapport 2010:42, Arkeologi, Norrbottens Museum.

Buchwald, V.F. 2005. *Iron and Steel in Ancient Times*. Det Kongelige Danske Videnskabernes Selskab: Copenhagen.

Doonan, R.C.P. 2013a. Recovering value in experimental studies of ancient metallurgy: a theoretical framework for future studies? In D. Dungworth and R. C. P. Doonan (eds.) *Accidental and Experimental Archaeometallurgy*. The Historical Metallurgical Society: London. pp. 17-24.

Doonan, R.C.P. 2013b. Monstrous fallacies and the assembly of archaeometallurgical experiments. In D. Dungworth and R. C. P. Doonan (eds.) *Accidental and Experimental Archaeometallurgy*. The Historical Metallurgical Society: London. pp. 93-98.

Gansum, T. 2004. Role the bones – from iron to steel. *Norwegian Archaeological Review*, 37(1): 41-57.

Hansson, P. 1989. *Samhälle och järn i Sverige under järnåldern och äldre medeltiden. Exemplet Närke*. Univeristy of Uppsala Aun 13: Uppsala.

Hjärthner-Holdar, E. 1993. *Järnets och järnmetallurgins introduction I Sverige*. Univeristy of Uppsala Aun 16: Uppsala.

Karjalainen, J. 2016. *The Spell of Iron. Iron smelting experiments with stone box furnacesof the Finnish Early Iron Age*. Master's Thesis. University of Oulu. Available at: <http://jultika.oulu.fi/files/nbnfioulu-201605261996.pdf> [Accessed 3 July 2016].

Kehusmaa, A. 1972. *Kemijärven Neitilä 4*. MA. *Helsingin yliopiston arkeologian laitos, Moniste no: 3* (Helsinki University, Department of Archaeology, Handout no: 3).

Keränen, J., Itävuori, E. and Kettunen, P. 1991. *Esihistoriallisten rautakuonien tunnistus faasirakenteiden pohjalta*. Tampere University of Technology, Institute of Materials Science: Tampere.

Kosmenko, M.G. and Manjuhin, I.S. 1999. Ancient Iron Production in Karelia. *Fennoscandia Archaeologica* 16: 31-46.

Kotivuori, H. 2014. *Rovaniemen ja Maununiemen raudanvalmistusuunit*. [Email] (Personal communication, 19 March 2014).

Kotivuori, H. 2013. Tidiga spår av järnhantering in Norra Finland. In B. Rundberget, J. H. Larsen, and T. H. B. Haraldsen (eds.) *Ovnstypologi og ovnskronologi i den nordiske jernvinna*. Kristianstad: Portal. pp. 55-58.

Kotivuori, H. 1995. *Rovaniemi 474 a-c, Korkalo Riitakanranta. Kivikauden ja varhaismetallikauden asuinpaikan, esihistoriallisen raudanvalmistuspaikan ja historiallisen ajan tupasijan kaivaus vuosina 1989 ja 1990.* Excavation report.

Kotivuori, H. 1996. Pyytäjistä kaskenraivaajiksi. Rovaniemen asutus noin 6000 eKr.-1300 jKr. In M. Saarnisto, H. Kotivuori, J. Vahtola and M. Enbuske (eds.) *Rovaniemen Historia Vuoteen 1721. Kotatulilta savupirtin suojaan.* Gummerus Kirjapaino Oy Jyväskylä. pp. 36-125.

Lavento, M. 1996. Varhaista Raudanvalmistusta Ristiinassa – muutamia huomioita Kitulansuon raudansulatusuunista ja siihen liittyvästä keramiikasta. *Sihti* 4: 64-75.

Lavento, M. 1997. *Ristiina Laasola Kitulansuo d 1995.* Excavation report.

Lavento, M. 1999. An Iron Furnace from the Early Metal Period at Kitulansuo in Ristiina, in the Southern Part of the Lake Saimaa Water System. *Fennoscandia Archaeolociga* 16: 75-80.

Lavento, M. 2003. Viipurin läänin pronssikausi ja varhaismetallikausi. In M. Saarnisto (ed.) *Viipurin Läänin Historia I. Karjalan Synty.* Gummerus Kirjapaino Oy: Jyväskylä. pp. 245-290.

Mäkivuoti, M. 1983. *Varhainen Raudanvalmistus Pohjois-Suomessa.* MA. University of Oulu: Oulu.

Mathieu, J.R. 2002. Introduction – experimental archaeology: replication past objects, behaviors, and processes. In J. R. Mathieu (ed.) *Experimental Archaeology: Replicating Past Objects, Behaviors, and Processes.* BAR International Series 1035: Oxford. pp. 1-11.

Nieminen, E.L. 1983. *Kajaani Äkälänniemi. Kertomus kivikautisen asuinpaikan ja keskiaikaisen(?) raudan valmistuspaikan kaivauksista.* Excavation report.

Peets, J. 2003. *The Power of Iron.* Tallinn: Research into Ancient Times 12.

Poutiainen, H. 2000. *Nastola Kilpisaari 1. Esihistoriallisen asuinpaikan arkeologinen koekaivaus.* Excavation report.

Puustinen, K. 2002. Kaivoslain mukaiset valtaukset, kaivospiirit ja tutkimustyöselostukset Suomessa vuosina 1811 - 2001: Tietokanta Internetissä. [pdf] Espoo: Geological Survey of Finland. Available at <http://tupa.gtk.fi/raportti/arkisto/m10_1_2002_3.pdf> [Accessed 9 May 2016].

Sarvas, P. 1963. *Kemijärvi Luusua Neitilä 4. Kaivaus vuosina 1962-1964.* Excavation report.

Shepherd, D.J. 1997. The ritual significance of slag in Finnish Iron Age burials. *Fennoscandia Archaeologica*, 14: 13-22.

[...] *quia pulvis es et in pulverem reverteris*" (Genesis, 3: 19)

Experimental production of Iberian iron and post-processing approach to the furnace structures

José Miguel Gallego Cañamero,

Manel Gómez Gutiérrez and Josep Pou i Vallès

Introduction

Since its excavation between 1996 and 1997 and, up to the moment of writing these lines, the Iberian-Cossetan archaeological site of Les Guàrdies (El Vendrell, Tarragona) has provided a *unicum* (a unique example) in the Iberian Peninsula archaeology. It presents comprehensive archaeological evidence of all processes of the ironworking chain, from the mine to the obtaining of metal as well as evidence related to peripheral elements such as the making of charcoal or the extraction of ore during the Full Iberian period (4th century BC to 2nd century BC, with special effect in the 3rd century BC).

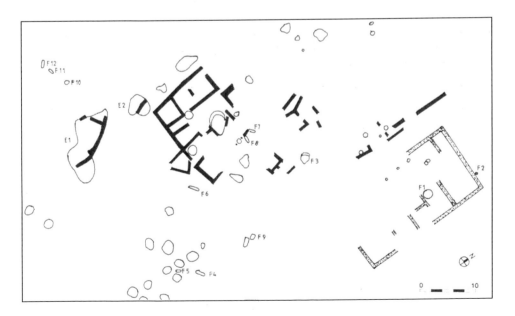

Figure 11.1: Floor of the site. Source: Gallego Cañamero, Gómez Gutiérrez and Pou i Vallès.

The site is unparalleled in the pre-Roman context of the Iberian Peninsula (Figure 11.1). All evidence indicates that, at least between 4th and 2nd centuries BCE, Les Guàrdies dwellers were involved in intensive and extensive mining development of iron-ore and its later insertion in the political and/or commercial networks at the local and regional level (Morer *et al.* 1997; Morer and Rigo 1999).

It was not until recent years that investigation on experimental paleo-ironworking in Spain has begun to enjoy an encouraging scenario, as a result of the development of diverse projects of experimental archaeology that have begun to shed light on the subject (Burillo and Rovira 2005; Gallego 2013; Gallego 2014a and 2014b, and Gallego in press) and within the fields of experimental archaeology and archaeometallurgy research (Pleiner, 1988; Reynolds1988; Madroñero de la Cal 1989; Rostocker & Bronson 1990; Crew 1984 & 1991a; Rostocker & Bronson 1990; Rovira & Solías1991; Mohen 1992; Mangin 2004; Manning 1995; Rovira 1993, 2000 & 2012; Dunikowsky & Cabboï 1995; Gómez Ramos1996; Boonstra *et al.* 1997; Serneels1997 & 1998; Ferrer 2000; Karbowniczek *et al.* 2009; Mata *et al.* 2009; Espelund 2010). It is within this dynamic that the experimentations presented here were carried out at La Ciutadella (Calafell, Tarragona), an enclosed area of the Iberian-Cossetan group, inhabited between 5th to 2nd century BCE. La Ciutadella is an EXARC member, where activities related to experimental archaeology and the dissemination of history are often developed. This site, of aristocratic character, exerted a political control over Les Guàrdies rural site, probably a decisive difference as regards to the distribution of the valued metal (Santacana *et al.*, 2005). This project, named *From evidence to facts. Iberian bloomery chain under an experimental perspective,* was developed with the EU Culture Programme funded project OpenArch, during April 2014 and it signifies a milestone in the history of the paleo-ironworking in Spain. This is due to the fact that besides the initiative developed in Segeda (Mara, Zaragoza) in 2005 on a small scale (Burillo and Rovira 2005), we are not able to mention any other proposals of a similar significance.

Because of this, we hope it contributes to widening the knowledge about Iberian ironworking, as well as to setting out supplementary hypotheses about technological knowledge, the social organisation and the territorial hierarchisation of the inhabitants of the Cossetan territory which have been outlined by diverse researchers (Asensio *et al.* 2001).

The presence in the aforementioned site of pyrotechnical structures include remains that were easily identified as bloomery furnaces and forges, in addition to ore remains, thermally-altered structural wall fragments, slags, and iron objects. All have allowed a hypothetical reconstruction of the comprehensive ironworking process developed in Les Guàrdies, during at least two centuries and it has greatly facilitated its practical comprehension. We refer to these elements as direct archaeological evidence. Nevertheless, despite the plentiful documentation emanating directly from the archaeological record, there were certain gaps relating to pre- and post-reduction processes that were filled with elements coming from other archaeological sites. In this sense, and in order to not distort the accuracy of the study, we have always tried to search material in the closest geographical and chronological proximity to those elements. That is what we name indirect archaeological evidence.

Although all the archaeologically documented ironworking chain was reproduced in total, this work discusses only the core part of it, that is, two of the Bloomery furnaces. These have been chosen because they provided greater information and because they were representative of two different occupation phases, separated chronologically.

The reproduction of the ironworking chain carried out in an experimental way at the Iberian Citadel of Calafell has allowed detailed explanations of the technological aspects which was understood and controlled by the dwellers of the Iberian-Cossetan site of Les Guàrdies, which was devoted to intensive production of iron between 4th and 2nd centuries B from the mine to the obtaining of iron.

Planning Phase

The works started with the documentation, classification and structuring of the so-named direct archaeological evidences, following the steps marked by the archaeologists who were in charge of the excavation[1], and later the construction planning of the central core of the ironworking chain, that is, the bloomery furnaces.

In this case they were inspired by two excavated structures in Les Guàrdies, in particular the structures SU-7438 (Figure 11.2) dated halfway through 4th century BC and the structure SU-7235 (Figure 11.3) dated halfway through the 2nd century BC. In

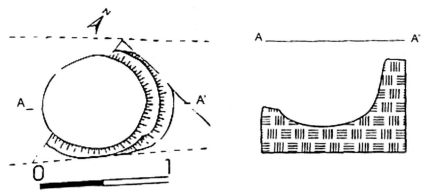

Figure 11.2: Plan and profile drawing of ELNOBE. Source: Gallego Cañamero, Gómez Gutiérrez and Pou i Vallès.

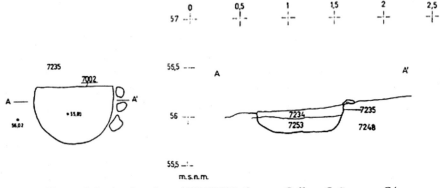

Figure 11.3: Plan and Section drawing of ELBUTIE. Source: Gallego Cañamero, Gómez Gutiérrez and Pou i Vallès.

both cases, the structures have been severely affected by farming activities carried out on the field for generations, so, in reality, from the original the structures only bases and slightly elevated excavated remains were preserved. Obviously, where reconstructions are based on findings that are known only from surviving archaeological elements, the hypothetical construction is an interpretation and, therefore, it might contain a certain controversy that, we hope, stimulates debate.

The noteworthy dimensions of one of the recovered bases, the SU-7235, with a maximum preserved diameter of 0.9 m, it brought us immediately to the suspicion that such a large combustion structure had presented serious issues and difficulties to be fed by bellows, probably meaning a decrease in its productivity owing to the need for more human resources would have been required to its functioning[2]. Due to no molten wasted slags being found in any part of the site, we think this structure could compare with various typologies of furnaces within the suggested classification by Pleiner (Pleiner 1978). However, we made the construction taking as a reasonable hypothesis its adscription to the 'domed furnace" typology, which were totally compatible with the physical laws that take part in the natural draw, according to our own research (Gallego, *in press*). The existence of intensive ironworking production centres found in the Mediterranean and trans-Pyrenean environments with similar chronologies[3], as the Clérimois ensemble (Yonne, France) (Dunikovsky and Cabboï 1995) or the Etruscan city of Populonia (Crew 1991), besides other examples documented in the La Tène world (Pleiner 1980), makes us think about the possibility that Les Guàrdies constitutes a settlement of equivalent typology and functionality. Therefore, a site devoted to the intensive exploitation of iron ore and its transformation *in situ* into raw iron (Gallego, *in press*, based on the assertions of Morer and Rigo 1999). Therefore it is possible that the economic activity of the Les Guàrdies dwellers, though not responding to current mercantilist parameters, nonetheless pivoted on the maximum profitability of efforts and resources, mechanical and human. Hence its location in the immediate proximities of the mineralogical geological surface outcrops. In this sense, and as we had extensively set out in a prior work whose conclusions we will not tackle here (Gallego, in press), we are persuaded that natural draft type furnaces meet these requirements and form a possibility that we consider should not be underestimated and which were likely to be even more used in the Ancient times than we currently believe, a question that has been set out by other researchers (Rehder 2000).

We will also not expand here on the thermo-dynamic of how these structures functioned as this has already been described (Gallego in press). We will just emphasise its high versatility and remarkable profitability and the benefits that it represents.

The lack of molten slag (referred to in the French literature as '*ecorie ecoulé*') among the material recovered from the SU-7438 (not only in this structure but also in the entire site) led us to explain the evidence as a more rudimentary structure type a 'slag pit furnace', not dismissing the previous option though. The maximum diameter which is preserved never exceeded the 0.65 cm in an area of the base that clearly corresponded to the central part of it and therefore, to the wider section. Its volumetric capacity was a fourth part of the previous furnace, around 140 l. according to what we could check from its hypothetical reconstruction, a datum that could imply, *a priori*, a lower productivity and a lower profitability as a result. Nevertheless, it is necessary to point out that the limited dimensions favour the controlled blowing of air, then the bloomery time lessens (in this case it took 26 hours of combustion, 4 of them for pre-heating, 13 of 'natural draught' and 9 of feeding with bellows) and therefore the effort investment, meaning that in a certain way, it could be affirmed that profitability would increase. We will also not expand here on this debate as this, too, has been set out previously (Gallego 2014a).

Construction Phase

For the construction of both structures various materials that had been documented during the archaeological excavation works were used. These materials, such as limestone blocks, clay and vegetable fibre are currently kept in the collection of the Government (*Generalitat*) of Catalonia's Service of Archaeology and Paleontology in the headquarters of Girona.

ELNOBE the reconstructed furnace was built taking advantage of a pronounced stepped slope of the land, in the same way as evidenced by the excavation of the SU-7438 that was partially truncated in the calcareous geology. Although a great part of the base perimeter had been cut off by the farming works, it was possible to deduce its diameter, because more than half of it was perfectly preserved. Due to the lack of the frontal part of the furnace in the archaeological record, we chose to build a small frontal aperture whose aim was to facilitate the extraction of the material obtained. The aerial part of the furnace was built using mortar made with local clay full of iron-staining coming from Tertiary floods (85%), ashes coming from the ore enrichment bonfire compounded by white pine (*Pinus halepensis*), holm oak (*Quercus illex*) and wild olive tree (*Olea europaea sylvestris*) (5%) and vegetable fibres coming from the late reaping of the wheat (*Triticum dicoccum*) (10%). Adding small local limestone blocks, very similar to those used in Les Guàrdies, it was constructed up to 1.3 m high (our objective was to study if the 'natural draught' system could have been used combined with the bellows, therefore we respected the minimum relation width/height of 1:2 that we have observed in previous experiments (Gallego 2014a) leaving an air duct of 0.2 m of maximum diameter. In addition, a 1 cm. thickness refractory layer was applied as internal covering of the furnace, with the intention to favour the refraction capacity and to generate a regular and homogeneous surface to favour the gas fluidity and to prevent the load obstruction. This mixture was also made with local clays that were sifted by flotation (80%), ashes with identical composition to the aforementioned ones (10%) and horse (*Equus ferus caballus*) manure (10%) to provide an endo-structure at once resistant and thermodynamic.

With the information recovered from the SU-7235 an interpretation of the structure that we named ELBUITE was built. This was a furnace with 0.9 m of internal maximum diameter and 2 m high[4] with a total volume of 430 l. that took outside air in a natural way through 16 D-section cylindrical tuyeres whose evidences were not found during excavation works, but they could be documented in the Iberian sites of La Fonteta (Guardamar de Segura, Alicante), in earlier chronologies though (8th century BC), associated with the development of ironworking activities

(Renzi 2007) and in La Torre dels Encantats (Arenys de Mar, Barcelona), associated with archaeological remains from 2nd cent BC (Garcès 2013). Likewise, the aerial structure of ELBUITE as well as the tuyeres was built with a mixture made with the same clays (85%), the same ashes (5%) and the same vegetable fibres (10%). The main difference is that, in this case, the mixture used for making the tuyeres was previously sifted through a flotation system, with the intention to eliminate limestone nodules that with high temperatures could have had micro-explosions that could have caused the fragmentation and blockage of the air duct.

The aerial part of the furnace was constructed from the positioning of medium-sized calcareous cores of local origin (up to 30 cm) thickened with mortar in a series of rows, respecting the minimum relationship height/diameter 2:1 in order to cause the 'Bernoulli effect', also named 'chimney effect', following the parameters that we set out in an aforementioned previous work (Gallego 2014a). Up to a 0.9 m- 1 m high, the basin was given a spherical volumetry aiming to cause, on the one hand, the rise in temperature and on the other, the acceleration of ascending gases to the chimney as a result of the evacuation of gas through a narrow duct, following the principle of fluid mechanics. To conclude, and taking as reference a furnace wall fragment, totally infrified, that was recovered during the excavations (although belonging to SU-7150), the internal wall was covered in its entirety with the same refractory layer of about 1 cm thickness as that in the prior example. In addition to this, a staircase formed by three large limestone blocks was built in the furnace wall with the aim to facilitate the load and the clearing activities and to avoid at the same time, leaning the weight of ladders against the wall and other elements for accessing to the chimney mouth.

Use Phase

The ELNOBE furnace was designed to work with a mixed system ('free breathing' and 'bellows'). We could differentiate three sub-phases in the structure 'use phase'. Firstly, a pre-heating sub-phase defined by the furnace firing and the introduction into the furnace of dry firewood of local origin, mostly white pine (*Pinus halepensis*), though holm oak was also used (*Quercus illex*). This first phase did not extended more than four hours and its goal, besides dehydrating and heating the structure, has as a purpose the generation of a carpet of embers and ashes that later would be used to favour the combustion of charcoal during the reduction process.

Next we proceeded to place four cylindrical tuyeres in opposite positions, with an inclination of about 30º, entering about 13 cm. inside the base.

The opening in the base of the furnace through which the load would be extracted, was closed with the same constructive materials. Straightaway, the furnace was completely loaded with wild olive tree (*Olea europaea sylvestris*) (90%) and holm oak (*Quercus illex*) (10%) charcoal, as documented in the archaeological record. This 'natural draught' sub-phase was kept going for thirteen hours until it was finally time to proceed to the positioning of the hand-operated bellows each to be used of 30 l. volume.

Figure 11.4: Reconstructed ELBUITE and ELNOBE in use. Source: Gallego Cañamero, Gómez Gutiérrez and Pou i Vallès.

The cadence was about 33.600 air litres per hour during ten hours. The thermal ceiling during the process did not surpass 1090 ºC. The ratio of ore:charcoal stood finally in a relation of 1:5,6.

The interpretative construction of the latest furnace, ELBUITE, was subjected to a prolonged bloomery process that encompassed a period of 82 hours, including 4 hours of progressive pre-heating with living flames of dry firewood from white pine (*Pinus halepensis*) and holm oak (*Quercus Illex*). From this moment on, we proceeded to close the aperture in order to extract the load, previously adjusted to the furnace base and filled in with charcoal, in this case only from holm oak (*Quercus illex*). Throughout 78 hours, in an uninterrupted way, the furnace was loaded in progressive cycles of charcoal and ore in a volumetric proportion of 1:3.1, until the load descended to the tuyeres level. In that moment, with the chimney air duct released from the load, the gas ascended in a dramatic way, making a huge flame. The peak temperature reached was 1283 ºC. (Figure 11.4).

In ELNOBE, 41 kg of iron ore was used coming from the same geological seam utilised in Les Guàrdies, in this case, coming from a tiny outcrop in Calafell. In ELBUITE, 85 kg of iron ore was used coming from the mine of Rocabruna (Gavà, Barcelona) that had already been utilized during the Iberian Age (Álvarez and Estrada 2009). In both cases, the ore was an iron hydroxide formed by limonite ($FeO(OH)nH_2O$) with small traces of hematite (Fe_2O_3) and goethite ($FeO(OH)$).

Conclusions

We are fully aware that limited experimentation does not constitute a definitive data basis. Nonetheless, we firmly believe that the implementation of data from previous experimentations performed by ourselves, elements recovered directly from Les Guàrdies site, together with some others coming from various protohistoric sites in which a transformation of ore also happened, allows us to complete the interpretative hypothesis of the archaeologists who excavated. In this way we contribute towards a more defined and structured for the interpretation of the ironworking chain developed in the Iberian site of Les Guàrdies.

As regards to the bloomery furnaces in the strict sense, the central axis of the present study, we are able to set out various hypotheses. For a start, we can affirm that the 'natural draught' furnace, ELBUITE, higher and bulkier, experienced a much more noticeable deterioration than the 'induced draught' (bellows) furnace, ELNOBE. With probability, its clayey structure contained a larger quantity of water that when evaporated in a short time lapse, it contributed to its own contraction.

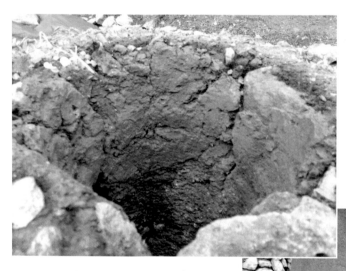

Figure 11.5: Current state of the furnaces.
Source: Gallego Cañamero, Gómez
Gutiérrez and Pou i Vallès.

We are convinced that these structures were not built for a single use only but that they could have been functioning throughout multiple smelting operations depending, obviously, on the intensity and the level of use by the Iberian-Cossetanian smiths. Furthermore, the rare thermal alteration of the inner surfaces, despite they reaching temperatures in the order of 1100-1300 °C, allows us to deduce that the glazed wall fragment from the SU-7150 could correspond to an isolated reduction which reached an upper thermal level or that the clay used in the furnace construction was easily changeable because of the thermal increase. The progressive vitrification of the inner surface due to high temperatures allows a continuing reutilisation of this type of structure because the friction level of the gases and the load decreases and besides, it structurally consolidates, homogenises and weathers the furnace, with all the advantages it brings.

During the pre-heating phase, the inner surface of the ELBUITE furnace experienced a series of micro-explosions in some calcareous cores that initiated the deterioration of the inner surface, but without structural implications. Later, the appearance of large fissures along the external surface, in some cases of a structural type[5], even before the completion of the experiment, constitutes another important datum to consider (Figure 11.5).

It should be mentioned that these fissures already started to appear already during the pre-heating process, but in a moderate way, when the temperature was around 850 °C. As the temperatures increase was produced, the furnace walls showed an abrupt dehydration and a resulting structural contraction that culminated during the last stage of the reduction, around 1280 °C, in the appearance of large cracks. Some of them corresponded very graphically with the constructive stages. This possibly happened due to the predominance of clays over calcareous blocks in the constructed surface; the higher hydration level of this material caused a contraction that it finally collapsed due to physical pressures, opening cracks that in some case surpassed 3 cm.

Along the inner air duct of the chimney, the change progressively happened with fissure development and the partial detachment of the inner refractory cover though improving. We believe this could be linked to a lesser thickness of the walls which affects their own contraction level, accentuating it. In fact, and as an argument in favour, we can mention that the more relevant structural cracks, transmitted to the external face, happened in this area. Regarding the cylindric tuyeres, of about 60 cm length, walls between 3 and 5 cm, and inner duct between 1.5 cm and 3 cm, it is important to point out that almost all of them were fragmented when put into the furnace and subjected to temperatures over 900 °C. The fragmentation line was situated 20-30 cm from the side kept inside the combustion base. It corresponded in most cases, with the level of thermal incidence, that is, the point where it did not produce an abrupt and noticeable contraction effect. On the other hand, this side experimented the vitrification at different levels depending on its position in the base and its thermal affects.

In both cases, in order to access the load and be able to extract it, it meant an aggressive activity that implied the literal destruction of the furnace aperture. Indeed, due to the difficulties of extracting the load that sometimes was fused to the inner walls, it was necessary to voluntarily destroy those obstructing areas. At times, the destruction happened accidentally, as a result of the fortuitous action of the iron tools used in the load extraction. Nevertheless, and foreseeing future smelts, it was tried to preserve most part of the structures, as much as possible; we think this rational behaviour was probably shared by the 'smiths' of Les Guàrdies, as in some aspects of sheer economic profitability it has been possible to document that they tried to optimise their effort; they could have proceeded to do the same by trying to preserve the structures.

Final Impact

The structure of the furnace has been exposed to the climate and only briefly but two months after it was abandoned, clear evidence of erosion can be observed, mainly due to the effects of heavy rains. These rains have superficially damaged both furnaces whose clay is deposited in its base, making a slight elevation around it on its external surface, involuntarily protecting it. The inner surface of the combustion bowl has not been much altered, because it was subjected to the higher temperatures and it has kept a better state than the outside. Instead, the inner chimney flue suffered a great deal of deterioration. In the light of the remains and with the available data, it is easy to foresee that if this situation extends, the external surface will progressively erode, jumbling together in the structure base, leaving the chimney duct that will disappear last into the combustion basin. The cooking and vitrification level of this area will determine its durability, though probably, exposure would disintegrate it in the end. Ultimately, the evidence that we would find archaeologically would be fragments of glazed wall and, perhaps, if the accumulation of constructive elements in the base it is not altered by the anthropic or natural action, the remains of the basin and of the aerial part of the furnaces.

In this sense, our intention is to continue studying the process for obtaining iron in the same used structures as well analysing their own degenerative progression, paying special attention to repairs, modifications and re-interpretations of the furnaces, the emergence of wild vegetation, or the effect that the very heavy rains, typical in the area have on the structures. In this way, the research will study not just the metal produced but the object biography of the structure.

Bibliography

Álvarez, R., Estrada, A. 2009. L'explotació de ferro en el complex miner de Gavà. La mina número 65, in *L'arqueologia a Gavà, Homentage a Alícia Estrada*, Collection "La nostra gent", 5, pp. 141-160.

Asensio, D., Morer, J., Rigo, A. i Sanmartí, J. 2001. Les formes d' organització social i econòmica a la Cossetània ibèrica: Noves activitats sobre l'Evolució i tipologia dels assentaments entre els segles VI-III a. C., in *Taula Rodona Internacional d'Ullastret: Territori polític i territori rural durant l'edat del ferro a la Mediterrània occidental*, Monografies d'Ullastret, 2, pp. 253-272.

Boonstra, A., Van de Manakker, T., Van Dijk, W. 1997. Experiments with a slag- tapping and a slag pit furnace. In Lars Chr. Nørbach (ed.) Early iron production. *Archaeology, technology and experiments. Nordic Iron Seminar, Lejre*, from July 22th to 28th, 1996. Technical Report. 3: 73-80.

Burillo, F., Rovira, S., 2005. Experimentos de fundición de minerales de hierro en la ciudad- estado celtibérica de Segeda (Mara, Zaragoza). *Avances en Arqueometría*, Universitat de Girona, pp. 137- 145.

Cleere, H.F. 1971. Ironmaking in a Roman furnace, *Britannia* 2: 203-217.

Cleere, H.F. 1972. The classification of early smelting- iron furnaces, in *The Antiquaries Journal II*: 8-23.

Crew, P. 1984. Bryn y Castell Hillfort. A late prehistoric ironworking settlement in North-West Wales. In Scott, B.G & H. Cleere, H. (eds.): *The crafts of the blacksmith*, Ulster Museum: Belfast. pp. 91-100.

Crew, P. 1991a. The experimental production of prehistoric bar iron, in *Historical Metallurgy* 25: 21-35.

Crew, P. 1991. The iron and copper slags at Baratti, Populonia, Italy, in *Historical Metallurgy* 25: 109-15.

Dunikowsky, M. and Cabboï, S. 1995. La sidérurgie chez les Sénons: les ateliers celtiques et gallo- romains des Clérimois (Yonne), in *Documents d'Archéologie Françoise* 51, Maison des Sciences de l'Homme, Paris.

Espelund, A. 2010. Experimental ironmaking once more: combining theory and find material, *EuroREA* 7: 4-8.

Ferrer, M.A. 2000. La metalurgia ibérica del hierro. Una aproximación a través de la interpretación arqueométrica, in Mata, C., Pérez, G. (eds.), Ibers. Agricultors, artesans i comerciants. III Reunió sobre Economia en el Món Ibèric, *SAGVNTUM Extra- 3*, Universitat de València, pp. 283-290.

Gallego, J.M. 2013. La siderurgia en el mundo ibérico. Primeros datos a partir de la experimentación arqueológica, in *Actas del III Congreso Internacional de Arqueología Experimental*, Banyoles, from october the 17th to the 19th, 2011, Museu d'Arqueologia de Catalunya, Barcelona.

Gallego, J.M. 2014b: Experimentando con armas ibéricas de hierro. La producción del metal en hornos de "tiro natural", *Gladius*, vol. XXXIV, CSIC, Madrid.

Gallego, J. M. 2014b: La producción de hierro entre los pueblos ibéricos septentrionales. Experimentaciones y primeros resultados, *Kobie, Anejo* 13, Diputación Foral de Bizkaia, 39- 58.

Garcès, I. (dir.) 2013: *Catàleg dels materials arqueològics de la Torre dels Encantats, Col·lecció del Museu d'Arenys de Mar, Ajmt.* d'Arenys de Mar.

García, G. 2006. *Entre iberos y celtas: las espadas de tipo La Tène del noreste de la Península Ibérica*, Anejos de Gladius, 10, CSIC/ Polifemo, Madrid.

García, G. 2012. *El armamento de influencia la Tène en la Península Ibérica (siglos V- I a.C.)*, Monographies Instrumentum 43, Éditions Monique Mergoil, Montagnac, 2012.

Gómez Ramos, P. 1996. Análisis de escorias férreas: nuevas aportaciones al conocimiento de la siderurgia prerromana en España. *Trabajos de Prehistoria* 53, vol. 2, 1996, pp. 145-155.

Karbowniczek, M., Weker, W. and Suliga, I. 2009. Experimental metallurgical process in a slag pit bloomery furnace, *EuroREA* 6, pp. 45-49.

Madroñero de la Cal, Á. 1989. Los hierros de la España prerromana, in C. Domergue (ed.), *Minería y metalurgia en las antiguas civilizaciones mediterráneas y europeas*, Ministerio de Cultura, pp. 109-118.

Mangin, M. (*dir.*) 2004. *Le fer*, Col. *Archéologiques*, Errance, Paris.

Manning, W.H. 1995. Ironworking in the Celtic World, in *The Celtic World* London, pp. 310-320.

Mata, C., Moreno, A. and Ferrer, M.A. 2009. Iron, Fuel and Slags: reconstructing the Ironworking Process in Iberian Iron Age (Valencian Region), *Pyrenae* 40, vol. II, pp. 105-127.

Mohen, J.P. 1992. *Metalurgia prehistórica. Introducción a la paleometalurgia*, Masson, S. A., Barcelona.

Morer, J., Rigo, A. and Barrasetas, E. 1997. Les intervencions arqueològiques l'autopista A- 16: valoració de conjunt, *Tribuna d'Arqueologia*, 1996-1997, pp. 67-98.

Morer, J. and Rigo, A. 1999. *Ferro i ferrers en el món ibèric. El poblat de les Guàrdies (El Vendrell)*, Aucat, Autopistes de Catalunya.

Pleiner, R. 1978. Comments on I. Martens: Some reflections on the classification of Prehistoric and Medieval Ironsmelting furnaces, in *Norwegian Archaeological Review* 11: 27-47.

Pleiner, R. 1980. Early Iron Metallurgy in Europe, in TA Wertime & JD Muhly (eds), *The coming of the Age of Iron* , New Haven; London, pp. 375-415.

Pleiner, R. 1988. Les primeres produccions de ferro a l'Europa Central i Oriental, *Cota Zero* 13, Vic, pp. 71-84.

Quesada, F. 1997. *El armamento ibérico. Estudio tipológico, geográfico, funcional, social y simbólico de las armas en la Cultura Ibérica (siglos VI-I a. C.)*, Monographies Instrumentum 3, Montagnac.

Rehder, J.E. 2000. *The mastery and uses of fire in Antiquity*, McGill-Queen's University Press Montreal: Canada.

Renzi, M. 2007. Estudio tipológico y funcional de las toberas del yacimiento de la Fonteta (Guardamar de Segura, Alicante), in *Trabajos de Prehistoria*, 64, 1, pp. 165-177.

Reynolds, P.J. 1988. *Arqueologia experimental. Una perspectiva de futur*, Eumo, Col. Referències 4, Vic.

Rostocker, W. and Bronson, B. 1990. Pre-industrial iron, its technology and ethnology, in *Archaeomaterials Monograph* 1, Philadelphia.

Rovira, S. 1993. La metalurgia de la Edad del Hierro en la Península Ibérica: una síntesis introductoria, in Arana, R., Muñoz, A. M., Ramallo, S. i Ros, Mª. M. (eds.): *Metalurgia en la Península Ibérica durante el Primer Milenio a. C. Estado actual de la investigación*, Universidad de Murcia, pp. 45-70.

Rovira, M.C. 2000. Los talleres de herrero en el mundo ibérico. Aspectos técnicos y sociales; in Mata, C., Pérez, G. (eds.), Ibers. Agricultors, artesans i comerciants. III Reunió sobre Economia en el Món Ibèric, *SAGVNTVM Extra- 3*, Universitat de València, pp. 265-270.

Rovira, M.C. 2012. La producció siderúgica en època ibèrica a Catalunya, in Boscos de Ferro, *Actes de les Primeres Jornades de Recerca i Desenvolupament de la Vall Ferrera*, Garsineu Edicions, Tremp, pp. 41-50.

Rovira, S., Solías, J.M. 1991. Iron minery and metallurgy in the lower course of river Llobregat (N. E. of Spain) during the Roman Republican period, in *Materialy Archeologiczne XXVI*, International Archaeometallurgical Symposium, pp. 53-57.

Santacana, J., Pou, J., Morer, J., Asensio, D. and Sanmartí, J. 2005. Evidències arqueològiques del procés d'emergència "d'élites" aristocràtiques a la ciutadella ibèrica d'Alorda Park (Calafell, Baix Penedès), in Mercadal, O. (coord.): *XIII Col·loqui Internacional d'Arqueologia de Puigcerdà. Homenatge a Josep Barberà i Farràs*, Puigcerdà, november the 14th and the 15th 2003, vol 1, pp. 597-614.

Serneels, V. 1997. L'estudi dels rebutjos metal·lúrgics i la seva aportació a la comprensió de la industria del ferro, *Cota Zero* 13, Vic, pp. 29-42.

Serneels, V. 1998. La chaîne opératoire de la sidérurgie ancienne, en Feugère, M., Serneels, V. (dir.) : *Recherches sur l'économie du fer en Méditérranée nord- occidentale, Monographie Instrumentum, 4*, Montagnac, pp. 7-44.

Endnotes

1 We want to express gratitude to the inestimable help of Jordi Morer, the archaeologist that provided to us the archaeological floors and additional information about the site.

2 Indeed, the maximum diameter documented in this structure was 0.9m. However, the fact that this diameter corresponded to the lower part of the 'base', made us think that perhaps this measurement could even be wider if it had been of spherical morphology.

3 The influence of La Tène culture on the Iberian people up north of the Ebre River is clearly reflected in many aspects and it has been studied in detail by various authors (Quesada, 1997; García, 2006 and 2012).

4 The functioning of 'natural draft' furnaces is ruled by the laws of the fluid dynamics and, especially, by the Principle of Fluid Mechanics and the Bernoulli's Law. This last one stipulates that the more height, the more effectiveness in the chimney flue. It is what we denominate the "Bernoulli effect" or "Chimney effect". According to these physical principles the height of the structure is determining and must keep a relationship with the combustion base width that, according to out hypothesis, it must be minimum 1 to 2, that is, height must be the double of the internal width. A more exhaustive development of this matter in Rehder (2000) and in Gallego (2014a and 2014b).

5 Some of them affected the structure of the chimney in a so intensive way that it seemed to predict the detachment of a part of the wall. However, the totality of the structure remained intact despite the high temperatures.

'Huize Horsterwold'

The reconstruction of a Neolithic houseplan using Stone Age equipment

Annelou van Gijn and Diederik Pomstra

Abstract

In the summer of 2012 the National Forestry Service (The Netherlands) and the Faculty of Archaeology of Leiden University built a reconstruction of a house plan from the Late Neolithic Vlaardingen culture. The objective was to combine the wish for a place to conduct educational activities on the part of the Forestry Service with the goal of professional archaeologists to carry out a scientific experiment. For the archaeologists the building process itself and the tools involved in it were the main interest, whereas for the Forestry Service it was the finished structure. This paper discusses the *chaîne opératoire* of the building process, the biography of the various tools used and the amount of building materials used. In fact, all tools were extensively documented to allow a functional analysis, which is currently being carried out. The paper will also briefly address the divergent expectations of the different interest groups involved (Leiden University, Forestry Service, local council, (knowledgeable) volunteers).

Introduction

The construction of a Neolithic house using only Stone Age equipment was a collaboration between the University of Leiden and the Dutch National Forestry Service. The Dutch Forestry Service wanted a small building to use for educational and other public activities, enabling them to integrate the past with their focus on experiencing and learning about nature (Figure 12.1a). Leiden University, specifically the chairgroup Archaeological Material Culture Studies, was looking for a place to do scientific archeological experiments. We also wanted to study the toolkit for house construction, what kind of tools were most effective for which part of the building process and which ones were selected by whom (for instance skilled versus unskilled workers, women versus men). The biography of all used implements was documented because all tools were studied for the presence of use wear traces and were to be incorporated in the experimental reference collection of the Laboratory for Artefact Studies in Leiden. Hans de Haas, Leo Wolterbeek

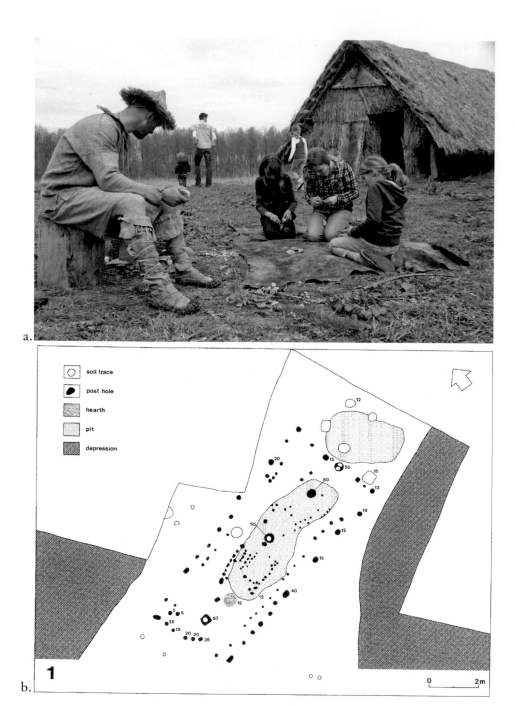

Figure 12.1: a). Huize Horsterwold just after it was finished when schoolchildren visited the place to learn about prehistoric crafts. b) The houseplan from Haamstede-Brabers on which the reconstruction is based (from Verhart 1992, fig. 10).

and Diederik Pomstra were involved respectively as architects and toolmaker. Archeology students would be learning neolithic skills, complementing their more theoretical education at the University with hands-on experience.

The main objective was to document the process in detail and to examine the building sequence from a tool's perspective. Documenting the biographies of the tools involved in the construction was especially important because we intended to study the toolkit holistically, to examine the interconnectivity of different components of the toolkit, and to give tools a place in the *chaîne opératoire* of house construction. Which parts of the building process would be visible in the archaeological record in the form of microwear traces? This way we wanted to combine mobile material culture with architecture. So each time a student took a tool to carry out a task, however short and unimportant, they had to take a new, uniquely numbered recording form to list the specifics of that experiment (duration, contact material, effectiveness and so forth). So each minute task was considered an experiment that needed to be recorded. All the forms for one experimental tool, collected together, reflected its entire biography.

The archaeological houseplan selected was House 1 from the site of Haamstede-Brabers (province of Zeeland, Netherlands), excavated in 1959 by Trimpe-Burger. The site dates to c. 2500 BC and is attributed to the Vlaardingen culture. It formed part of a small cluster of structures and was situated on a dune (Verhart 1992, fig. 10) (Figure 12.1b). This plan was selected because it was relatively small (9.10 m. long and 3.8 m. wide); as this was the first construction most of us were involved in, it was achievable. Another important point was that the plan was not crosscut by earlier or later structures However, even though the house plan was relatively simple, a number of issues had to be solved like the lack of clear entrance ways and the large depression present in the center of the house which more or less overlapped with a rectangle of small postholes in the middle of the house.

Tools and materials

The tools used for the construction were made of a variety of materials. All were replicas of Mesolithic or Neolithic archaeological examples. These tools included ground stone and flint axes and adzes, tranchet axes, bone adzes and chisels, chisels and wedges of antler and wood and uretouched flint flakes and blades (Figure 12.2a). The students received instructions on how to use these tools so that the axes would not break immediately. In total 120 tools were used.

Most tools were made beforehand by Diederik Pomstra apart from some of the simple wooden implements that were made in an ad hoc fashion. They were for the most part produced using Stone Age technology only. If short cuts with modern technology were taken because of time limitations, the surfaces of the implement were carefully finished with Stone Age techniques in order to remove all traces from metal tools. The only exceptions are the handles for the axes and other implements, all of which were made with modern tools.

The time involved in tool production is not included in the calculations of the time required for the house's construction. All tools were documented photographically in the laboratory prior to use. Their surfaces were studied by means of a stereomicroscope (magnifications 10-64x) to detect traces of manufacture and an incident light microscope (100-500x) to document the surfaces prior to use (Van Gijn 2010). Casts were made during the building process whenever a tool

Figure 12.2: The tools in action. a) an overview of the tools used; b) a digging stick in action, note the perfectly straight posthole; c) chopping trees; d) placing the batten onto the rafters before the reeds were folded over them. Source: Annelou van Gijn and Diederik Pomstra.

changed use in terms of motion or contact material. The casts were made by Provil dental casting material. In this way we obtained a record of the use wear traces for the entire biography of the implement.

All building materials were quantified. We relied on locally available material only. For the posts and larger building elements like wall plates and ridge poles we selected oak (*Quercus*), ash (*Fraxinus*), hazel (*Corylus*) and alder (*Alnus*). Rafters were largely made of ash, whereas many of the laths were willow (*Salix*). We also included one poplar tree. As binding material we chose limebark to test how this material would perform as a lashing material in a larger, permanent structure (Pomstra and Van Gijn 2013). We used both retted and unprocessed bark. The wattle and daub walls were made with willow shoots and clay that was locally available. We used a mixture of equal amounts of clay and sand. As roofing material we choose summer reed (*Phragmites*), harvested in late August when it attained an average length of c. 2.5 meters. The two short ends of the house were made by woven mats of reeds, plastered on the inside with loam. The doors and air vents were constituted of deerskins tied onto a wooden frame. Most of the collection of building materials took place in spring: felling the trees for the posts, collecting willow shoots and harvesting the lime bark. The posts were kept in the local lake to keep moist. The wood for rafters and laths was cut in late August when the actual construction took place. This was also the time that we harvested the reeds for the roof.

The building process

Although the house plan was relatively simple, the location of the entrance way was not obvious. In the first instance we designed it along the southern wall but even when making a porch, the entrance would always be relatively low. Because the house was going to be used by groups of small children, two entrance doors were placed in the short ends of the house. The advantage here was that it was easy, due to the absence of wall plates, to make a relatively high doorframe. These would create two easy and fast escapes in case of fire. However, it should be stressed that the archaeological substantiation of this choice is not very strong.

The second choice we had to make was the placement of the outer walls. There were two options: first along the wall posts, making the inside of the house c. 3.5 meter wide, or alternatively, along the two rows of stakes which lined the wall posts. We opted for the latter, because the outer walls would be better protected from the weather being completely covered by the roof's overhang. It did however, result in a very narrow living space (Figure 12.3a). On the houseplan published by Verhart (1992, fig. 10), the two rows of stakes seem to veer towards the outer wall posts in the eastern side of the house. For this reason we did not create a wattle and daub wall to the very eastern end of the house but instead stopped where the rows of stakes seem to merge with the wall posts. The last two metres of the house were then covered with two movable walls made of a wooden frame with skins lashed on. These walls could be removed to create a covered but airy "veranda" for domestic activities where daylight could easily penetrate. Nevertheless, when we finally got hold of the original excavation drawings, the rows of stakes seem to be running parallel to the wall posts although they do stop before the eastern end of the house. So, despite of the fact that the "veranda" is indeed very practical in case of rainy or very hot weather, in our next reconstruction we will not make this choice again because in wintertime the house becomes much harder to heat.

The last choice to make was what to do with the large pit in the centre of the houseplan. Was this a storage pit covered by planks or was it indeed used as a seating and sleeping area? We decided to leave it as a depression and use it to sit around or sleep in. For our experimental campaigns involving groups of students, this was highly practical but, in combination with the limited width of the house, it limited the floorspace and access to other parts of the house (Figure 12.3a). So, in our next reconstruction we will cover this depression and use it as a storage area.

The building process of Huize Horsterwold is described in detail in a previous publication and is only summarized here (see Pomstra and Van Gijn 2013 for more details). First, on the basis of the house plan, the holes for the posts were measured in and dug with digging sticks. The digging sticks proved to be highly effective in making perfectly straight postholes that could be fitted exactly to the diameter of the post (Figure 12.2b). The trees for the posts were felled in spring time (Figure 12.2c) and shaped as much as possible when the wood was still fresh and thus more easily worked. During the August construction campaign, the posts were shaped by fire when they turned out not to be fitting. We controlled the extent of the burning by applying wet mud to those parts that needed to be retained. After all the poles and the wall plates were fitted, the ridge pole was lifted on top of the centre poles. In a house this size, with a height of a little over three

a.

b.

Figure 12.3: a) The inside of the house; b) Overview of the "hamlet" in 2015 with the original house in the top right hand corner, showing the additional structures that were built in subsequent years. Source: Annelou van Gijn and Diederik Pomstra.

metres, this was actually far easier than expected: some forked poles were used for this purpose. Afterwards the rafters and A-poles could be placed, the batten could be tied to the rafters with lime bark (Figure 12.2d) and the wattle and daub walls could be erected. For the roofing material we choose summer reed (*Phragmites*) which was folded over the batten. This is a very fast way of roofing and we managed one row of 9 metres in an hour with one person on the roof and one handing the bundles over. The top of the roof was filled with bundles of reed covered with a last row of reeds and loam. The two short ends of the house were made by woven mats of reeds, plastered on the inside with loam. The doors, movable walls and air vents were constituted of deerskins lashed onto a wooden frame. Last we dug a depression inside the house where this was indicated by the excavation data and lined this pit with hazel shoots. Finally a hearth was constructed according to its location in the archaeological plan.

Quantification

All building material was quantified. We cut down 87 trees (*Fraxinus, Alnus, Corylus* and *Quercus*) but not all of the wood was actually used. By better planning we could have reduced this number substantially.[1] We stripped the bark of c.8 lime trees as lashing material, used both in untreated and retted state. A total of 246 armfuls of summer reeds (*Phragmites*) (circumference c. 67 cm, c. 2.5 m long) was collected as roofing material and to create the two short ends of the house. For the wattle and daub walls we used c. 400 willow shoots and 2386 litres of loam. To line the pit inside the house 50 hazel shoots were inserted around the circumference of the depression. Finally, we scraped six red deer skins for doors, air vents and for the movable walls.

It took about 4 weeks for 2-3 experienced builders and 10-15 students and volunteers to finish the house, working c. 40 hours a week. We estimate that this can be reduced to c. 2-3 weeks if not spending so much time on documentation and with people who are more used to manual labour. Our students all went through a few days of blisters. We are convinced that this type of simple house can easily be built by a small family, without a great deal of expertise. All of the tasks, even erecting the centre poles, can be done with 2-3 persons, both men and women.

In total 120 tools were used for a total of 19.602 minutes of real contact time (we did not include resting breaks). Surprisingly, the contribution of wooden tools in the construction is higher than of any other material category (25%) (Table 12.1). Wooden tools were very effective for all sorts of tasks. Interestingly, many wooden tools were unmodified pieces that we picked up from the forest and used directly because of their appropriate shape (*pièces de fortune*, or naturefacts as Oswalt (1976) called them. Such tools are expediently used, thrown away quickly and probably ending up as fire wood. The wooden tools being involved in a lot of stages of the *chaîne opératoire*, a quarter of the total working time is a lot of information to loose. The six stone axes and adzes, made of quartzite and basalt represent 12% of the total contact time. The flint axes and adzes were used longer but this is almost entirely due to the important role of tranchet axes and one flint adze. Flint flakes were selected as expediently used general cutting tools but were actually used a very short time. Their contribution was quite minor.

Total tool use Horsterwold House	Total min. used	% of total time	n=
wood	5076	25,90	25
flint axes, adzes, tranchet axes or choppers	4397	22,43	17
flint, other	2755	14,05	46
antler	2182	11,13	10
bone	1370	6,99	7
stone axes	2416	12,33	6
stone, exluding axes and adzes	1406	7,17	9
total	**19602**	**100,00**	**120**

Table 12.1: The contribution of the different tool types in the building process, measured in minutes used.

Some observations

The construction of Huize Horsterwold was a tremendous learning experience for all participants. Foremost we became more familiar with the properties of materials, occasionally being confronted with unexpected difficulties or pleasant surprises. For example, harvesting the reeds for the roof turned out to be the most time consuming, tedious and painful task of the entire building process. It almost provoked a strike amongst the students and, in combination with lack of time due to the eminent start of the academic year, forced us to harvest the last quarter of the reeds in a mechanical fashion. On the other hand, felling trees with axes turned out to be easier and faster than expected. We learned that hazel is easily cut, but the fact that it is multi-trunked makes the removal of individual stems nearly impossible due to the interlocking of the canopy. We realized the importance of planning because once a building element is in place, it is virtually impossible to modify. We learned this when some of our rafters were a little too long and we had trouble incorporating them in the roof cover as chopping them off was not an option anymore.

As to the tools, we were surprised to find that the quartzite and basalt axes and adzes could function for the entire campaign without having to be resharpened. They continued to be effective, in contrast to the fine grained flint axes which became blunt quickly. Students had difficulties cutting down trees with tranchet axes but these light tools were frequently chosen to make slots in rafters to fit batten (Figure 12.2d) or for other light wood working tasks. Antler axes functioned well but were slower than the stone axes in felling trees and generally were not the preferred tools. This also pertained to the big bone adzes which were also used to fell trees.

Having a range of people on the site, skilled, unskilled, women, men, young and old, made us reflect on learning curves and individual technological choices. All students were taught how to use the unfamiliar tools. A stone or antler axe has to be moved in a different way from a metal one. However, although students never became "experts" and despite blisters, several became very proficient lumbermen and women. Digging postholes required some practice but in due time all were capable of creating perfectly straight and narrow postholes, raising the question as to why archaeological postholes are frequently so wide: is this due to repair? Allowing everyone to choose the tools for the task also gave us some insights in choice. People clearly had their favourite tool and women more frequently opted for adzes, whereas men preferentially choose axes.

Conclusions and future plans

The house is situated in a very beautiful spot in the polder of Zuidelijk Flevoland and is gradually becoming a little hamlet (Figure 12.3). It is used regularly to host school classes by the Forestry Service. Leiden University uses it as an experimental station for conducting field experiments with students and to run long term experimental programs on taphonomy, the use of fire and pottery making. Whenever scientific experiments are conducted these are announced and reported in the local newspaper and on our Facebook page. The local community stops by on their Sunday cycle trips and enjoys the open days. Here they can participate in Stone Age crafts and learn about the uses of the plants in their forest.

Somehow it has become a magical place for locals and students alike.

Performing microwear analysis of the entire toolkit was one of the objectives of this project. Because we also had accumulated hundreds of dental casts of the various use stages of the tools, this turned out to be a tremendous task. It will form the focus of a separate publication. The same pertains to the other goal of the project, mapping the interconnectivities of tools, materials and people into one comprehensive *chaîne opératoire*. The widespread press coverage the project had, has resulted in an increased interest in experimental house construction. The possibilities for a successful collaboration of scientists and local volunteers has been widely recognized and has resulted in a new initiative in the town of Vlaardingen where a group of inhabitants, joined in the Federatie Broekpolder, has joined forces with the Leiden University to construct another Vlaardingen house.

Acknowledgements

We thank the National Foresry Service at Horsterwold, particularly Hans-Erik Kuijper and Andre Wels for their enthusiasm and cooperation. The same applies to the Council of Zeewolde who has facilitated the construction. We are grateful to our close collaborators Tobias Buitenkamp, Hans de Haas, Annemieke Verbaas, Leo Wolterbeek and countless students and volunteers. The Prins Bernhard Cultuurfonds generously financed the project.

Bibilography

Kroon, E. & van Gijn, A.L. in prep. A *chaîne opératoire* approach towards experimental house construction with Stone Age tools.

Oswalt, H.W. 1976. *An anthropological analysis of food-getting technology.* Academic Press: Calgary.

Pomstra, D. and van Gijn, A.L. 2013. The reconstruction of a Late – Neolithic house; combining primitive technology and science. *Bulletin of Primitive Technology* 45, pp. 45-54.

Van Gijn, A. 2010. *Flint in focus: lithic biographies in the Neolithic and Bronze Age.* Sidestone Press: Leiden.

Verhart, L.B.M. 1992. Settling or trekking, the Late Neolithic house plans of Haamstede-Brabers and its counterparts. *Oudheidkundige Mededelingen Rijksmuseum van Oudheden Leiden* 72, pp. 73-99.

Endnotes

1   We are currently working on a second reconstruction based on the same excavation plan in the town of Vlaardingen near Rotterdam. Although not yet finished, we have created the basic house frame using only 14 trees which were carefully selected to size, straighness and suitability for specific building elements.

Part Four

Structures in life

Testing the indoor environment and personal health in an inhabited reconstructed Viking Age house during winter

Jannie Marie Christensen

Introduction

An archaeological indoor environment experiment was conducted in two inhabited reconstructions of the same Viking Age house from Haithabu built at two museums in Denmark during 15 weeks in wintertime in 2011 and 2012 respectively. The purpose of the experiment was to examine the indoor environment of the two houses, the living conditions and the health effects on the inhabitants living in the houses. Both houses had wattle and daub walls with thatched roofs and a fireplace in the centre of the house. Exposure to smoke from solid fuel used for cooking and heating in open fireplaces in homes, is currently to blame for about 3.5 million deaths each year globally, due to lower respiratory infections of the trachea and bronchus and it is also known to cause lung cancers, ischaemic heart disease, cerebrovascular disease, and chronic obstructive pulmonary disease. The magnitude of the disease burden from household air pollution from solid fuels accounts for 5.4 % of disability-adjusted life years globally (Lim *et al.* 2012, 2227-2251). The experiment was in the framework of my master's thesis at Medieval and Renaissance Archaeology at Aarhus University, Denmark and was called *Mennesket og huset – levevilkår og eksperimentelarkæologiske undersøgelser af indeklima i et rekonstrueret vikingetidshus* [Man and House – Living Conditions and Experimental Archaeological Studies of the Indoor Environment in a Reconstructed Viking House] (Christensen 2013C, 1; Figure 13.1). The purpose of this paper is to introduce the experiment and present the results achieved. The differences between the houses, health risks, use and misuse of these houses and how this could improve the environment will also be discussed.

The houses

The houses used in the experiments were chosen due to their type and structure. Both houses are reconstructions of a Viking Age house excavated in Haithabu [Hedeby], Germany dated 870 AD. In the excavation the walls of the house were

Figure 13.1: Smoke seeps out of House 1. Source: Jannie Marie Christensen.

found fallen inwards, which made it possible to see the height and structure of the house. In addition the position of the fireplace, a domed baking oven, and low plateaus were found. The roof, its height and the position of a possible roof hole for the smoke to get out, was not found in the excavation (Roesdahl 1987, 51).

The experiment started on the 24th of October and lasted until the 28th December 2011 in the older reconstruction. It was built in 1972 at Moesgård Museum on the east coast of Jutland, (House 1) (see Figure13.2). It has been used in periods for the museum visitors and school classes but was seldom heated for longer periods. The second house was used from the 6th of February to the 16th of April 2012 and had just recently been completed at Bork Viking Harbour at the west coast of Jutland (House 2) (see Figure 13.3).

At the time of the experiment, both reconstructions measured approximately 5x12 meters and 3.3-4.3 meters at the highest points. The buildings were divided into three rooms; the east end was possibly a workshop, the middle room was the living room and the west end was the kitchen. The outer walls were wattle and daub and the partition walls were wooden. Both houses had thatched roofs with a hole for the smoke in the middle. The thatching at House 1 was old, moist and thinner at the northern side, while House 2 had a new thick layer of thatching. House 2 had an additional hole above the kitchen and both holes had adjustable plates on top, the goal being to lead the smoke out of the house more efficiently. House 1 had a door at the south side of the east room, while House 2 had a door at the east gable. Both houses had doors to both north and south in the west room. Furthermore, the rooms had door openings between them as well, the western door opening was only closed with a blanket and the northern door opening was

| THE LIFE CYCLE OF STRUCTURES IN EXPERIMENTAL ARCHAEOLOGY

Figure 13.2: House 1 located at Moesgård Museum built 1972. Source: Jannie Marie Christensen.

Figure 13.3: House 2 located at Bork Viking Harbour built 2012. Source: Jannie Marie Christensen.

closed with a wooden door. Both houses had window openings in the east wall in the east room. House 1 had one additional window opening to the north in the east room and one to the south in the west room. House 2 had a window in the middle room. All the windows in House 2 were closed with wooden shutters. The east room in House 2 was not in use during the experiment and was not accessible. In both houses there was a fireplace elevated slightly from the floor in the centre of the middle room. In addition, plateaus ran along the sides of the middle room in both houses, making a low corridor for the draft to pass by the fireplace at the floor. In house 1 the plateaus were solid clay, while in House 2 they were wooden and hollow and used for storage. Above the plateaus there were ceilings running along the room, but not at the centre part of the room so the smoke from the fire could get past them.

Inhabitants

In an attempt to achieve as realistic measurements and results as possible, the experiment was conducted under conditions as close to our knowledge of the Viking Age as possible. This meant that inhabitants were chosen to live in the houses during the experiment, to have the houses function as was expected in the original time of use. During their stay, the participants wore clothing similar to clothes found in the Viking Age, so the participants had to use the fire for heat when necessary due to the materials of their clothes and the realistic temperatures inside the house. The fire was also used for cooking, while additional light came from either candles or the small amount of light leaking through the smoke holes. The items of furniture were reconstructions of what could have been in use in the time period of the house. The bed was made from hay, wool and sheep skins sewn together and used as blankets.

Smoking was prohibited inside the houses due to proximity to, and possible interference, with the measuring equipment. Between three to five participants lived in the house during each of the inhabited weeks. The participants were between 19 and 51 years old except one child, age nine, who was there with a parent. Among them about half wore glasses/contacts lenses. All participants volunteered and were informed in writing and at a meeting of possible health risks involved. Most of the participants had little experience with the use of a fireplace, reconstructed houses, and/or archaeology.

Measurements

The houses were heated and measured during all 15 weeks, though for the first week the house was not inhabited. This was due to fact that the house needed to be properly heated, making the walls and roof dry as they would be, were the fire in regular use.

The parameters monitored during the experiment were air quality (combustion products; fine particles $PM^{2.5}$, carbon monoxide (CO), carbon dioxide (CO^2) and nitrogen dioxide (NO^2)), climate (temperature and relative humidity) and the air change rate. Light, firewood consumption, and humidity, use of the adjustable roof hole plates, and weather conditions were registered. Each week two

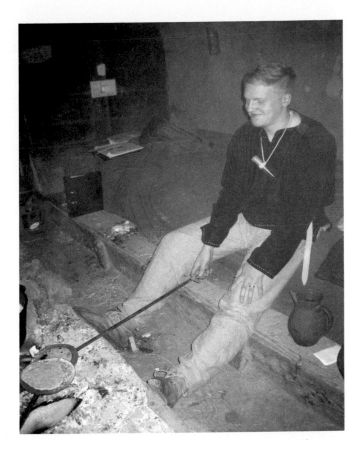

Figure 13.4. Participant with CO monitor inside House 1.

participants were equipped with monitors for carbon monoxide (CO) exposure (see Figure 13.4). During the day all participants filled out questionnaires about their health and activities that might be useful to support the measured conditions. The participants in House 1 had additional physical health tests done (exhaled nitrogen monoxide (NO), lung function, blood samples, nasal lavage and allergy). The indoor environment measurements were conducted roughly in the same method as in an earlier experiment in Danish farmhouses from the 17th to 19th century (Ryhl-Svendsen *et al.* 2010, 736-738).

Results

Daily levels of particles ($PM^{2.5}$) were in the order of 0.80 – 3.4 mg/m³ with short-term peak concentrations of up to 22 mg/m³. The daily mean carbon dioxide concentration was 554 – 737 ppm (see Graph 13.1) and the weekly average nitrogen dioxide concentration was 55 – 80 ppb in House 1 and 160 – 380 in House 2. Daily levels of carbon monoxide were in the range of 5.5 – 22 ppm in the occupied area around the fireplace.

There was a daily fuel consumption of about 50 kilos of dried hardwood used for cooking and heating and the temperature distribution was very asymmetric (see Figure 13.5). The mean temperature inside House 1 was 17.5 °C and 15 °C in House 2. The mean outside temperature was 10 °C lower at both locations (see

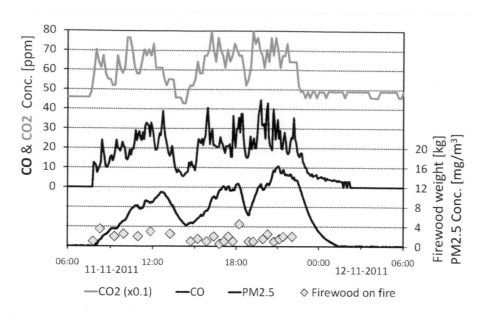

Graph 13.1: Combustion products and fuel consumption for 24 hours in House 1. Source: Jannie Marie Christensen.

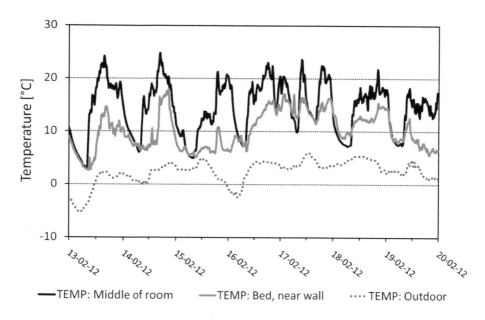

Graph 13.2: Temperature in House 2 during one week. Source: Jannie Marie Christensen.

Graph 13.2). The air change rate was 10 – 15 per hour, which is very leaky. The absolute humidity was the same as outside, typically 40 – 60 %.

Only certain aspects of physical health deteriorated, when it came to both the exhaled nitrogen monoxide and the white blood cell count from the blood samples and the nasal lavages. In general lung function was declining which shows a negative effect on the bronchi. Other aspects stayed the same or even improved, making the deterioration equally divided between smokers and non-smokers,

| THE LIFE CYCLE OF STRUCTURES IN EXPERIMENTAL ARCHAEOLOGY

Figure 13.5: Thermal image showing the asymmetric surface temperature on a person's clothes (approximately 15-50 °C) and on the interior (down to 10-25 °C). Source: Jannie Marie Christensen.

males and females, and participants with allergies. The carbon monoxide exposure tests of the participants showed an average exposure of 5.8-7.7 for one woman and 6.6-9.5 for one man in House 1, while the average exposure was 4.3-9.5 for one woman and 3.5-12 for one man in House 2 (Christensen 2013 C, 77).

Comparison of the two houses

It was decided to examine the houses during wintertime, when the houses would be most exposed to cold from the outside, thereby increasing the use of the fire as a primary source of heat in the daytime (see above Figure 13.4). House 1 was measured in early wintertime with the temperatures getting lower during the period. The measurements in House 2 started in wintertime with the outdoor temperatures getting warmer during the period. The two houses were located in different environments; House 1 was situated in a forest area with less wind around the house, making it easier for the house to become damp, rotten and eventually start to decompose. The almost 40-year-old house had at the time of the experiment already sunk in a bit due to decomposition in the wooden frame and the roof was thin and soggy. Conversely, the newly built House 2 was situated in a flat, windy area with nothing to shelter the house from the weather.

In trying to build the most accurate reconstructions from the excavated finds, the archaeologists often only find the outline of the houses, and never the roofs, which means they do not know the pitch of the roof or how the smoke escaped from the house. We tend to give qualified guesses to these unknown factors from ideas of how modern houses functions best. However, occasionally we forget the fact that we are building reconstructions of older houses with different needs and functionality than modern houses. Today most houses with straw roof are built after modern standards, which make the thatching rather thick. This is done to insulate the houses better. However, in houses with no chimney, this can be a problem since the roofs need to be able to breathe. If not then the smoke can have difficulties getting out through the thick roof.

In the construction of the two houses, there were a few differences in the design. House 1 had one open roof hole extended a bit from the roof and it was situated above the fireplace in the middle room. From here the wind could easily drag the smoke from the room, thus leaving the middle room less smoky. House 2 had two slightly extended roof holes, one being situated above the middle room fire and the other above the kitchen room at the west end of the house. Both of these roof holes were designed with an adjustable plate that can be regulated with a string from the underlying rooms to make the drag more efficient. This construction primarily works if the wind comes from the east or west. When it does the wind hits the side of the house, putting more pressure on the house, than if the wind were to hit at the gable. Another miscalculation in building the roof holes with the adjustable plates was that the wind primarily comes from the west in this area. This means that the wind faces the gable of the adjustable roof hole constructions, with just a small chance of dragging the smoke from the rooms below. Additionally the two holes seemed to let the indoor smoke circulate more between the two rooms due to the multiple exits, than it did in House 1, where there was just one roof hole. It seemed that the solution of two roof holes and adjustable roof plates worked very poorly when the wind blew from different directions than north or south. Other openings in the houses, such as open windows and doors, seemed to have a similar effect of making the smoke escape by these alternative routes, and these routes were usually close to where the participants were situated, thus exposing them to even more smoke.

Both houses seemed to take advantage of the indoor ceilings, situated along the top sides of the middle room leaving the centre part of the room open. It seemed that the smoke in the house that did not leave, cooled down and circulated back down from the roof. This was caught on top of these ceilings and from there circulated back up with the warm smoke from the fire, instead of circulating down into the occupied area.

The leakiness of the houses was confirmed in several ways both by air change tests, comparison of air humidity inside and outside the houses, and by the carbon dioxide concentrations. During daytime the highest concentrations in the house were measured close to the fireplace. However, due to the house being so leaky and changing the air so rapidly at night when the fire was out, the highest carbon dioxide concentration in the house was measured in the sleeping area because of the respiration of the participants.

Comparison with WHO Guidelines

The experiments were all done in wintertime with the worst possible scenario in two houses not regularly heated. This was when it was least healthy to stay inside the houses and where the air quality was dominated by wood combustion products. Whether high levels of smoke were realistic for a house in use in the Viking Age is difficult to say since there can be construction errors in the reconstructed houses. Other difficulties and variations could be caused by the inhabitants not being accustomed to living in the houses and using the fire properly. During summertime, the exposure to smoke would probably be much lower, since there is a smaller demand for heating from the fire and people would tend to work outside. The concentrations measured in the two houses are comparable to similar houses in for example South Asia and sub-Saharan Africa that have a fire or a stove in the primary room. Here mostly women and children get acute lower respiratory infections and lung diseases in homes where cooking and heating are done with the use of a fire made from solid fuels (Lim *et al.* 2012, 2247-2249).

The main health risks stem from fine particles (PM$^{2.5}$) and carbon monoxide. The WHO guidelines for exposure to particles PM$^{2.5}$ are 0.025 mg/m^3 for 24 hours (WHO 2006, 278-279). In House 1 the average particle PM$^{2.5}$ concentration was 3.382 mg/m^3 near the fire in the middle room and 0.789 mg/m^3 near the bed. This is a ratio of 135 times above the WHO guidelines for 24 hours near the fire and a ratio of 31.5 near the bed in house 1. In House 2 the particle PM$^{2.5}$ concentration was not measured but instead approximated from the carbon monoxide measurements in the house. From these approximations, the particle PM$^{2.5}$ level in House 2 was a ratio of 149 times higher than the WHO 24 hour guideline near the fire and a ratio of 25 times higher than the 24-hour guideline at the bed.

Carbon monoxide is a non-irritating, colourless, odourless, and poisoning gas. The WHO guidelines for exposure to carbon monoxide is 86 ppm for 15 minutes, 30 ppm for 1 hour, 8.6 ppm for 8 hours and 6 ppm for 24 hours (WHO 2010, 55-87). In both House 1 and 2 the WHO guidelines of short-term exposure for a 15 minutes period were never exceeded, showing that the risk of short-term carbon monoxide poisoning was low. In both houses, the participants were only briefly,

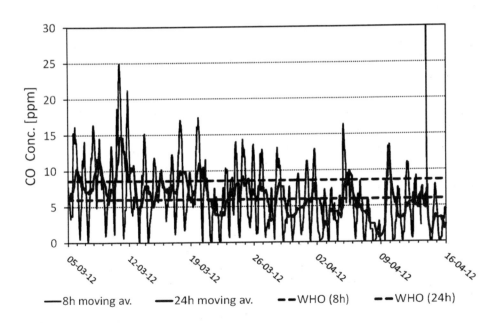

Graph 13.3: *Personal exposure to carbon monoxide during six weeks for one woman in House 2 versus WHO guidelines for 8 and 24 hours. Source: Jannie Marie Christensen.*

but on a daily basis, exposed to close to or above the guidelines of an average 6 ppm carbon monoxide for 24 hours (WHO 2010, 55-87) (See Graph 13.3).

The WHO guideline for exposure to nitrogen dioxide is 105 ppb for 1 hour and 21 ppb in a year (WHO 2010, 201, 246, 248). The concentrations in the houses were measured on a weekly basis making comparisons more difficult. In House 1 these were between 55-80 per week, which could be above the WHO guideline. In House 2 on the other hand the weekly concentration was between 160 – 380 ppb, which was well above the guidelines.

It was probably during cooking and tending to the fire that the participants were exposed to the highest concentrations of particles, carbon monoxide and nitrogen dioxide. During the day the participants also stayed outdoors and were therefore not exposed to as high concentrations as in the house itself. In spite of the air quality being so poor, it only showed sometimes in the weekly physical tests, which often were supported by the questionnaires. But even smaller concentrations of long-time exposure to particles PM$^{2.5}$ and carbon monoxide will still have a negative effect on human beings.

A hypothetical day versus today

The houses used for the experiments both had flaws in construction and use that we first registered after using the houses and presumably some that we still have not found. Besides tending to the fire and cooking, the participants spent the day doing smaller Viking Age crafts and additional manual measurements.

During the stay, the participants quickly started using the lower part of the house more due to the lower concentration of smoke there. Not all the smoke exited through the roof hole or the roof, some of it cooled off and eventually circulated in the room. The concentration of carbon monoxide above the ceilings in the middle room was much higher than below them, suggesting that the ceiling worked as a trap for the smoke that had cooled off and prevented it from descending to where the participants stayed. This indicates that the ceiling probably was not used for example as a sleeping area, but could very well have been used as storage for food or firewood. It is also possible that the ceiling worked as insulation, helping the heat to stay below the ceiling where the participants stayed (Christensen 2013A, 73 – 74).

Also the participants tended to stay near the fire, where there was less smoke and more light and heat. Tending the fire made a rather big difference on the environment inside the two houses. When the fire was left for too long it was smokier and died out. To be able to keep warm, have light and less smoke, wood was put on the fire several times per hour. If it was done less often, this would either cause the fire to die out or larger pieces of wood would have to be used, giving less light and more smoke due to incomplete combustion. A fire with smaller and drier pieces of wood and enough air around the fire will produce the smallest amount of particles compared to a smouldering fire.

It also quickly became clear that the radiant heat from the fire was great, making the participants warm where they faced the fire, but cold where they did not face it. Tests were also done on the use of wall blankets showing a slight tendency towards the house staying warmer during the night when the wall blankets were not in use, compared to when they were, due to the wall blankets having a lower heat capacity than the walls themselves (Christensen 2013B).

Before the participants moved into the houses both houses had had a lit fire for one week to dry the house walls and roofs. This was done since the smoke seemed to leave the house more effectively through the hole in the roof and the roof itself, when the house and roof were heated and dry after having a fire lit for a while.

Often the houses at the museums are not heated regularly which results in the house walls and roof being cold and damp, and making a worse indoor environment where the smoke would be trapped. To prevent this, the obvious thing is to open the doors and windows often, but this leads to the smoke trying to escape via these routes instead, causing more smoke in the lower parts of the house (see above Figure 13.1). Using wet wood, or larger pieces, or the wrong types of wood will also cause more smoke. It is also possible that there are types of fires or ovens used in the houses that cause less smoke.

People in the Viking Age did not have measurement equipment but must have known many of these simple rules – and probably more – to keep the houses working in the best possible way. The measurements and this experiment of course only shows what the reconstructed houses, not the prehistoric houses, do when they are used by modern re-enactors and not prehistoric people. Either way the indoor environment is unhealthy to stay in for a longer period today or it most likely was for the Vikings as well. Due to this, it is reasonable to suspect that the women and children in the Viking Age were living under roughly the same conditions as people in homes with fires for cooking in Third World homes today.

Today House 1 has been demolished due to the construction of new museum buildings at Moesgård Museum, while House 2 is still in use and can be visited at Bork Viking Harbour.

Conclusion

From the indoor environment experiments in two inhabited reconstructions of a Viking Age house conducted during the winter of 2011 – 2012, it is clear that the houses can be used for inhabitation during wintertime. Comparisons between the two houses showed several differences due to location and construction, and several health factors exceeded the WHO guidelines. Some of these factors can be improved by changing the construction of the houses or the use of them.

New studies of household air pollution from solid fuels in reconstructed houses will give us a better knowledge of the indoor environment in the prehistoric and reconstructed houses.

Acknowledgement

All measuring equipment and firewood was either borrowed or sponsored by the two museums, Committee for Reconstruction and Terrain, Moesgård Museum; the Danish National Museum, the Department of Conservation; Technical University of Denmark, Indoor Centre; Aarhus University, the Department of Public Health – Environmental and Occupational Medicine; Aarhus University, Department of Chemistry and University of California, Berkeley.

Bibliography

Christensen, J. M. 2013A. Hvornår var det mindst skadeligt at opholde sig i et vikingehus?, *Vikingetid i Danmark*, Copenhagen University: Copenhagen. pp. 73-76.

Christensen, J.M. 2013B. *Living Conditions and Indoor Air Quality in a Reconstructed Viking House*, EXARC 2013(3) http://journal.exarc.net/issue-2013-3/ea/living-conditions-and-indoor-air-quality-reconstructed-viking-house (Accessed 21 November 2013).

Christensen, J.M., 2013C. *Mennesket og huset – levevilkår og eksperimentelarkæologiske undersøgelser af indeklima i et rekonstrueret*, Master Thesis in Archaeology, Aarhus University: Aarhus. pp. 1-270.

Lim. S.S., Vos, T., Flaxman, A.D., Danaei, G. and Shibuya, K. 2012. *A comparative risk assessment of burden of disease and injury attributable to 67 risk factors and risk factor clusters in 21 regions, 1990-2012: a systematic analysis for the Global Burden of Disease Study 2010.* 380: 2224-2260. www.thelancet.com (Accessed 10 July 2013).

Roesdahl, E. 2001. *Vikingernes Verden* (7th edition). Gyldendal: Copenhagen.

Ryhl-Svendsen, M., Clausen, G., Chowdhury, Z., Smith, K.R., 2010. Fine particles and carbon monoxide from wood burning in 17th-19th century Danish kitchens: Measurements at two reconstructed farm houses at the Lejre Historical-Archaeological Experimental Centre. *Atmospheric Environment* 44: 735-744.

World Health Organisation, 2006. *WHO Air Quality Guidelines: Global Update 2005: Particulate Matter, ozone, nitrogen dioxide and sulphur dioxide.* Copenhagen.

World Health Organisation, 2010. *WHO Guidelines for Indoor Air Quality: Selected Pollutants. World Health Organization, Regional Office for Europe*, Copenhagen. pp. 55-101.

Experiences concerning Stone Age building constructions in Finland

Eero Muurimäki

Introduction: Experiences in the Stone Age village of Saarijärvi

The reconstructed Stone Age village of Saarijärvi (founded in 1980) is located in middle Finland, about 350 km north of Helsinki. The Stone Age village is a popular tourist attraction presenting the results of archaeology to the public. However, there has been no professional archaeologist attached to the museum to run the Stone Age village and consequently, there has been few opportunities for systematic experimental archaeology, but over time, data has been collected through the construction and maintenance of the buildings. This paper focuses on the experiences and the knowledge gained by the author especially relating to house structures and the roofing materials.

My working periods have been from 5 months to 2 months of the year. During longer work periods, I have also planned archaeological exhibitions for the Museum of Saarijärvi. I began my work as an archaeologist at Saarijärvi Museum in 1989. At that time

Figure 14.1: Saarijärvi Stone age village in the year 1990. Source: Eero Muurimäki.

there were six buildings planned and some structures partly built by Simo Vanhatalo in 1980. There was only one reconstruction illustration of Stone Age buildings in Finland at that time: the hut of Räisälä, therefore huts of Byske (Sweden), Västerbotten and Narva (Estonia), alongside a shelter, a hut covered with hides and a small pit dwelling were constructed to create the village (Figure 14.1). This was the first time that full-size reconstructions of prehistoric buildings were accomplished in Finland.

A short history of Stone Age building reconstructions in Finland

The first illustrated reconstruction of a Stone Age building was proposed by Sakari Pälsi in 1916. It was based on the observations he made from an excavation in the Karelian Isthmus, Räisälä Pitkäjärvi, now part of Russia (Pälsi 1916, 1918). Pälsi discovered a circle of twelve dark spots on the ground which he interpreted as postholes, nine of them forming a circle about 5 metres in diameter. In profile, the postholes seemed to be upright, indicating that the structure was not a conical hut, but a structure where upright posts created a frame that supported slanting poles. Two postholes outside the circle are interpreted to be the vestiges of an entrance. The structure is similar in form to dwellings found at Giulyaks (Nivkhs) in Northern Sakhalin Island and the Amur area in eastern Siberia (Pälsi 1918, 28-31; Figure 14.2).

In his 1918 scholarly publication Pälsi did not mention the material used in the construction. However, despite no remains of roofing material found during the excavation, he suggests that the roof could have been made from hides, birch bark, or spruce sprigs (Pälsi 1916).

In the following decades, there was little interest in researching Stone Age houses in Finland. In the 1950s, interest resurfaced when some archaeological sites, such as Madeneva, Middle Finland, large round or oval depressions, referred to as "House pits of Madeneva type" were excavated. Nonetheless, these findings were not published until 1976 (Meinander 1976). According to Meinander (1976)

Figure 14.2: The hut of Räisälä according to Sakari Pälsi. Source: Eero Muurimäki.

the depressions were about 6-8 m in diameter which suited the idea that they represent structures similar to a conical Sámi "kota" type of tent.

Markus Hiekkanen excavated house pits in Evijärvi, Isokangas, Ostrobothnia, in late the 1970s. He found seven pits on one site, which were like the depressions of the "Madeneva" type, but much larger; up to 20 m in diameter. The plan of the buildings were roundish. No vestiges of the structures could be found, not even fireplaces. Although they are referred to as hut bases of Madeneva type they were much larger than the previous structures of this type. Furthermore, the large size indicates that these buildings could not be like tents of the Sámi's or Indian tepees (Hiekkanen 1984).

Not huts but houses

Until the 1980s it was thought that Stone Age huts were always round or elliptical by their plan. The first observation that there could also have been right angles was put forward by Matiskainen & Jussila (1984). Their excavation in Pieksamäki Naarajärvi, Savo, exposed a depression, which had a "parallelogrammatic" form. There was a large number of dark spots inside the excavation area, which they interpreted as postholes. Meinander (1976) was very sceptical about the possibilities of finding postholes in Finnish soil. Matiskainen and Jussila did not describe the structural features of the house but from the excavation plan it could be seen that the supposed postholes were randomly distributed, without any regular pattern.

In the beginning of the 1990s it was apparent that the new finds from Evijärvi Isokangas and Pieksamäki Naarajärvi were challenging our understanding of the size of structures from Stone Age Finland. In addition, a seal net from the late Stone Age site of Pori Tuorsniemi (Kauhanen 1974) indicates that not everything was small in the Finnish Stone Age. The preserved part of the net indicates that the net had been about 1.6 km long.

New reconstructions – new village

The question we have to ask is what kind of houses were there and what did they look like? Which one to choose as the basis of reconstruction? Naarajärvi had no structure, only a random collection of possible postholes in an indefinite form of depression. In Isokangas there were only big round or oval depressions, without any information of the structure of the houses. What is clear is that there were more than one type of house structure in Finland. The excavated postholes suggest that they were not conical huts, which would be too high based on the vertical orientation of the postholes. But by lowering the tent-model by folding the roof so that the angle of the upper part is smaller than on the lower part, the reconstruction fits the archaeological evidence and the proposed roof is not too high (Muurimäki 1995). The result was a yurt-like structure similar to the earth lodges of Mandan-Indians (Nabakov & Easton 1989). It is in principle the same structure as Pälsi proposed for his Stone Age hut, but there are two or three "rounds" of the horizontal framework instead of one.

Figure 14.3: Saarijärvi Stone Age Village in the 1990´s. The "yurt-like" buildings planned according to the house-pits of Evijärvi Isokangas. Source: Eero Muurimäki.

Figure 14.4: The house of Rusavierto reconstructed according to the house-pit which is found 800 m from Saarijärvi Stone Age village. Source: Eero Muurimäki.

The new large houses were built on to 'The Strand' of the Stone Age village, the older huts were rebuilt further away from the shore. Three new houses were built on 'The Strand', based on the depression in Isokangas (Figure 14.3). They were 12 m, 16 m and 20 m in diameter however, there was only enough birch bark to roof only the smallest of the structures.

During the planning phases of these reconstructions new excavations in Finland and Sweden revealed large, rectangular log structures from the Late Stone Age. None of these excavations supported the theory behind the "yurt-hut" reconstructions. Jukka Moisanen excavated a Stone Age settlement in Kerimäki Kankaanlaita, where he exposed a rectangular stripe of light earth and stones. The form of the possible house was mentioned briefly in publications without any detailed discussion relating to the construction of the house (Moisanen 1991). Some years later, Taisto Karjalainen found rectangular features in the pits. He also stressed that the oval form of the pit does not testify that there had been an oval building instead when sand pours in to the depression the corners fill and the pit settles in an oval form (Karjalainen 1996, 15-17; Räihälä 1997, 379).

More profound evidence concerning the structure of the buildings came from Sweden. The Finnish middle Neolithic is characterised by comb ceramic culture, which is an eastern phenomenon. No comb ceramic sites were known in Sweden until Ove Halén excavated house pits in Kalix, about 50 km west from the Finnish border to the west in Southern Lapland. He found a group of nine rectangular houses, five of them forming a row house. He found coloured soil features which he claimed to be all that remained of logs. There were also upright poles supporting the log walls. He also noticed that birch bark was probably used as roofing material. The reconstruction building is more like a log cabin than a hut because the walls are high. He thought them to be high because there were fire places located near to the walls where the roof above a more modest log structure would have burnt (Halén 1994). In his reconstruction picture the house had a smoke hole in the middle. But if the house had been gabled, as in the later reconstructions in Finland, there is no need for high log walls.

It was evident that the reconstructions at Saarijärvi had no relevance to the new archaeological evidence. How to proceed? The Finnish National Board of Antiquities arranged funds for individuals who were unemployed to work as diggers on archaeological excavations. The Board made a project to resolve the structure of Finnish Stone Age buildings. A team of excavators came to Saarijärvi with Sirpa Leskinen as the leader. They choose Rusavierto settlement, about 800 m from our Stone Age village, as their focus for excavations in 1999 and 2000. During the excavation the team excavated a rectangular house pit found some years earlier by Hans-Peter Schulz. They found the burnt foundations of a house where remnants of its lowest log preserved in situ. The house was quite big, 12 x 8 m (Leskinen 2002). Leskinen was leading the reconstruction work according to her plans (Figure 14.4) when an excavation conducted in Uimaranta, discovered a "new" site which was about 300 m from Stone Age village. There she found a pit dwelling, which she also reconstructed the following year when excavating at Uimaranta. The excavation suggests that this building was supported by four posts and it was smaller and older than Rusavierto (dated to the Stone Age, c.2200 cal BC whereas Uimaranta is dated c.3000 cal BC).

On excavation there were seen very faint postholes in profile. If the structure had been symmetrical, it had been based on four upright posts. In principle, this is similar to the Räisälä hut, the difference is that in Räisälä the hut had nine upright posts, in the Uimaranta House there were only four. The reconstruction,

Figure 14.5: Uimaranta house, reconstructed after house-pits and postholes found 300 m from Saarijärvi Stone Age village. Source: Eero Muurimäki.

located on 'The Strand' of the Stone Age village, does not include a log frame (Figure 14.5). When the Rusavierto and Uimaranta houses were built, the "old" yurt-like buildings were dismantled. The finds after their reconstruction did not support the idea of large round or oval buildings.

Experiences of roofing materials

When beginning my work in Saarijärvi Stone Age village, I paid attention to the roofing materials. How plausible are they? There were three kinds of roofing materials used: turf on the Räisälä hut, Byske hut and the pit "house" ("house" in quotation marks because the structure was a little more than 2 m in diameter) – the pit finds on which it was based were probably for refuse or a larder of beets (Muurimäki 2012). The Narva structure was covered with birch bark and the conical framework was covered with elk hides.

Birch bark

The Narva hut was covered with birch bark according to a suggestion by N. N. Gurina, the excavator of the original Narva hut. It was based on ethnographic parallels from Siberia; no organic material was found during the excavation (Gurina 1967). Birch bark is a very good material if the building is used only in the warm season. It keeps water and moisture out and offers a shelter against wind. If there is a fire inside, it keeps the interior quite warm down to exterior temperatures of 0°C according to our experience.

In Denmark, the floors of a Mesolithic hut at Åmosen have been interpreted as having been covered with birch or pine bark (Andersen 1981, 41). Although it is thought that the bark would keep moisture out of the floor this is not a credible assumption. Birch bark is not a suitable floor material, because it is very brittle, breaking immediately if stepped upon. It is very probable that the bark covered the walls of the huts and had fallen down.

Hide

The hide tent was very problematic in the Stone Age village. The first skins used were tanned using modern methods and lasted for about three years. After which elk skins were obtained directly from hunters. To prepare the skins they had to be cleaned by removing the flesh – a job that took two weeks of normal working days. It was not possible to do that for all seventeen hides which the small structure required. Therefore, some hides were put on the frame without cleaning. The smell was so offensive that it is hard to believe that anyone could live in such a structure not even in the Stone Age. It is of course possible to tan the hides but the amount of work involved with old fashioned methods makes it a lot of work. Ethnographically, hides are used in the Arctic, where tree bark is not available. There is no reason to suppose that they were used in Stone Age Finland during the warm period.

Turf

Three of the buildings of the original Stone Age village were covered with turf only. There are two types of turf used: "real turf" from bogs but it is very unlikely that this kind of turf was used by Stone Age people. Bogs and settlements were normally far away from each other and turf is very heavy to carry. But in all coniferous forests there is a layer of moss about 5 cm thick, of which the upper part is alive and the lower part is dead. This is called "kuntta" in Finnish (perhaps moor turf in English). The settlements were on sand beaches near pine forests therefore there was "kuntta" very near and it was easy to obtain. However, when dry, the turf drops in small pieces inside the hut leaving behind small holes that let rain water in. After about one hour of rain, water will penetrate through the wall of the hut almost like outside. When the rain is over the turf drips water for hours afterwards.

Birch Bark and Kuntta

Even without taking ethnographic data into account the most probable coverings of the buildings were birch bark for protection against rain, and moor turf offering insulation against the cold when the building was used in the cold season. The combination of moor turf and birch bark was experimented with when we made a reconstruction of a hut of the "North Osthrobotnian" type according to Kotivuori (1993) in the so-called "Upper Village". We used them for a hut made according to his drawing and it worked well. The huts do not last many years and how long they will last depends on the covering. The frameworks which were covered only with turf were un-usable within three years. Constructions with birch bark only or with turf coverings can survive from 10 to 15 years. We can assume that if the huts are kept dry with heating inside, they can remain in a good condition for a much longer time.

Reed

In Kierikki Stone Age Centre there are buildings covered with reed (see Inga Nieminen's paper). The collecting of reeds was not based on experiences or archaeological evidence, however, reeds would have been available nearby. The reeds used in the reconstructions at Kierikki were imported from Estonia.

In Saarijärvi reeds or straws were not used, because there are good reasons to argue, that their use was not possible for hunter-gatherers before the advent of agriculture. In April of 2004, I visited Kierikki Stone Age Centre when there was still a lot of snow on the ground. Inside of a reed covered building I had a feeling of glowing warmness as there was no draft of air. This is in contrast to the birch bark and turf covered buildings. *If I were a Stone Age man I would not hesitate, I would absolutely choose a reed roofed building.*

The crucial question is, did the hunter-fishers have suitable equipment for cutting reeds. The best tool or apparently the only possible tool for cutting reed is the same as for cutting corn, a sickle. The first sickles from Finland coincide with the first traces of agriculture from the Kiukais-Culture, beginning about 2300 cal BC. There is one pollen grain of buckwheat about 5100 cal BC and one pollen grain of wheat from about one thousand years later (Alenus *et al.* 2012), but there are no agricultural tools. It is very likely that the use of reeds as a covering material began first after corn had been cut, or reeds have never been used for roofing in Finland. The use of reed for covering buildings is ethnohistorically not known in Finland. There is also no evidence that the Eurasian hunter-fisher had used it in times of the historical sources (Sirelius 1906, 1921; Vuorela 1998). Historically, straw roofs have been in use, but only in the westernmost parts of Finland, from the 17th century straw was used as a roofing material on rectories. The use of straw was influenced by the Swedish tradition of using straw for roofs in upper class buildings. The straw as a roofing material was very rare among peasant buildings until the 19th century and is virtually unknown in eastern Finland (Sirelius 1921, Vuorela 1998).

Of course there is a theoretical possibility that bone, which does not preserve in Finnish soil had been used as sickles. As far as I know there are no bone sickles know from Northern European chalk lands where bone artefacts are preserved. Straw and reed contain silica cells which are very hard. A bone sickle would have to be sharpened after a few strokes when in use perhaps making harvesting very slow.

This question is interesting because it reveals what kind of limits there are if you use only experiments or experiences as the basis of reasoning. We have to take a broader view that incorporates ethnographic data and considers the technical possibilities of a variety of materials that may have been used by hunter-fishers in their structures. The conclusions are formed in the intersection of all these factors.

Bibliography

Alenius, T,. Mökkönen, T. and Lahelma, A. 2013. Early Farming in the Northern Boreal Zone: Reassessing the History of Land Use in Southeastern Finland through High-Resolution Pollen Analysis. *Geoarchaeology: An International Journal* 28: 1-24.

Andersen, Søren H. 1981. *Stenalderen: Danmarkshistorien*. Sesam: Viborg.

Christiansson, H. and Knutsson, K. 1985. Bjurselet – Gamla nya experiment. Finn forntiden. Västerbottens norra fornminnesförening. Skellefteå museum. *Meddelande XLVII* 1985.

Gurina, N.N. 1967. Iz istorii drevnih plemen zapadnóh oblastei SSSR. *Materialó i issledovanija po arheologii SSSR, 144*, Moskva – Leningrad.

Halén, O. 1994. Sedentariness during the Stone Age of Northern Sweden in the light of the Alträsket site, C. 5000 B.C., and the comb ware site Lillberget c. 3900 B.C. Source Critical Problems of Representatively in Archaeology. *Acta Archaeologica Lundensia. Series* 4 (20):1-163.

Hiekkanen, M. 1984. Otlitsitelnnye osbennosti postroek tipa Madeneva. otnosjastsihsja kammenomu veku. *Novoe v apheologi CCCP i Finljandii*: 46-53.

Karjalainen, T. 1996. Outokumpu Sätös ja Orov Navolok 16, talo 3. *Muinaistutkija* 1: 13-18.

Kauhanen, I. 1974. Porin Tuorsniemen verkkolöytö. *Karhunhammas* 1: 25-38.

Kotivuori, H. 1993. Kivikauden asumuksia Peräpohjolassa – vertailuja ja rakenteellisia tulkintoja. Selviytyjät. Näyttely Pohjoisen ihmisen sitkeydestä. *Lapin maakuntamuseon julkaisuja 7:* 120-160.

Leskinen, S. 2002. The Late Neolithic House at Rusavierto. In Ranta, R. (ed.). *Huts and Houses. Stone Age and Early Metal Age Buildings in Finland*. National Board of Antiquities. Helsinki. pp. 147-170.

Matiskainen, H. and Jussila, T. 1984. Naarajärven kampakeraaminen asumus. *Suomen Museo* 91: 17-52.

Meinander, C.F. 1976. Hyddbottnarav Madeneva-typ. *Iskos 1*. Helsinki.

Moisanen, J. 1991. Tutkimuksia Kerimäen kivikautisilla asuinpaikoilla. *Sihti* 1: 25-32.

Muurimäki, E. 1995. Saarijärven museon kivikauden kylän rakennusennallistukset – teoreettista taustaa. *Muinaistutkija* 2: 3-11.

Muurimäki, E. 2012. Teemu Mökkönen, Studies on Stone Age Housepits in Fennoscandia (4000-2000 cal BC): Changes in Ground Plan, Site Location, and Degree of Sedentism. Reviewed by Eero Muurimäki. *Fennoscandia archaeologica* 29: 133-137.

Nabakov, P. and Easton, R. 1989. *Native American Architecture*. Oxford University Press. New York – Oxford.

Pälsi, S. 1916. *Kulttuurikuvia kivikaudelta*. Otava: Helsinki.

Pälsi, S. 1918. Kaivaus Pitkäjärven kivikautisella asuinpaikalla Räisälässä v. 1915. *Suomen Museo* 25: 25-34.

Räihälä, O. 1997. Kuoppatalon "merkitys". *Muinaistutkija* 4: 37-44.

Sirelius, U.T. 1906. Über die primitive wohnungen der finnischen und ob-ugrischen völker. *Finnisch-ugrishe forschungen. Sehester band.* Helsingfors.

Sirelius, U.T. 1921. Suomen kansanomaista kulttuuria II. Helsingissä.

Vuorela, T. 1998 (4th edition). *Suomalainen kansankulttuuri.* Werner Söderström Osakeyhtiö: Porvoo, Helsinki & Juva.

Part Five

Decline of structures

Blackhand Kiva

Biography of a replica ancestral Pueblo subterranean masonry-lined structure, Montezuma County, Colorado, USA

Bruce Bradley

Introduction

Cultural sensitivity dictates that early period open air museums in the USA do not exist in the same way as seen in Europe. Some reconstructions of archaeological structures do exist but the immersive experience offered by European Union Archaeological OpenAir Museums (AOAMs) is rare except in those representing post contact era sites, such as, Colonial Williamsburg or the Jamestown settlement in Williamsburg (USA). However, this paper presents a biography of a replica ancestral subterranean structure from the early period.

A replica kiva was built, used, maintained, used for experiments and then abandoned. This process is described and some preliminary observation presented. The object biography of the structure demonstrates the implications for archaeologists seeking to understand the use and maintenance of resources for structures and of the structures themselves.

A kiva is a chamber/structure, built wholly or partly underground, used by Pueblo Indians in the northern American Southwest for habitation and/or religious rites (Figure 15.1) (Vivian & Reiter 1965; Rohn & Ferguson 2006; Mertens 2000). As a building form, kivas developed from subterranean structures (pithouses) with primarily variable domestic features into more formalised structures with sets of repeated internal features (Gonzalez 1953; Gillman 1987). At the same time as these changes took place, from the second through the 13th centuries A.D., these pit structures changed from earthen-walled to masonry-lined constructions (Figure 15.1).

As an archaeologist, over decades of digging, I was involved in the excavation of numerous kivas as well as the pithouses that preceded them. While each was unique in its own way there were certain characteristics of their construction, use and disintegration that I wanted to better understand. As with many other technologies I decided that the best way to get this understanding was to build, use and abandon a pithouse; then a kiva. Initially these were not designed as experiments but as experiences from which to learn.

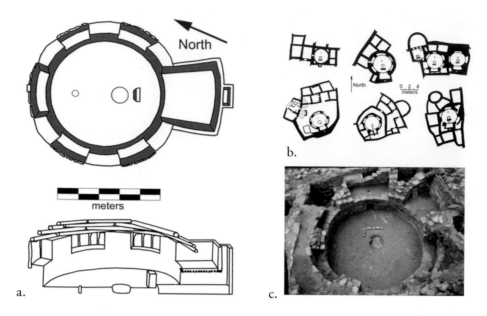

Figure 15.1: Kivas: a) plan and cutaway of 'ideal' kiva; b) kiva unit plans at sand canyon Pueblo; c) excavated kiva at Sand canyon Pueblo. Source: Bruce Bradley.

In the 1980s, the United States Park Service commissioned me to build a pithouse and associated features on our family property in south western Colorado, to be used as a set in a docudrama. This was an ideal opportunity and the result was used in the docudrama to great effect (Hisatsinom 2006). After the filming the structure and features were maintained and the pithouse used off and on for a decade. During this time several experiments were undertaken to better understand how it worked. In the early 1990s, I decided to build a full-scale masonry-lined kiva, however, as this was unfunded, construction lasted for several years. The object biography of Blackhand Kiva (as it came to be known) is presented here.

The design was based on my general knowledge of archaeological Kivas and was not a copy of a specific archaeological structure. There were no drawn plans nor was there any use of modern measuring equipment. Construction materials were gathered from various locations, including the reuse of archaeological stone, beams and posts salvaged from the pithouse (Figure 15.2) and on-site stones, sediment and fresh beams (Figure 15.3). Although there was occasionally some assistance with labour, for the bulk of the effort, I was on my own.

Originally it was planned to make the kiva entirely subterranean but after encountering the major power line going to our house, the design had to be adjusted to avoid it, so the structure became semi-subterranean. In consequence, the roof had to be partly redesigned; which ultimately proved to be a weakness.

Figure 15.2: Pithouse material source; a) uncovering juniper shake level; b) exposing juniper roof 'leaners'; c) preparing to recover main posts; d) pulling main post using a lever. Source: Bruce Bradley.

Figure 15.3: Building materials preparation: a) stone shaping: b) debarking pine beam; c) charring ends of juniper beams; d) juniper beams ready for use. Source: Bruce Bradley.

Construction

Pit

The pit was first dug using digging sticks and baskets. After doing this for about a quarter of the pit work continued with modern tools (a shovel) but work switched back to the digging sticks for the finishing work. The general orientation was lined up with a prominent horizon feature at the edge of the cliff to the south. No attempt was made to orient it to the cardinal points or sunrise-sunsets of any specific dates (e.g. solstices and equinoxes). The importance of this is discussed later.

Walls

The sandstone masonry was a simple pit lining below the encircling banquette and the walls of the 'southern recess' and solid blocks of masonry for the six pilasters. Mortar was mud made from the on-site silt sediment and was kept to a minimum. It was hand-mixed to a stiff consistency to minimize drying shrinkage. The upper walls behind the banquette segments were formed with vertical sandstone slabs (Figure 15.4).

Several niches were built into the walls as construction proceeded. The number, size, form and locations were based on my generalised personal knowledge and not copied from any particular archaeological structures. Once the structure was roofed, the lower walls and pilasters were coated with a thin layer of mud plaster as seen in the archaeological samples (Mindeleff & Mindeleff 2014). This had to be continually smoothed as it dried to reduce cracking. Eventually, the walls were coated with a thin whitewash of burned gypsum and painted designs were applied with natural pigments. This is also when individuals who helped with the construction applied painted hand prints to the walls.

Floor

The floor was levelled, features were added including a subfloor ventilator tunnel, a sipapu and a central hearth. Their locations, sizes and forms were also based on my subjective knowledge and not based on any particular archaeological structure. The floor was finished with a thin layer of mud plaster, which like the walls had to be continually worked as it dried.

Roof

There are several intact archaeological kivas and an abundance of other archaeological data indicating how the roofs were made (Lightfoot 2008). Juniper beams were used to build the main roof by using a cribbing method (Figure 15.5a). This was done for three layers then two long ponderosa pine beams were used to span the remaining roof area, parallel to the structure's axis, one on each side of a roof hatchway (Figure 15.5b). The main roofing was then made by extending juniper beams from the top of the cribbing to the pine spanning beams (Figure 15.5c). Openings between the beams were covered with split juniper shakes and these were

*Figure 15.4: Masonry construction; a) lower lining wall; b) pilaster construction on banquette;
c) floor-level vent tunnel and lining of southern recess; d) wall lining behind banquette segment.
Source: Bruce Bradley.*

*Figure 15.5: Roof construction: a) cribbed juniper beams; b) ends of central pine beams and
layer of secondary beams; c) split juniper shake layer (on left); d) mud daub sealing spaces
between secondary beams on banquette segment roof. Source: Bruce Bradley.*

also used to cover the banquette segments (Figure 15.5d). Mud daub (the same as the mortar and plaster) was pressed into any remaining cracks and openings (Figure 15.5d). A central hatchway was constructed, directly above the central hearth, by spanning the central pine beams and building up masonry walls around it (Figure 15.6a). Again, the size and height was based on my generalised archaeological knowledge and subjective sense of what would work. Finally, the entire roof was covered with a layer of loose dirt, which in turn was covered with a layer of juniper bark strips and a final layer of dirt to form a flat 'courtyard' surface.

Enclosing wall

Because it was not possible to dig the pit deep enough to make an entirely subterranean structure as originally planned a wall had to be added around the outside to hold in the roof materials. This wall was made by dry-laying large pieces of sandstone two to three high (Figure 15.6b).

Use

I used and maintained the kiva over about a decade, finally abandoning it in 2004 when I accepted a permanent position at the University of Exeter in the UK. It was used in a number of ways, including some 'experimental' work, but mainly

a.

b.

Figure 15.6: Other construction: a) hatchway; b) enclosing wall. Source: Bruce Bradley.

a.

b.

c.

Figure 15.7: Location use for documentaries: a) transporting large central pine beam; b) meat processing in kiva; c) 'mystical' man. Source: Bruce Bradley.

for exhibition to interested visitors. It also served as the location for one television show (Nickelodeon: a USA channel focused on programmes for children) and a couple of documentaries (Figure 15.7). Three family pets were also buried under the floor; a parakeet, a small dog and a cat.

Maintenance

Through the decade of use I occasionally did basic maintenance consisting mainly of minor replastering and filling shallow subsidence on the roof to maintain adequate run-off. After one heavy rain I had to replaster a section of the north wall where accumulated water broke through (Figure 15.8a). The hearth, being directly below the hatchway, tended to weather and needed remodelling several times (Figure 15.8b). I also added some wall paintings, some to correspond with where sunlight struck the walls on special occasions such as birthdays and solar events.

Abandonment

The kiva was abandoned with many replica artefacts left in their last position of use or storage. Since then I have been monitoring the structure's deterioration and roof collapse. The roof held up well for the first couple of years with the main

a.

b.

Figure 15.8: Maintenance: a) washed-out area before replastering and repainting in 1999; b) remodelled hearth in 1996. Source: Bruce Bradley.

a.   b.

c.   d.

Figure 15.9: Structure collapse and weathering; a) main chamber floor in 2006 (note drip marks); b) collapse after main beam breakage in 2009; c) roof collapse in 2010; d) roof collapse in 2012. Source: Bruce Bradley.

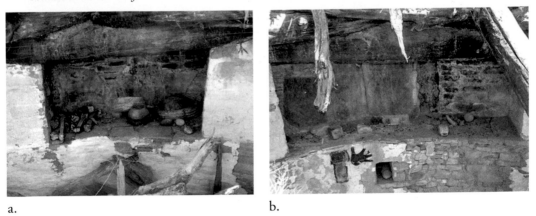

a.   b.

Figure 15.10: Artefact preservation on banquette segments: a) banquette segment 2 in 2010; banquette segment 3 in 2012. Source: Bruce Bradley.

deterioration being wall plaster (Figure 15.9a). This corresponded with erosion of the roof and slight subsidence so that rain and melting snow penetrated the roof and dripped onto the main chamber floor producing distinctive drip marks (Figure 15.9a). This interior moisture resulted in a substantial seasonal growth of mould inside the structure. Dry rot seems to have attacked the two pine central spanning beams but had no effect on the juniper beams. Ultimately, one of the central spanning beams broke producing a hole in the roof adjacent to the hatchway (Figure15. 9b). Once this started, deterioration continued until the whole central area of the roof collapsed (Figure 15.9c-d). However, the cribbed juniper beams around the periphery have remained in place, effectively protecting the banquette segments, including the southern recess, and the artefacts sitting on them (Figure 15.10).

Experiments

The main 'experiments' had to do with ventilation. Although there was a built-in ventilator system, it was difficult to keep the smoke produced from the central fire from making the structure uninhabitable. I had built the kiva with both floor-level and subfloor vent systems and found that they were equally functional/dysfunctional. The features which deal with controlling fire and smoke are clearly an important part of the structure (see Christiansen's chapter).

The other major experiment is the documentation of the deterioration of the kiva through natural weathering. Along with documenting the process of the structure becoming 'archaeological' there is a long term plan to someday excavate it as an archaeological feature so that it may be compared to prehistoric examples

a.   b.

c.   d.

Figure 15.11: Rabbit carcasses and steel replacements: a) main chamber floor in 2006; b) main chamber floor in 2010; c) southern recess in 2010; d) steel cut-outs in 2010. Source: Bruce Bradley.

| THE LIFE CYCLE OF STRUCTURES IN EXPERIMENTAL ARCHAEOLOGY

to better understand their origins. The processes of disintegration have been interesting. I had not predicted that the central pine beams would break first and the roof periphery has lasted longer than expected with the artefacts left on the banquette segments remaining basically unaltered.

Of particular interest was the inadvertent capture of a number of rabbits. These started to fall into the structure in the first year and there being no way out they perished (Figure 15.11a-c). This unfortunate circumstance also served as a source of desiccated rabbits for a PhD student's research project. To maintain the locational information in the kiva each removed rabbit carcass was replaced with a sheet steel cut-out (Figure 15.11d). After 2 years I erected a rabbit-proof fence around the outside of the kiva halting its function as a rabbit trap. While this was an unexpected consequence, it has served to question why, to my knowledge we have never found rabbit skeletons on the floors of archaeological kivas or pithouses nor has there been any mention of this in any archaeological reports.

A cautionary result

As stated above I added features to the wall and floor as I constructed the kiva. These were not calculated to be related to any outside phenomena nor to line up with anything. However, totally coincidently, some of the features turned out to be illuminated on particular solar events (Figure 15.12). In some ways it may have been inevitable as the southern orientation would allow the sun to shine on the north lower lining wall at times in the summer. Exactly where this would happen

a.

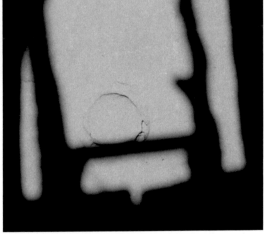

b.

c.

Figure 15.12: Fortuitous astronomical alignments: a) north wall on winter solstice; b) sipapu at noon on equinox; c) northeast niche on equinox. Source: Bruce Bradley.

and on what days was dependant on the placement and height of the hatchway. That all but one of the built-in features (two of three niches in the north wall and the sipapu) aligned with the sun on the solstice and equinox would be considered significant if found in an archaeological structure. Perhaps, but in this case it was totally fortuitous.

Acknowledgements

Over the years many people helped with construction and maintenance of the structure; I thank them for the assistance. My family also 'tolerated' the many hours I spent on this project. I am especially indebted to the many friends who helped with the re-enactments for the various documentaries that were shot 'on location'.

Bibliography

Gilman, P.A. 1987. Architecture as Artifact: Pit Structures and Pueblos in the American Southwest". *American Antiquity* 52.3: 538-564.

Gonzalez, A.R. 1953. Concerning the Existence of the Pit House in South America. *American Antiquity* 18: 271-272.

Interpark 2, 2006. *Hisatsinom the Ancient Ones (Anasazi)*, National Park Service DVD.

Mertens, C. 2000. Kivas of the Anasazi. https://www.uwec.edu/math/journals/Ethnomath/christina.html.

Mindeleff, C. and Mindeleff, V. 2014. *A study of Pueblo architecture, Tusayan and Cibola.* Karan Kerry.

Lightfoot. R.R. 2008. Roofing an early Anasazi Great Kiva: analysis of an architectural model." *Kiva* 74(2): 227-246. DOI: 10.1179/kiv.2008.74.2.009.

Smith, W., Ewing, L.H. and LeBlanc, S.A. 2006. *Kiva mural decorations at Awatovi and Kawaika-a: with a survey of other wall paintings in the Pueblo Southwest* Vol. 37. Harvard University Press: Harvard.

Rohn, A.H. and Ferguson, W.M. 2006. *Puebloan Ruins of the Southwest.* University of New Mexico Press: New Mexico.

Vivian, G. and Reiter, P. 1965. *The great kivas of Chaco Canyon and their relationships.* University of New Mexico Press: New Mexico.

The day the house sat down
The deterioration and collapse of the Ferrycarrig roundhouses

Tríona Sørensen

Introduction

Houses, like most other things we create, can be seen to have a clear life cycle. They are conceived of as an idea, planned, constructed, used and maintained, and when time and the elements begin to take their toll and old age sets in, they deteriorate, collapse and decay. The stages involved in this process are crucial to our understanding of how houses and other built structures were utilised in the past, and have the potential to shed light on key issues such as the longevity of structures, patterns of wear and decay and how these processes may be identified archaeologically.

The four early medieval house reconstructions situated on the crannóg at the Irish National Heritage Park, Ferrycarrig, Co. Wexford, were built during the 1980s and 1990s and formed the basis for a doctoral research project carried out from 2006-2011. The houses had by this stage reached 'old age' and offered a unique opportunity to document and explore the decline and collapse of post and wattle roundhouse structures. This paper will present the biography of these houses, looking briefly at their construction and use before focusing on the processes involved in their deterioration and eventual collapse.

Where the houses have a home: the Irish National Heritage Park, Ferrycarrig

The Irish National Heritage Park (Hereafter referred to by its more well-known title, Ferrycarrig) was established in 1987 with two express aims, namely,

To enhance direct and indirect employment by attracting visitors to a unique, interesting and pleasant place by demonstrating the original purpose and methods of construction of certain man-made features of the Irish landscape and by showing how people lived, worshipped and buried their dead at different times in our history.

To educate Irish people, particularly young people, concerning their rich material heritage of which they are both guardians and heirs.

This mission statement, drawn up by Ferrycarrig's founder, Dr. Edward Culleton, indicates clearly that experimental archaeology was never part of the agenda (Culleton 1999, 77). The various reconstructions at Ferrycarrig were, however, built as accurately as possible, with leading Irish experts advising on the design, layout and construction of each site. Recent growth of interest in experimental archaeology in Ireland has lead to an awareness of experimental methodologies, and while Ferrycarrig has no research agenda of its own, the management have been extremely co-operative in terms of opening up the park as a research base for researchers wishing to use the reconstructions.

An island in time: the reconstructed crannóg at Ferrycarrig

Crannógs are a typical early medieval settlement type consisting of an artificial platform or island built on a lake. They are usually enclosed by a palisade and contain a number of structures, including houses, workshops, storage pits and hearths (O'Sullivan 1998). The crannóg at Ferrycarrig was based on the early medieval crannóg excavated by John Bradley at Moynagh Lough, Co. Meath, and Bradley acted as archaeological advisor during its construction (Bradley 1991, 1997). Twenty-seven acres were set aside for the construction of the heritage park and the crannóg was located in an area of wetland next to the Slaney estuary. An island was constructed, surrounded by a natural lake as water levels rose in the excavated areas, and a drainage system was put in place to allow the lake to drain under the newly constructed road and out into the estuary (Figure 16.1).

Figure 16.1: The reconstructed crannóg at Ferrycarrig (Photo: Tríona Sørensen).

Construction of the roundhouses

Early medieval Irish roundhouses conform to a fairly homogenous pattern. The majority are between 3-6 m in diameter, though larger examples have been found, including the 8th century the 11.2 m roundhouse from Phase Y at Moynagh Lough (Bradley 1991, 15) Roundhouses are predominantly constructed from post and wattle, and most have a single doorway, oriented towards the east or southeast, generally interpreted as an attempt to avoid prevailing south-westerly winds while capitalising on the early hours of daylight (Lynn 1994, 92: Nicholl 2011, 91). One important characteristic, which sets the Irish roundhouses apart from their British counterparts, is the lack of internal ringbeam to support the roof: the full weight of Irish early medieval roundhouse roofs rested solely on the walls.

Over a period from 1987 – 1997, four roundhouses were constructed on the Ferrycarrig crannog (Table 16.1).

All four of the houses were built using the same methodology, inspired by the model developed by Peter Reynolds at Butser (Reynolds 1967). The walls were constructed of a ring of oak posts, ca. 10 cm in diameter, set at intervals of 30 cm and filled in using a simple weave of hazel rods. The roofs were all thatched with river reed and topped with a roof cone.

Life: daily use – or lack thereof – of the Ferrycarrig roundhouses

The houses were initially fitted out with basic furnishings such as benches and stools and each structure – except for the Weaver's Hut – was equipped with a centrally located hearth. This was, however, essentially the full extent of their daily use. Although students and crafts people were employed to occupy and work in the houses during the summer months, they were basically empty structures. Due to stringent Irish health and safety rules, fires were rarely lit in the houses and the wet Irish climate began to make its presence felt on the superstructure of the reconstructions.

During the 1990s, steps were taken to address the 'emptiness' of the houses – something visitors frequently commented negatively upon – and funding was acquired to equip the reconstructions with furniture, cooking utensils, textiles, tools and other items. The refit was a disaster: rather than sourcing accurate period equipment, the then management settled on what might best be called film props, such as plastic fish, fruit and bowls, sound effects of crackling fires and voices and, worst of all from the point of view of the maintenance of the structures, the internal hearths were removed and plastic, imitation fires were installed.

Structure Name	Construction type	Shape	Orientation	Size	Built
The Forge	Post and wattle	Round	West	5m diameter	1987
The Weavers Hut	Post and wattle	Round	West	4m diameter	1987
The Kitchen	Wattle and daub	Round	North	5m diameter	1987
The Main House	Wattle and daub	Round	East	6m diameter	1997

Table 16.1: Construction details for the Ferrycarrig roundhouses.

The years after the refit highlighted yet another problem facing the Ferrycarrig reconstructions, namely vandalism and theft. A decade later and virtually none of the props remained within the houses: everything that wasn't physically nailed or glued in place – and indeed, much of what was – had been stolen, and so the houses continued to stand, relatively empty and unused.

Age and decay

Weather, wattle and weakened walls

In 2005, the author began a doctoral research project, which involved the use of the Ferrycarrig reconstructions (Nicholl 2011). By this stage, they were rapidly approaching the end of their days. The study therefore included an analysis of the final phases of the life of a roundhouse reconstruction. This was important as at the majority of heritage and experimental archaeology centres, when reconstructions become too dilapidated, they are generally replaced and we rarely get to witness their decay. At Ferrycarrig, there was no funding available for replacement, and so the reconstructions continued their gentle decline into old age.

This decay affected the reconstructions as a whole. Due to the overhang that the eaves of a conical roof creates, post and wattle walls – at least their upper portions – are relatively sheltered from wind and rain. The lower sections of the wall however, must contend with sun, rain, frost, and in the case of the Ferrycarrig roundhouses, floodwaters, and as a consequence of this, the lower halves of the walls were consistently the first place where serious decay and deterioration occurred. As the weight of the house and principally of the roof began to settle, the base of the posts was the point where the greatest stresses were concentrated.

The 'settling' of the Ferrycarrig roundhouses manifested slowly as each house gradually began to lean to one side. The crannóg's levels had no doubt shifted and sunk in the years since its construction, contributing to the destabilisation of the houses. The Weavers Hut, Main House and Forge had all been affected by this process, with each structure adopting their own particular angle and speed of decay. The Main House had listed to the south, the Forge to the north and the Weavers Hut to the northeast. The Kitchen remained largely unaffected by this, perhaps due to its location on the slightly higher, southern side of the island, the area least prone to flooding.

This leaning can be seen to affect the house in two distinct ways. One side of the house is being required to stretch, the other to compress. Wooden posts can in reality do neither and so stresses begin to appear on the building. Post and wattle walls can be seen to respond to these stresses in an unexpected way. Rather than buckling and bending with the upright posts breaking along their midsection, the woven wattle panels remain intact and the shift in the angle occurs at the base of the wall. The position of the posts within the ground starts to change: packing around the section of the post below ground level starts to loosen and crumble and posts can be seen to lean, often dramatically, within the below ground features which might now better be described as a 'post gully' rather than a posthole. As yet, there have not been any excavations carried out in and around the Forge (the only remaining example of the Ferrycarrig roundhouses, the others having been removed in 2012 to allow for renovation of the crannóg itself) though this would certainly be a useful exercise at a later date.

The immediate point of weakness is therefore the junction between the posts and the socket that contains them. As the angle of the posts increases, eventually the stress becomes too great and this is where they shear and break. However, prior to the final breakage of the posts, the post and wattle walls demonstrate incredible resilience in the face of what look to be overwhelming pressures and the walls can continue to defy gravity for much longer than expectation would allow. The strength of these walls lies in the method of their manufacture. The overlapped and interlocked layers of wattle support and strengthen the post along its length, increasing the stability of the structure as a whole. The degree to which these houses can lean without collapsing is quite staggering. The question is of course, for how long?

The roof as an active architectural element

Roundhouse roofs play an integral role in determining the lifespan of the structure. When used properly, they can prolong the years of its use and are an integral and dynamic part of the superstructure, shielding the interior from the elements while at the same time removing smoke from within the house. Conversely, if used incorrectly, that is to say, if no fires are lit within the house and the thatch becomes waterlogged, the roof and its increased weight will be one of the key factors involved in the eventual collapse of the house.

When a fire is lit within a roundhouse, the smoke generated by the fire spreads throughout the interior and rises upwards. The circular draught that is created speeds up this process and the smoke can be seen swirling towards the apex where it gathers and hangs in a smoke ceiling before slowly percolating out through the hollow reeds of the thatch. This percolation can be seen from the outside of the structure as a light haze of smoke trickling from the thatch as, slowly but surely, smoke is drawn down through the reeds. Percolation not only clears smoke from the interior, it also has the extra advantage of aerating the roof and maintaining a dry thatch, thus slowing the onset of floral and faunal infestation and prolonging the lifespan of the roof.

Despite being regularly depicted in reconstruction drawings of early medieval settlements, it seems highly unlikely that Irish early medieval roofs would have included smokeholes. If a smokehole were located in the apex of the roof, it would be impossible to completely secure the thatch at the highest point of the roof as the strength and stability of the roof cone or ridge requires the entire surface of the apex to be covered (Seán Savage, pers comm.). Experiments have also shown that smokeholes located centrally above the hearth can increase the risk of the roof catching fire, as the updraught it creates carries live sparks into direct contact with the dry underside of the roof covering (Harrison 1984, 109). Without a smokehole, the gentle draught that rises from the hearth gives sparks time to burn out before coming in contact with dry and dusty thatch. Smokeholes have been used successfully at Butser in their Iron Age roundhouse reconstructions where the use of a internally supported ringbeam allowed for the creation of an aperture in the roof covering but again, the lack of internal ringbeam in Irish early medieval roundhouses precludes this kind of design.

Delaying the ageing process: archaeological evidence for the use of ageing structures

Budget constraints at Ferrycarrig meant that reconstructions that are past their prime have not been demolished and replaced; rather, efforts have been made to keep them standing. This has been an unexpected boon for research into how these structures can be used and for how long they can conceivably last and valuable lessons have been learned along the way. No attempt was made to halt the leaning of the Weavers Hut and so that was the first of the reconstructions to collapse in 2003. As a result of this, efforts were made to reinforce the Forge, the next of the crannóg reconstructions in line to collapse. Additional posts were inserted on the inside of the structure, directly against the inner face of the wattle wall at an opposing angle and lashed to the top of the original post in an effort to counter the pressures and weight of the roof as the house continued to lean to one side (see Figure 16.2). On the exterior, extra posts were added in the same manner in an attempt to buttress the structure.

There are parallels for this kind of buttressing attempt within the archaeological record. The trapezoidal early medieval house at Garryduff I, Co. Cork had an extra row of posts on its western side, presumably in an attempt to support a decaying structure (O'Kelly 1962a, 26). A similar sloping posthole found at the north-western corner of the rectangular house at Béal Boru, Co. Clare, may also have served the same function (O'Kelly 1962b, 6). The success of the approach is

Figure 16.2: Buttress posts were inserted in 2003 in an effort to slow the decline of the Forge. Five years later, they too had been pulled out of their sockets: note the fire-blackened ends, which had previously been below ground level (Photo: Tríona Sørensen).

limited however. The inexorable march of decay continued and five years after they were installed, the buttress posts, along with the rest of the house were dragged to the north, lifting them out of their sockets and rendering them obsolete. However, it had prolonged the life of the house. The buttressing came into effect in 2003 after the collapse of the Weavers Hut and while it failed to halt the decay of the building, it certainly helped slow it down. It should be noted that even after that the buttress posts failed, the house remained upright – albeit at a decidedly drunken angle – for a further 12 months.

Migrating hearths: keeping the home fires lit

One curious feature of a number of early medieval hearths is the fact that they seem to migrate over the course of the use of the house. The roundhouses at Moynagh Lough, Co. Meath are a perfect example of this phenomenon. During Phase Y, the large 11.2 m roundhouse began life with a centrally located, undefined hearth. Later, a new sub-rectangular hearth was added to the east of the original hearth and the central hearth was abandoned (Bradley 1991, 16; Nicholl 2011, 110). Experimental archaeology may perhaps have provided an answer to this problem. At twenty-two years of age, the post and wattle Forge finally collapsed in 2009. As the house began to lean, the roof moved with it and so the original, centrally located hearth was no longer beneath the apex – the point where the flammable underside of the thatch is at the safest and furthest remove from stray sparks. As the house leaned further, the underside of the roof came ever closer to the original hearth site and if knocking and rebuilding the house were not an option, moving the hearth would be. As of the summer of 2007, twenty years after the construction of the house, this centrally located hearth was deemed to be too close to the underside of the thatch to be used in safety and a new hearth had to be inserted, further to the north.

While this is not to suggest that all migrating hearths are due to this effect, it is certainly a sound proposal for at least some of them, particularly those on crannogs where the damp conditions and shifting foundations would have sped up the process of decay and collapse in timber-built structures.

Collapse

The hazards of island life: the impact of floodwaters on the Ferrycarrig roundhouses

Archaeological evidence has shown that occasionally, early medieval settlements were damaged or destroyed not just by the slow march of time but also by more immediate and catastrophic occurrences such as floods (Van de Noort and O'Sullivan 2006, 109-111). Unfortunately for Ferrycarrig, the same is also true of reconstructed early medieval settlements. During the spring of 2004, high spring tides and torrential rain resulted in the Slaney bursting its banks, inundating Ferrycarrig and much of the surrounding area. The higher levels in the estuary caused the drainage system at the crannóg lake to fail, creating a deep and dangerous rise of over five feet in water level.

Added to the damage the floodwaters would inflict was the extra destruction caused by tidal action. The Slaney estuary is tidal at the point where it snakes past Ferrycarrig and so twice a day, the levels of the floodwater rose and fell as the tides swept in and out of Wexford harbour. Once the waters had finally drained away, the effect of this tidal action was dramatically displayed. The crannóg palisade had been entirely washed away on its western side where the floodwaters had broken through the post and wattle and sections of the broken palisade could be seen lying intact on the lakebed. The houses suffered considerable damage, especially the Main House, which stands slightly lower than the Kitchen and Forge. Whole sections of daub on the Main House had been washed away or damaged to such an extent that it simply crumbled away as it dried out in the days after. The interior of the house was also severely damaged. The swirling floodwaters had scoured the inner face of the walls, causing much of the daub to break up and fall off.

It became obvious that the daub had become so waterlogged that it was not going to dry out again. Sections of the walls that had been wholly submerged for days were drying out on their exterior surface, but remaining damp and wet at their centre. Amid fears over the destabilisation of the structure if the wooden frame was to be exposed to this damp for a prolonged period, it was decided that the best course of action would be to remove what was left of the daub, allowing the wooden superstructure to fully dry out. Once this had been done, the frame dried out and was successfully daubed again.

This flood had demonstrated an aspect of the use of daub that had not previously been considered. We think of it solely as an insulating material, one that increases heat and warmth and not as one that could potentially cause serious damage to the overall structure. The incident suggested something that would not otherwise have come to mind – the fact that in wetland locations or areas prone to flooding, daub is simply not an advantageous building material.

The collapse of the Ferrycarrig roundhouses

The failure of the woven walls Part I – the Weavers Hut

The Weavers Hut was the first structure to be built on the crannóg in 1987 and also the first of the roundhouses to collapse, sixteen years later. Perhaps 'collapse' is too strong a word to use in this case; what actually happened was far slower, far gentler. Over a period of three years, the strength of the wall posts started to fail as they shifted in their sockets and began to lean backwards. The house continued to lean at increasingly extreme angles until one day Ferrycarrig staff opened up in the morning to find the house had finally just sat down (see Figure 16.3 below).

Its arrival at the point of collapse was the result of a number of factors, one of these being the manner in which the house was used. During the sixteen years of its life, no fire was ever lit within the Weavers Hut. Essentially, the house was the equivalent of an abandoned early medieval structure. The lack of fire led to the roof becoming waterlogged and heavy and the increased weight of the thatched roof seems to have been more than the wattle walls could support. The house began to

Figure 16.3: The Weaver's Hut after its collapse in 2003 (Photo: Tríona Sørensen).

lean, greatly increasing the stresses on the wall posts, which simply sheared at the base, causing the wattle to compress and condense and the house to fall backwards.

The wattle walls proved to be highly resilient in the face of these stresses. Rather than breaking or bending along their midsection above ground, the woven structure of the wall provided it with a fierce rigidity that maintained a straight surface, even after the posts had sheared at their base. The roof frame was also unaffected by the collapse, remaining vertical throughout the slow process of the collapse. Essentially the collapse resulted in a lowered version of the original building but one that was once again stable and in theory, could still function in some capacity. Two years after its collapse, the house began to be used as a storage space for the various craftspeople working on the crannóg and it seems probable that early medieval houses could also have continued in use in a similar way.

The failure of the woven walls Part II – the Forge

The Forge was completed shortly after the Weavers Hut in 1987 and its decline followed much the same process but with a greater degree of intervention. The Forge began to settle and lean sixteen years into the life of the building, and this phase of decline and collapse lasted six years. The Forge – as its name suggests – was intended to represent a blacksmith's workshop. To that end, a hearth and anvil were installed and used periodically during the summer season. Thus the roof of the Forge was occasionally aerated and warmed from within, which helped keep the thatch dry for longer. The larger diameter of the Forge also seems to have increased its stability. Measuring 5 m across, the extra length added to its circumference in comparison with the Weavers Hut seems to have allowed the structure to more successfully absorb some of the stresses of the leaning and settling.

The speed of the buildings eventual demise was slowed by the insertion of buttressing both inside and outside the structure. However, the buttressing was only ever going to be a stopgap measure and the end finally came for the Forge in November of 2009. Once again, the crannóg found itself under water as another period of heavy rains and high tides inundated the Slaney estuary and this second period of sustained flooding proved too much for the Forge. The combination of the action of the flood and the prior weakness of the posts resulted in the house finally settling quietly onto its northern side (Figure 16.4). None of the wall posts broke at their midpoint and so the walls can be seen to have shifted and compressed rather than breaking.

One difference between the manner of the collapse of the Forge and the Weaver's Hut is the way in which the roof frame of the Forge could be seen to warp as the angle of the lean increased. The roof on the southern side of the house was raised up at the same time as the northern side of the frame was edging slowly closer towards the ground, something that did not occur in the Weavers Hut roof, which sat vertically until it was dismantled. Perhaps the buttressing of the wall posts of the Forge can be held to account here; while they slowed the movement of the posts, gravity was still clearly taking its toll on the roof frame which warped accordingly.

The failure of the woven walls part III – the Main House

The flood of November 2009 that claimed the Forge would also complete the decline of the Main House. In the years since the 2004 flood, the superstructure of the Main House had begun to show the most serious signs of decay of the four houses. The damage sustained by the posts and wattles during the days following the flood when the daub hindered their drying out began to manifest further. The Main House walls are the only post and wattle walls that fractured and broke along their midsection. The southern section of the wall developed a bulge, which pushed the lower sections of the wall towards the interior of the house and the upper sections outwards. The wall could literally be seen to be folding on itself, as wall posts broke along their midsection within the daub. This bulge caused the roof frame to warp and change its shape considerably, as the rafters struggled to maintain the span of the interior with walls of two different heights. No attempt was made to buttress the Main House as it began to collapse: as the Main House had in essence buckled, rather than leaned, internal buttressing could do nothing to prop the structure back up again.

The Main House finally collapsed during the flood of 2009 (Figure 16.5). Of the three structures to collapse on the crannóg, the Main House was the only one to have partially failed; the Forge and Weavers Hut both suffered a total collapse in that their wall posts were damaged and broken around the length of their circumference whereas the Main House could be seen to have failed in specific areas. The southern wall was the most significant point of failure and the resilience of the northern wall, even in the face of the distortion of the roof frame and the eventual collapse of the southern side, is astonishing. Post-flood, the northern side could be seen to have sustained damage; daub had once again begun to crack and

Figure 16.4: The Forge, after its collapse in 2009 (Photo: Tríona Sørensen).

Figure 16.5: The Main House, after its collapse in 2009 (Photo: Tríona Sørensen).

flake away and the line of the eaves was more uneven than before but otherwise, the northern side stood firm.

And so the Main House with its wattle and daub walls has become something of a paradox; did the daub help strengthen the walls or did it weaken them when the floodwaters rose? It is difficult to answer this question as the house has essentially suggested both alternatives, the daub helped keep the structure of the northern wall coherent in the face of structural stress, but the manner by which it locked in damp and moisture depleted the strength of the southern walls when challenged by the flood. It is the view of the author that although daub may provide a level of extra support, the risk involved in using it in wetland environments far outweighs the benefit. Just twelve years old at the time of collapse, the Main House was a full decade younger than the Forge when its structure failed, suggesting that daub may have been a contributing factor in this accelerated decline.

The eventual collapse of the Forge and Main House underlined the crucial, uniting factor in the manner of the use of the Ferrycarrig reconstructions and its influence on their collapse; lack of internal fire had caused the structures to become damp and waterlogged, and the delicate symbiosis between the different construction materials that makes this a potentially successful house-type, was lost.

The failure of the woven walls – part IV?

The Kitchen remained the last standing of the four crannóg houses. It too had contended with two floods and the many other challenges that weather and the passage of time had sent its way. Constructed in 1987, the Kitchen had enjoyed a somewhat more favourable location than the other three reconstructions, located as it was on the slightly higher, southern side of the crannóg. By the time it was dismantled in 2012, the house had not yet begun to lean but had certainly begun to settle. This could be seen in the line of the eaves of its lichen covered roof, which rose and pitched, most noticeably on its western and southern sides, suggesting that even though movement of the wall posts could not be observed externally, it was still taking place nonetheless.

Lifespan of early medieval roundhouses: revision of old interpretations

The standard maxim in Irish archaeology is that early medieval houses would have lasted for between fifteen and twenty years before needing to be demolished and replaced. The Ferrycarrig roundhouses fly in the face of this claim, surviving as they did for up to twenty-two years. There is no reconstructed house in Ireland or Europe that can claim to have been used in a realistic way – all are colder, damper and emptier than their early medieval counterparts would have been and so their lifespan presents us with the lowest possible denominator – build an early medieval house and essentially leave it abandoned, and it can survive for up to twenty-two years. Build an early medieval post and wattle house and treat it correctly, heat and aerate it daily and in response to the demands of the seasons and the elements and it will survive for…? That is the challenge that is open to us now.

Conclusions

The future for the Ferrycarrig roundhouses

The crannóg underwent a major rebuild in 2012 after funding was acquired to carry out a much-needed renovation of the heritage park's reconstructions. The funding came at a price however, and strict conditions were imposed which demanded that the new buildings have modern additions such as steel cable ties and cement post pads in order to ensure a longer lifespan. While this is understandable in an economic context, it has however rendered the new Ferrycarrig houses unusable in terms of experimental archaeology. This makes the biography of the Ferrycarrig roundhouses all the more important as it records a process that we are not likely to witness again in Ireland.

That biography is not entirely finished, however. It has been agreed that the Forge will be allowed to remain in place and that the processes involved in its decay will continue to be recorded, creating a more accurate picture of how the superstructure behaves over time. It is also planned that a number of small-scale excavations will take place, to explore the archaeological footprint of the structure, which may help identify incidences of the use of ageing structures within the archaeological record.

This paper has presented the last years of the lives of the Ferrycarrig roundhouses, which is just one chapter of their story. However, the various insights that this chapter has afforded, from the use of buttressing posts to the possible repositioning of hearths in early medieval contexts, highlight once again the importance of building and interacting with reconstructions as a methodology for exploring past built environments – an apt reminder at a time when straightened economic circumstances across Europe threaten this very practice.

Acknowledgements

Sincere thanks to Maura Bell and the staff of the Irish National Heritage Park for their co-operation and support over the course of the study conducted there.

Many thanks to Dr. Edward Culleton for providing access to his archive from the construction of Ferrycarrig.

Many thanks to Seán Savage, Thatcher, for information and advice.

Financial support from the Irish Research Council for the Humanities and Social Sciences is gratefully acknowledged.

Bibliography

Bradley, J. 1991. Excavations at Moynagh Lough, Co. Meath 1985-87. *Riocht na Midhe* 8: 21-36.

Bradley, J. 1997. Archaeological investigations at Moynagh Lough, Co. Meath 1995-6. *Ríocht na Mídhe* 9 (3): 50-61.

Culleton, E. 1999. The origin and role of the Irish National Heritage Park. In Planel, P. and Stone, P. (eds.) *The Constructed Past: Experimental Archaeology, Education and the Public*. Routledge: London. pp. 76-89.

Harrison, J.M. 1984. Smokehole experiments at Craggaunowen. *North Munster Antiquarian Journal* 26: 108-9.

Lynn, C.J. 1994. Houses in rural Ireland, A.D. 500-1000. *Ulster Journal of Archaeology* 57: 81-94.

Nicholl, T. 2011. *Houses, dwellings and daily life in early medieval Ireland: perspectives from archaeology, history and experimental archaeology*. Unpublished PhD Thesis, School of Archaeology, University College Dublin: Dublin.

O'Kelly, M.J. 1962a. Two ringforts at Garryduff, Co. Cork. *Proceedings of the Royal Irish Academy* 63C: 17-125.

O'Kelly, M.J. 1962b. Béal Ború, Co. Clare. *Journal of the Cork Historical and Archaeological Society* 67: 1-27.

O'Kelly, M.J. 1962. Two ringforts at Garryduff, Co. Cork. *Proceedings of the Royal Irish Academy* 63C: 17-125.

O'Sullivan, A. 1998. *The Archaeology of Lake Settlement in Ireland. Dublin*: Discovery Programme Monograph no. 4.

O'Sullivan, A. and Nicholl, T. 2011. Early medieval settlement enclosures in Ireland: dwellings, daily life and social identity. *Proceedings of the Royal Irish Academy 111C*: 59-90.

Reynolds, P. 1967. Reconstruction of an Iron Age Hut. *Evesham Historical Society Research Papers* 88: 29-33.

Van de Noort, R. and O'Sullivan, A. 2006. *Rethinking Wetland Archaeology*. Duckworth. London.